APACHE
AT WAR

Steve Jones spent twenty-seven years in the military, earned his stripes as a ferocious war pilot, and has been decorated eight times. He fired the UK's first controversial thermobaric missile; helped track and kill Most Wanted Taliban commanders in Afghanistan; and taught Prince Harry to wage war from an attack helicopter.

Jones had been the UK's youngest trainee military pilot when he signed up. He went on to serve with the Army Air Corps in the Balkans, in the Gulf War, twice in Northern Ireland, and three times in Afghanistan. Along the way he secured the Queen's Commendation for Bravery after pulling comrades from the burning wreckage of a crashed helicopter.

Steve Jones left the army in the rank of Warrant Officer Class 1, the highest non-commissioned rank in the British Army. Based in Aberdeen, he now flies helicopters servicing the North Sea oil industry.

APACHE
AT WAR

Flying the world's deadliest
attack helicopter in combat

STEVE JONES

elite pilot, Army Air Corps

First published by John Blake Publishing
an imprint of The Zaffre Publishing Group
A Bonnier Books UK company
4th Floor, Victoria House
Bloomsbury Square
London WC1B 4DA
England

Owned by Bonnier Books
Sveavägen 56, Stockholm, Sweden

www.facebook.com/johnblakebooks
twitter.com/jblakebooks

First published in hardback in 2024

Hardback ISBN: 978-1-78946-720-8
Trade paperback: 978-1-78946-776-5
Paperback ISBN: 978-1-78946-773-4
Ebook ISBN: 978-1-78946-774-1
Audiobook ISBN: 978-1-78946-775-8

British Library Cataloguing-in-Publication Data:

A CIP catalogue record for this book is available from the British Library.

Design by www.envydesign.co.uk

Printed and bound in Great Britain by Clays Ltd, Elcograf S.p.A

1 3 5 7 9 10 8 6 4 2

MIX
Paper | Supporting
responsible forestry
FSC® C018072

Every reasonable effort has been made to trace copyright-holders of material reproduced in
this book, but if any have been inadvertently overlooked the publishers would be glad to hear
from them.

John Blake Publishing is an imprint of Bonnier Books UK
www.bonnierbooks.co.uk

'When once you have tasted flight, you will walk the earth with your eyes turned skyward; for there you have been, and there you long to return.'
John H. Secondari

CONTENTS

✳ = CONTACTS.

RECORD OF LIVE WEAPON FIRING

Date	Aircraft Type	Missile Hit	Missile Miss	FFAR	A-A	Cannon	Door Gun	Day/Night	Seat	Remarks
OCT 14	Apache AH1					20		DAY	R.	Gun DH
OCT 22	Apache AH1			8RA		303		DAY	F.	CASF
OCT 30	Apache AH1					10		DAY	R	CASF
NOV 1	Apache AH1					130		DAY	F.	Gun DH.
NOV 4	Apache AH1					60		DAY	R.	Gun DH
NOV 8	Apache AH1					20		DAY	R.	Gun DH
NOV 2	Apache AH1					130		DAY	R.	Gun DH.
MAY 11	Apache AH1			4FL 4RA		110		DAY	R.	Ranges.
✳ MAY 16	Apache AH1	1				180		DAY	R.	CONTACT RdS
✳ JUNE 6	Apache AH1	1		16FL		276		DAY	R.	CONTACT GSK.
✳ MAY 17	Apache AH1	1				40		DAY	R.	CONTACT SGN
JUNE 11	Apache AH1					220		DAY	F.	Gun DH.
JUNE 21	Apache AH1			6RA		80		DAY	R.	CASF.
JUNE 26	Apache AH1					180		DAY	F.	Gun DH.
JULY 10	Apache AH1			6RA		210		DAY	F.	Gun DH - FCX.
JULY 20	Apache AH1					140		DAY	R.	Gun DH.
JULY 22	Apache AH1		1	10RA		80		DAY	F	FRNT SGAT CX
✳ JULY 23	Apache AH1			16FL				DAY	R.	CONTACT GSK.
✳ JULY 26	Apache AH1	6	6	28FL		270		DAY	R.	CONTACT GSK.
✳ JULY 27	Apache AH1	3		23FL		450		DAY	F.	FRNT SGAT N/SHOOT.
AUG 1	Apache AH1	1		10RA		300		D/NIGHT	F.	AE CX RUN.
DEC 5	Apache AH1	1		16RA 8FL	8FL	500		N/NIGHT	F/R	CALFEX.
2008 JAN 17/08	Apache AH1					1200		DAY	F	CRIMSON EAGLE DH
MARCH 7	Apache AH1					44		DAY	F	CRIMSON EAGLE DH
MARCH 18	Apache AH1			40FL 8MB		440		DAY/NIGHT	F/R	CRIMSON EAGLE.
MAY 09	Apache AH1			8FL 4RA		110		DAY	F.	Op HERRICK 8D.
TOTAL		14	1	205		8542.				

A page from the author's logbook recording live firing on operations in Helmand, including the types of weapons and the number of missiles, rockets and rounds of cannon ammunition fired. The asterisks in the left-hand margin indicate sorties to support troops in contact.

GLOSSARY

AAC – Army Air Corps, the combat aviation arm of the British Army

AK – AK-47, a Soviet Russian-designed 7.62mm fully automatic assault rifle; also called a Kalashnikov

Aldergrove – Joint Helicopter Command Flying Station Aldergrove, Co. Antrim, Northern Ireland. A former RAF station about 21 kilometres north-west of Belfast, it shares runways with Belfast International Airport

ally – slang for scruffy, run down

ANA – Afghan National Army

ANP – Afghan National Police

APU – auxiliary power unit

ARP – aviation recce patrol

autorotation – engine-off condition in which a helicopter's rotors are turned only by the flow of air over them, used for emergency landings following engine failure

AW – air warning

AWACS – airborne warning and control system; high-flying surveillance and reconnaissance aircraft equipped with special radar systems

AWS – area weapon system; in the Apache, this is the 30mm automatic M230E1 chain gun mounted beneath the aircraft

azimuth – type of bearing used in navigation

'Bag, the' – initial instruments-only training for the Apache

BATUS – British Army Training Unit Suffield, Alberta, Canada

BDA – battle damage assessment

bergen – large load-carrying rucksack issued to British troops

bingo (fuel) – the calculated minimum fuel level needed for an aircraft to return to base or other destination

Blue Eagles – the AAC's helicopter aerobatics team, disbanded in 2010

bunt – aerobatic manoeuvre, one half of an outside loop

C-130 – Lockheed C-130 4-engined transport aircraft; the C-130 Spectre is a heavily armed gunship version

Card A – under ROE, permission to act on imminent threat to life

casevac – casualty evacuation; *see also* medevac

CFI – chief flying instructor

CGTW – Command Ground Training Wing

CO – commanding officer

Cody – callsign for a UAV, also known as a drone

collective – a helicopter's collective-pitch control

CPG – co-pilot/gunner

CTR – conversion to role training

CTT – conversion to type training

cyclic – a helicopter's cyclic pitch control

deconfliction – military term for action to lessen the risk of friendly fire, or of collision between two friendly aircraft

DFC – Distinguished Flying Cross

DHFS – Defence Helicopter Flying School, based at RAF Shawbury in Shropshire; now No. 1 Flying Training School

dicker – term for a watcher, observer

DShK – Soviet Russian 12.7mm belt-fed heavy machine gun, also known as a 'Dushka'

Dude – callsign for a fast jet

EF – enemy forces

EW – electronic warfare

famil – flight area familiarisation sortie

FCR – fire-control radar

FF – friendly forces

FHT – final handling test

FLIR – forward-looking infrared

FOB – forward operating base

GOA – ground observation aid

Good Friday Agreement – agreement signed in Belfast by all the principal parties on 10 April 1998 – Good Friday – that brought to an end most of the sectarian violence of the Troubles

GPMG – general-purpose machine gun; belt-fed 7.62mm gas-operated weapon, the British Army's standard infantry machine gun

groundie – member of the ground crew

gunship – heavily armed helicopter or fixed-wing aircraft

HALS – hardened aircraft landing strip

HCR – Household Cavalry Regiment

HEISAP – high-explosive incendiary semi-armour piercing, a type of 70mm rocket warhead

Hesco – brand name of a type of defensive barrier used to protect against blast, gunfire etc.

HIDAS – helicopter integrated defensive aids suite

HLS – helicopter landing site

HMD – helmet-mounted display

HVT – high-value target

IAT – image auto-track

IED – improvised explosive device

IHT – intermediate handling test

INLA – Irish National Liberation Army; Irish republican paramilitary organisation in Northern Ireland during the Troubles

IR – infrared

IRA – Irish Republican Army, the principal republican paramilitary organisation in Northern Ireland during the Troubles

IRT – immediate response team

JDAM – joint direct-attack munition

jingly lorry – also jingle truck, jingly truck; locally owned lorries in Afghanistan and Pakistan so-called from the chains and pendants hanging from their bodywork, causing a jingling sound when they move

JMB – joint mission brief

JTAC – joint terminal attack controller

Kalashnikov – *see* AK-47

leaker – term for a known enemy who leaves an area of interest

GLOSSARY

LS – landing site

LZ – landing zone

medevac – evacuation, usually by air, of sick or wounded for medical treatment. *See also* casevac

MANPAD – man-portable air defence system

Mastiff – 6-wheel-drive infantry mobility vehicle, or PPV, designed to be resistant to landmines and IEDs

MOD – Ministry of Defence

Mosquito – Taliban nickname for the Apache

MPD – multi-purpose display

MSQ – Musa Qala, town in Helmand Province, Afghanistan, a hotbed of Taliban insurgency

nap-of-the-earth flying – flying very low to avoid attack from the ground

NAAFI – Navy, Army and Air Force Institutes; official organisation that provides canteens, shops and other facilities for the British armed forces

NCO – non-commissioned officer

NVG – night-vision goggles

OC – officer commanding; *see also* CO

okta – measure of cloud cover; one okta is one-eighth of the visible sky

OP – observation post

Operation Herrick – codename for all British military operations during the war in Afghanistan from 2002 until the end of combat operations in 2014

pad brat – a child one or both of whose parents are in the military

pax – passengers

PD – point-detonating, a type of 70mm rocket warhead

PFL – practice forced landing

PKM – Soviet Russian-designed 7.62mm belt-fed, tripod-mounted machine gun

PNVS – pilot night-vision system

PPV – protected patrol vehicle

PRT – provincial (originally provisional) reconstruction team; military units with a civilian element deployed in Afghanistan to assist local government with security and reconstruction

PWRR – Princess of Wales's Royal Regiment

QHI – qualified helicopter instructor

quick stop (QS) – coordinated manoeuvre when a rapid decrease in forward airspeed is required to bring a helicopter to the hover; also called 'rapid deceleration'

RAC – Royal Armoured Corps

RCIED – remote-control IED (q.v.)

red airspace – airspace in which it is too dangerous to fly

red, to talk in – phrase indicating that comms may be insecure and that other parties could be listening in

REME – Corps of Royal Electrical and Mechanical Engineers. Described as 'the Army's professional engineers', they service and repair the AAC's aircraft

RF – radio frequency

ROE – rules of engagement; official orders that define when, where, how, and against whom military force may be used

Rolex – adjustment to the timeline of an operation or exercise

roulement – troop movement, usually of short duration, to relieve another unit

GLOSSARY

RPG – rocket-propelled grenade

RSC – rocket-steering cursor

RTB – return to base

RUC – Royal Ulster Constabulary, the established police force of Northern Ireland; replaced by the Police Service of Northern Ireland (PSNI) in 2001, following the Good Friday Agreement

RV - rendezvous

SAL – semi-automatic line of sight (missile)

SAM – surface-to-air missile

Scud – Soviet-designed medium-range ballistic missile; dozens were fired by Iraq into Israel and Saudi Arabia during the Gulf War

SF – Special Forces

SH – support helicopter(s)

sim – (flight) simulator

shock and awe – military strategy to deploy overwhelming force in dramatic fashion designed to demoralise an enemy before engagement

slave, to – in this context, to subject a device to control by another

SLR – self-loading rifle; 7.62mm gas-operated, magazine-fed semi-automatic rifle, the standard infantry rifle of the British Army from the 1950s to the 1980s

Spectre – *see* C-130

spot turn – a turn made while a helicopter is hovering

sprog – army slang for a recruit; otherwise, a baby or child

Squirrel – Squirrel HT Mk 1 light training helicopter, a variant of the Eurocopter AS350 (now Airbus Helicopters H125) single-engine light utility helicopter

Sultan – British Army tracked command and control vehicle based on the CVR(T) series of light tanks

TACEX – tactical exercise

TADS – target acquisition and designation system

TIC – troops in contact (with an enemy)

TLZ – tactical landing zone

TOW – tube-launched, optically sighted, wire-guided missile system

Troubles, the – violent sectarian conflict between loyalist and republican factions in Northern Ireland from c. 1968 to 1998

UAV – unmanned aerial vehicle, also known as a drone

UDA – Ulster Defence Association; loyalist paramilitary organisation in Northern Ireland during the Troubles

UGV – Upper Garesh Valley, Helmand Province, Afghanistan

UVF – Ulster Volunteer Force; loyalist paramilitary organisation in Northern Ireland during the Troubles

Viking (BvS10) – armoured amphibious all-terrain vehicle consisting of two coupled tracked units

VHR – very high readiness

VW – voluntary withdrawal

WHT – weapon-handling test

Widow – callsign for a JTAC

Winchester – out of ammunition

wings – flying badge usually awarded for completing flying training, or a significant part of it

WO1 – warrant officer class one, the highest non-commissioned rank in the British Army

WSF – Worcestershire and Sherwood Foresters Regiment

PROLOGUE

THIS PLACE WAS peaceful five minutes ago.

Just a warm breeze and a whisky-coloured sunrise, another desert day coming to life. It seemed a shame to fuck that up. But that was why we were here. Our job was to turn aviation fuel into noise, disperse sand, brown out the sun and think of war. Al Qaeda had attacked New York. No one was thinking of anything else.

Two Lynx parked face to face on bare desert, a hundred metres apart. Another crew had just got into the first aircraft. Andy B and I started checks on the second.

The other machine came to life, engine churning, rotors blurring, downdraught encasing it in a bubble of sand. Our eyes narrowed and we watched it lift. Andy turned away, got into the cockpit, pulled on his helmet. We were next to depart.

Then something I'd never seen before. That big, dark, churning cloud stopped, just thirty feet up. I could see the Lynx's nose dip and watched as the whole bloody thing started coming back down.

What the hell?

It hammered nose-first into the desert, the tips of four blurred blades red hot as they slammed through sand. The Lynx bounced upwards, punched down again. I was looking at a giant version of a Bonfire Night sparkler twirling around in a child's hand, a huge, screaming wheel of fire in the dark. And this 5-tonne, rotor-legged catastrophe was somehow stumbling towards us.

Too late to board our aircraft. I shoved Andy deeper into the cockpit, some instinct saying he'd get at least some refuge from this imminent disaster.

The nose struck ground again, bounced back, sparks flying, blades buckling. That steel was not designed to carve up desert. The immense torque driving it towards us would rip it to pieces from the inside out.

Something came my way like a meteorite, a chunk of aircraft careering out from wailing darkness. It thumped the sand to my side with freight-train force. I knew there'd be more as this mangled mess crashed again.

It was like my boots were glued to the earth. I was bursting with adrenalin yet fastened by fear. I'd no idea what to do, no time to do it. Without thinking, my eyes closed, my hands went over my ears and I turned. I put my back to it all, left it to fate.

And everything stopped.

Not even the sound of the desert any more...

I couldn't tell my story before. A first attempt, back in 2008, didn't work out. I was still serving at the time and every word was scrutinised by my commanding officer (CO). I was banned from revealing material that would have helped put a reader in the picture. I was forbidden from detailing involvement with Special Forces and other combat actions. I had to avoid operational data, various parameters, flying heights, intel, mission briefs. I couldn't have even told you my name (although that was only sensible at the time). Some material from my second Afghan tour was carried in another book, published in 2008, but my story was not told. So I decided to wait and try again.

PROLOGUE

That proved to be a good idea. At the time, both the war in Afghanistan and my military career had some distance to run and plenty of surprises to deliver. And I've come to realise that my transition to civilian pilot has been an important, though turbulent, part of the process of repurposing my military mindset.

Much of this book comes from diaries I kept while deployed and much comes from vivid memories. It is the story of my journey from airsick boy to airman, from Gazelle to Apache, from Northern Ireland to Afghanistan, from training to survive to training a prince to attack, from unleashing a genuine dream to unleashing verifiable hell.

Apache at War is the story of my decisions both in life and in combat, decisions that made me who I am today. Right decisions; wrong decisions; split-second decisions; decisions that changed things in ways that were good, bad or otherwise. It tells of being the youngest, of being the first, of refusing to fail, of refusing to become inhuman when humanity seemed hard to find. It is about looking at the options and taking the decision to become as ferocious and professional as possible at the same time.

I've included all the details I can to tell you this without putting any individual, organisation or military operation at risk. And I've written it under my own name.

In my career I have been fortunate enough, and trained hard enough, to pilot and fight the most fearsome, state-of-the-art search-and-destroy flying machine on the planet. On every occasion I took to the sky, there were those out there who wanted nothing more than to bring down one of those highly prized helicopters with me inside. Luckily enough, despite a few close shaves, they didn't succeed. In fact, some of them didn't survive. My story includes part of their story.

I'll start by telling you that my work with the British Army, with the very best of the very best, is something of which I am immensely proud. At all times in the text ahead, you should consider me immensely proud too of all those I've had the privilege of serving alongside.

I'm thinking now of those heroes who made it home and, sadly, those heroes who did not. This book is for them all.

We will remember them.

Chapter One

POLICE COLLEGE, SCOTLAND, 2015

I HAD A COFFEE and, as instructed, went off to watch the police officer speak in the briefing hall. He arrived, full-dress uniform, medal on, chest puffed out. Looking very pleased with himself, he strode about for a while, getting in the zone to deliver his message. When he was good and ready he moved centre stage, stood firm.

He said nothing.

People were still chatting in some of the seats behind me. He cleared his throat. Then, louder than you'd expect, he bellowed it.

'Right! Quiet now.'

And, as the chit-chatters fell silent, he did it again.

'That's it,' he yelled. 'Enough!'

I could see that medal now. The red, white and light blue ribbon. It was the Queen's Diamond Jubilee Medal from 2012, struck to mark Her Majesty's sixty years on the throne. Not testament to anything he might have done.

There were maybe seventy of us tuning in, all new recruits to Police Scotland, all fresh from passing the entrance tests. Twelve weeks of training lay ahead. I'd come this far, been selected to police the streets. Yet I still wasn't entirely sure how I'd ended up here, dressed in a copper's garb, learning to enforce the laws of the land. Anyway, it was time to listen.

He gave his name, a couple of other details about himself, said he would be going over some general principles about conduct, about the career we were embarking on, about his own experiences, even though he was only in his thirties. I couldn't help thinking he was a bit scruffy looking, that he'd let himself get a bit 'ally', as we called it in Afghanistan.

He took a deep breath, that small chest rising once more, that lone medal dangling and sparkling before us all again, and the spiel began.

'Look at me,' he said, and everyone was already looking at him. 'I am immaculate,' he said.

And my eyebrows went north. Now that's what I would call an opener.

Immaculate, my arse.

I wasn't the only ex-forces there. There were a handful of us dotted among the group. I'm sure they were behind the gentle, sincere chuckles I could hear.

Double creases on one of his trouser legs. If you're going to stand in front of people and tell them something, at least try to make it the truth. If I had to stand up there and say 'I am immaculate' I'd be bloody immaculate. And, if it was in the presence of a few seasoned veterans, I wouldn't be getting overly showy about that medal either. I'm pretty sure they dished out a few hundred thousand. Half the Commonwealth got them. Loads of UK cops and prison staff got them. Twenty quid on eBay would bag you one of those things.

I'd have to adjust my attitude about all this. The poor guy was just doing his job and, at the first opportunity, I was sitting there full of cynicism. He didn't deserve my scorn. He needed a dictionary, but not the scorn.

I made the decision to tune back in, let him say his piece.

Because, for reasons that must have made sense at one point, I was becoming a police officer.

Ten minutes later and I'm troubled once more. Another dubious pronouncement from Mr Immaculate. No police officer, he said, can wear 'any jewellery or adornments' while on duty. And from this day forward, he said, it all had to go.

I was at that very moment, as I am now, wearing a Help for Heroes wristband. It indicates, innocently enough, my support for wounded British military veterans. Back in that briefing hall I was sure Help for Heroes was an acceptable charity for a British veteran and/or police officer to endorse. I'd need to double-check what he meant.

A few minutes later he was mingling among the students and taking questions. So I asked him.

'That is correct,' he told me, loud and clear. 'You must remove it.'

And, as far as he was concerned, that was the end of that.

I wasn't happy. In fact, you could consider me pissed off. A thoughtless, blanket position had been taken on a significant issue. I wasn't the only one who felt that way. I wasn't even the only one wearing a Help for Heroes wristband. Looks were exchanged among veterans.

A few breakout group meetings later and we're back in the briefing hall, back to hear what more Officer Immaculate had to impart. This time he kicked off before most of us had even taken our seats. There was something on his mind.

'I'm informed,' he said, 'that this morning someone gobbed off to one of the café staff.'

Sounded bad.

He went on, 'The member of staff does not have a name for that person, but they said they would recognise him by the distinctive tattoo on the inside of his right forearm.'

Sounded like it was bang to rights for the guilty man.

'They had purchased a coffee,' he said.

Sounded exactly like what I did that morning.

'That person should report to the staff office immediately after this session.'

Wait. That could indeed be me. I had been in the café earlier, buying a coffee, and there is a distinctive tattoo on the inside of my right forearm.

Yet it couldn't be me because I didn't 'gob off' to anybody. I'd need to check this out, eliminate myself from enquiries, so to speak.

An hour later and I was in the intake sergeant's office.

'Sir,' I said, 'just wanted to make myself known as I was in the café this morning and I have a tattoo on the inside of my right forearm. But I think ... '

One tattoo inspection later and there's no doubt – I'm the guy the staff member complained about.

'Sir,' I said, almost tempted to laugh, 'I assure you I didn't gob off to anyone.'

I explained I'd appeared at the open side door of the café after seeing the shutters were down. I'd asked a lady there if the café was open and she'd said no, but that it would be in a few minutes. No problem. I said I'd wait. I milled around for five minutes and, when the shutters went up, walked over, got a coffee, said 'thank you' and went off to the briefing hall.

'No,' the sergeant advised. What I had done was enter the café 'through a locked door'. I had then proceeded to cause the lady there some concern by loitering. As for the 'gobbed off' bit, I was left in the dark. And as for the locked-door breach, I'm pretty sure the open door I walked through wasn't locked.

'Okay,' I said. 'I regret that any of my actions may have given her cause for concern.'

I could only think the woman must be nuts.

'Go back to the café,' the sergeant said, 'and apologise.'

I took a deep breath, told him I would and went on my way.

But what kind of bullshit was this? Entering through a locked door? Loitering with some kind of menace?

'Excuse me,' I said to the lady, as politely and softly as possible in case she misinterpreted my approach as attempted murder. 'Could I speak with you for a minute?'

I told her I'd spoken with the sergeant and he'd asked that I apologise. And then I apologised for any distress I had unknowingly caused. She seemed happy enough with that. Job done, back I went to my lessons on how to be a policeman.

A couple of hours later and I'm advised I need to call on the sergeant once more. This time he was with the inspector. I had a sinking feeling.

They explained they had been in the café since my apology and had spoken with my traumatised victim. They told me of their disappointment that I had told her I had been 'asked to apologise'. My regret at what I had put her through, the sergeant said, should have come only from me. Apparently I should have made it more clear that I wanted to say sorry as a result of searching my own conscience.

By now I'm getting close to losing the plot. Was this a wind-up? Is this the kind of shit that goes on in the civilian world?

The answer to that question is, I suppose, that I didn't really know. I knew the general trend in society had, for years, been moving towards ensuring no one said anything mean, but I'd no idea that intimidation now extended to asking a café employee for a cup of coffee. I'd been expecting to learn things that day but, between the coffee and the wristband, I hadn't expected it to be this.

But it was I who would have to do the adjusting, who would have to try to make sense of everything that was going on in this new world of social media and anti-social people. Truth was, I'd never really been part of civilian society before and was going to have to find my way. I'd been born into a military family, moved from base to base as a child, joined the army aged sixteen and a half, six months after leaving school. Since then, I'd been busy learning how to start things, stop things, fly things, survive things, save things, break things, fight things. I'd been busy in the Balkans, the Persian Gulf, Afghanistan and Northern Ireland. I'd been helping out in Brunei, France, Poland and other places. A lot of it involved war. It even involved my receiving, all in all, eight medals. Proper ones. And if I was ever to have been in the situation where I had been identified by a tattoo, where I was being sought for capture and interrogation, I would never have thought it would have been at a policing college near Fife.

In an Apache your words and actions are recorded. Every decision in terms of flying and fighting the aircraft is available for download, for analysis, for critique and, if appropriate, as evidence for sanction. I had become used to being observed, to operating efficiently, confidently and resolutely enough not even to think about how it might all look on screen in my CO's office. I suppose I might have assumed that, given the rising prevalence of CCTV across the UK, and the endorsement those systems have from law enforcement, that such cameras might be all over the place in a policing college. Anyway, the point is I did not, on the morning in question, feel it was wise to intimidate and/or 'gob off' to a café worker. It didn't happen.

I'll admit I've loitered with intent before, but usually while piloting an attack helicopter. I've loitered in the air while escorting or defending British troops or while seeking out enemy targets and gunning them down or blowing them up.

And I'll admit I've entered through a few locked doors before and that I wasn't always welcome. Indeed, I've torn a few doors and walls open with 30mm cannon rounds. I've certainly shifted some timber, metal and masonry around with Hellfire missiles to secure access to buildings, or just to level them. Truth be told, I've sent the sort of specialist artillery into places which takes out bad guys in ways you don't want to know.

What I'm saying is that when ranking police officers were accusing me of not issuing the right kind of apology for something I did not do, I somehow couldn't find a way to make it feel as important as they thought it was.

What bothered me more was that the same officers who didn't respect my word were telling me I should not be wearing a wristband in support of men and women wounded in our nation's service. That was a weightier matter in my book. When I got thinking about it, I had the feeling they should be the ones apologising to me and the rest of the veterans.

So it was towards the end of that same, stupid day when I began wondering if my policing career would be the shortest in British history.

I knew I had to go and I knew what I had to do.

I needed to fly again.

Chapter Two

'REMAIN OUTSIDE OF SMALL-ARMS RANGE' – NORTHERN IRELAND, 1998

THAT TATTOO ON the inside of my right arm is about four inches long. A single word and a paw print. It says Minty. She had been my second wife's dog when we met. I fell in love with Tracey and I fell in love with Minty. Tracey and I were heartbroken when we had to say goodbye. That dog helped get me through strange times. I'd get back home after a hundred days of war and kind of crash into both. Tracey, as a loving, understanding wife, was incomparably brilliant. Minty, in her own way, was brilliant too. If you've been lucky enough to know the perfect love and loyalty of a great dog, then you'll know what I mean. I lost a good friend when she went. Her name has been on my arm ever since.

I like loyalty. I like that it always feels right, that it's there when it counts and there when it doesn't. I like that it can survive everything, even death. When I say I have loyalty to the British military, I mean it – the living and the dead, the wounded and the lost, the young and the old. If I have a tribe, they're the guys.

Loyalty, respect and admiration for my fellow soldiers is at the core of what makes me tick.

There was a Grenadier Guardsman called Captain Robert Nairac. He was undercover in South Armagh, Northern Ireland, in the seventies. Sizeable parts of South Armagh, if you didn't know, were solid IRA turf. The place was lethal for police and army, deadly for those who stood against the terrorists. It got nicknamed Bandit Country for good reason. Landmines and mortars meant troops moved around by helicopter instead of road. Picture the scene, in among all that, of a lone Englishman, a soldier, having a few drinks in an isolated pub called The Three Steps Inn. That was Robert Nairac, undercover with 14 Intelligence Company. And if ever a man had balls of steel, he was the guy. In a learned Belfast accent, he would tell local people he was called Danny McErlaine. One night in 1977 it all went wrong.

Nairac was abducted from that pub in the village of Dromintee. He was taken over the border by the IRA's notorious South Armagh Brigade, interrogated, tortured and shot dead. One of the men who did that later said Captain Nairac told them nothing. And none of the men who did that have ever had the backbone to say where his remains are.

In 1998 I found myself flying low and fast in a Lynx, nap-of-the-earth, skimming wires and trees, slaloming over the badlands of South Armagh. The advice was to keep down and move quick to avoid attack, to ascend rapidly when the moment came. But, my co-pilot Rory B advised, I was not to ascend until we had buzzed by The Three Steps Inn. We would be making some noise around it, a forthright act of respect for Captain Nairac. It would serve as a reminder to whoever needed to know that we had not forgotten. I was advised on that day it had been a tradition for a while. As someone who likes the idea of standing by your comrades, who likes loyalty, I was happy to do it. And I did it some more too.

This wasn't the first time I'd been to Northern Ireland. My dad was in the Cheshire Regiment, his battalion stationed in Ballykelly, Co. Londonderry, in the early eighties. At the time it seemed like all hell was breaking loose. In December 1982, I was a twelve-year-old pad brat living on base at Shackleton Barracks. A phone call came in to say the nearby Droppin Well pub had been bombed. I remember clearly the phone ringing some more, ringing long into the night as news of the mounting death toll kept coming. Eleven soldiers and six civilians were killed and many more injured in an attack claimed by the Irish National Liberation Army (INLA). All the victims had been at a disco.

I had been enrolled into a largely Protestant school in Limavady, about four miles from Ballykelly. I remember the tall fence that separated it from the Catholic school next door. It wasn't tall enough to stop the stones flying over from either side at breaktime. To the best of my knowledge no one had their skull smashed open in my time there, which is amazing really. All of that was just accepted as part of normal life at the time.

In 1998 a voluntary three-month roulement tour for Northern Ireland came up as part of Operation Banner. I went for it, no hesitation. I was hungry for experience, eager to build flying hours. And I was curious, too, about taking a look at my old stamping ground when in a different kind of uniform. The Good Friday Agreement was up and running. IRA, UVF and UDA ceasefires were in place (the INLA were still getting around to it) and a fractured society was finally on the mend. Yet the peace was fragile. Hardliners on both the republican and loyalist sides were pissed off. From a security point of view, as events that year would prove, this was no time to get complacent. As ever, the army was around in case it all went tits up again.

I was posted to 655 Squadron based at RAF Aldergrove, fifteen miles north-west of Belfast. I'd been around a year or two and knew a few of the characters but, as a fresh-faced pilot newly arrived into the established military culture of Northern

Ireland, I had the strong sense I had to prove myself. I decided I'd do just that. I'd avoid the macho bullshit, build hours and learn what I could.

Duties were assigned by number. So, for example, Lynx 6 would be assigned general tasking, Lynx 10 assigned air testing. Taskings included surveillance, resupply, troop extraction and drop-off. Most would be flown from Aldergrove with the exception of Lynx 5 and Lynx 7 which operated out of Bessbrook Mill down in South Armagh. And, as I would soon find out, Bessbrook was a place with a character all of its own. It was a grey, grim sprawling old fortress with multiple concrete structures and tarmacked surfaces. Its role was not just as a barracks but also as the main supply base for other military outposts in the area. Landing pads there served Lynx, Gazelle and also Puma helicopters on high readiness. When things were at their worst in Northern Ireland, that old converted linen mill hosted arrivals and take-offs every eight minutes, making it one of the busiest heliports in the world. The coordination of all that traffic was seriously impressive.

I learned that Lynx 5 and Lynx 7 were the duties to get, where the real flying took place. Their primary task was to provide overwatch for support helicopters (SH) or other Lynx during landing or departure. Experience had been a great teacher. The IRA had secured themselves arms from Libya's Colonel Gaddafi which included eighteen Soviet 12.7mm DShKs heavy machine guns. One of them had taken down a Lynx in 1988. It was hit by fifteen armour-piercing rounds and had to land hard en route to Bessbrook from the IRA hotspot of Crossmaglen. Twelve men had tried to get to the downed craft to kill all the military on board, but thankfully couldn't find it in time. Although there were no casualties, for the IRA's South Armagh Brigade it was quite a coup. All in all, they had carried out twenty-three attacks on British Army helicopters in South Armagh. It wasn't until the early nineties that Lynx were finally fitted with general-purpose machine guns (GPMG) as both a deterrent and for fighting back. But the IRA weapons were still out there and to that point no ceasefire had been permanent. It was something I'd bear in mind.

So while the politicians and paramilitaries did their thing, the army kept on doing its own work. Military manoeuvres continued, troop drops and extractions were taking place all the time.

After about a week, I was in Bessbrook – nicknamed Battlestar Galactica due to the amount of air traffic. I'd been assigned to Lynx 7 and tasked with providing overhead cover for an SH dropping troops at Romeo 20 – codename for one of the observation posts (OP). Romeo 20 overlooked Drummackavall, south-east of Crossmaglen and just a couple of hundred yards from the South Armagh border with Co. Louth in the Republic. Like many OPs, it had a tall observation tower and was heavily fortified. Multiple cameras watched both the local area and the cars, trucks and people coming into and leaving Northern Ireland.

And Bessbrook certainly was active. The 'thwap' sound of Lynx helicopters seemed constant. They would arrive to get swapped out with one requiring maintenance work, the same crew departing. Or they would arrive for handover from ongoing crew to offgoing crew. As part of all of that, Army Air Corps and RAF crews had accommodation at the heliport building, which was about as basic and cramped as it gets. Rooms that were about the right size for a single man had three double bunks with delightful plastic mattresses. There was a TV room down the hall and across from that was the operations room. All the comms, planning and maps for tasks came from there.

So, ahead of my first trip out of Bessbrook, I attended the standard pre-flight brief. It was led by the very self-important commander of Lynx 5 who clearly liked the idea that although he was only a sergeant, he would be leading a flight of three aircraft. He seemed thrilled that one of them was the Puma crewed by RAF flight lieutenants. You have to laugh...

On take-off, I noticed graffiti on a wall overlooking the mill. Its purpose was to advise that the IRA and its supporters were never far away. Unfortunately, it raised more laughs than worries.

'Snipper at work.'

Pretty sure that was meant to say 'sniper.'

As we were lifting, Rory, my captain in the left seat told me to get more aggressive and pull all available power. I did. It sent us rocketing up to 2,000 feet in no time. I enjoyed it. I wanted to do it again and knew I'd get the chance. A top tip I'd been given on the first briefing came to mind: 'Remain outside of small-arms range.' It needed to be kept in mind going up and coming down. It might not seem obvious, but one well-placed bullet can spark massive damage to a helicopter.

So off out into Bandit Country for the first time as one of three aircraft. From above, it was hard to believe this picturesque land had seen so much bloodshed, yet that same pretty scenery was home to many who would have relished seeing us blasted out of the sky.

Rory launched into a running commentary on what a newly arrived pilot needed to know. He pointed out various hotspots such as Jonesborough, Silverbridge, Forkhill and, most notorious of all, Crossmaglen. He drew my eye to the hedgerows, streams and fields that make up the unclear border between Northern Ireland and the Republic of Ireland. I was glad he was there to keep me right. It would be too easy to fly into the Republic's airspace and spark a diplomatic shitstorm.

At Romeo 20, the Puma commenced its descent. The two Lynx were to orbit overhead, eyes locked on the landing aircraft as it got smaller and smaller. It was vital to hold the orbit, not to take too much angle in the turn and end up being directly above and unable to see the Puma.

A call from the rear gunner, the third crew member who was manning the GPMG at the door. 'Okay,' he said, 'he's running in on finals.'

It meant the Puma was on its final approach, that it would be going low and slow and therefore in maximum danger.

And then, 'Touchdown.'

Good news. But now every second counted. The idea was to get in and out as fast as possible. And, like a Formula One pitstop, that OP burst into life. Running men and materials were moving in all directions in some kind of organised chaos. In a moment, everyone was gone. The Puma's doors closed and it lifted, climbing rapidly on a predefined heading. We were to rejoin and follow back to Bessbrook.

On the approach, we were given the call to enter the Tube, basically the point at which aircraft get in line ahead of landing. On touchdown, there was a message to get to Forkhill Barracks, about ten miles away. We were to collect six personnel, drop off at Golf 40, refuel then on to nearby Romeo 23, collect four, then back to Forkhill and back to base. A little bit of coming and going in the danger zone. I was up for it, ever keen to fly some of the more interesting profiles when possible.

Lynx 5 would lead and, once at Forkhill, would remain overhead while we completed pickup and drop-offs. This time I was going for that aggressive ascent. A fast climb means building acceleration when low, effectively revving the engine before engaging the gear. I sent that Lynx roaring skywards pulling an armful of collective lever until reaching maximum power available. In fact, in the last second, I felt it was too fast, going too high. Some kind of minor panic took hold. Had I pushed this too much?

Rory turned to me.

'Better,' he said, although still not overly impressed.

Minutes later and we were approaching Forkhill.

'Okay, descend,' he said. Chuffed with my ascent, despite Rory's poker face, I was going to give this one very skilled descent. I pushed the cyclic forward, throwing the aircraft into a steep dive. At the same time, to confuse any hostile armed observers,

15

I rolled on a high angle of bank, first to the right then to the left. I banked hard left again, then right, sped up, slowed down. Still no reaction from Rory. What did I have to do to impress him? As far as I was concerned, to enemy eyes this Lynx was unpredictable, fast, uncatchable.

The location was certainly dodgy. The small town of Forkhill sat at the base of two mountains, Croslieve to the north and Tievecrom to the south-east. Ambitious terrorists could have found themselves a cosy spot to wait for an aircraft just like ours to enter a channel that reduced operating space. To my mind, however, any observer must have recognised that I was on top of my game.

By now, below the mountain tops, I was having to get slow and low ahead of landing. But I wanted to be slow and low for as little time as possible.

The rear door slid open, the wind bellowing in. The gunner had that GPMG ready to rock if required. Ahead were the drab high walls of the barracks... but they really were a fair distance ahead. I'd dropped too far too early and was going to be low and slow for way too long. Those fancy aerobatics of mine weren't much use if they meant I was just going to crawl along in the crosshairs of some armour-piercing monster.

'Shit,' I said.

Not another word was spoken as we trundled between the hills.

Like a guilty dog, the Lynx slowly skulked over the perimeter wall and dropped down.

'Well hello, Miss Daisy,' was all I heard from the back.

A fair point.

Troops bounced in, strapped on to the inner six-man seat, rifles pointed at the floor. It took seconds. Rory was already running through departure checks and made the call to Lynx 5 above. Now to rocket up out of there. I was really going to go for it, really going to learn to give these set pieces some welly. I thought it went well.

A little later, after that first Three Step Inn flyover, Rory took control. He said he wanted to show me what he meant by 'rapid'. I had a feeling this was going to be interesting. A minute later and I had a feeling I was about to throw up. Luckily enough, I hadn't eaten. There had been no warning. The Lynx went almost vertical. I shot upwards, grabbed the handrail above for security.

'Christ!' I gasped.

It was like the aircraft was in freefall, plummeting towards little Golf 40. And then, in a flash, we were recovering the descent, establishing our final approach. We'd dropped twice as fast as what I thought was fast. Now I'd got it. Fast meant something different when the right skills were in play, when there was a full understanding of the aircraft's capabilities. The lesson: be bold, push that thing to its limits, move faster than everyone else is thinking, be hard as hell to hit.

Further into my tour I was tasked to fly alongside Dave K, a seasoned pilot and old hand in terms of Northern Ireland's geographical and human terrain. I'd heard of him before, mostly about his scalding sense of humour, but also about his skill. I couldn't wait to get on board.

The job was to conduct dummy or fake drops in various fields around Jonesborough. The goal was to confuse anyone interested in army movements, get them wondering if we did or did not set down troops. Once we were pretty sure we'd made a mess of any plans, we were to collect four passengers from Crossmaglen and get back to Bessbrook.

The drops were among many tactics in the constant cat-and-mouse game between the army and the IRA. Typically, they took place on dead ground, a good distance from any habitation, to keep risk to life as low as possible. But the ground hadn't always been well-staked out in advance. I know, because when I landed in what I thought was an open field in the middle of nowhere, it turned out to be grassland at the back of a pub. I'd no clue until I looked left and noticed a huge bar behind the tree line. And it wasn't far away either, probably about three hundred metres. Within seconds, like a dam bursting, the clientele came piling out to witness the Brits landing beside their local. Up went a dozen or more middle fingers while pint glasses and whatever else came to hand were pelted our way. I'd been a bit startled at first, but when one of the three of us started laughing, all of us did. And what a waste of good beer. That said, rapid ascent required.

It wasn't long after that when I was due to land at Crossmaglen Barracks, right in the centre of the most hostile little town of them all. Five years earlier in what was called the Battle of Newry Road, the IRA attempted to ambush three helicopters lifting off from there. It kicked off a massive twenty-minute firefight. No troops were wounded or killed and the army took a decent weapons haul, including a heavy machine-gun (12.7mm DShK or 'Dushka'), two GPMGs and plenty of ammo. Shortly after the ambush, Shaun Wyatt, one of the Lynx commanders, was awarded the Distinguished Flying Cross (DFC). Years later I would have the pleasure of being taught by Shaun on my Apache course.

Dave was alongside me as I approached. By this stage I was confident (again) that my rapid climbs and drops were doing the job. Although it was a bit off-putting to have my sarcastic co-pilot always staring at me, a smile on his face, when I was giving it some rapid. So I ignored him, shuffled the aircraft around in the sky, adjusted turns and angles of bank. The final path was over a sports pitch before descent behind base walls. If there was a potshot coming, this was the time. If so, I was ready to abort and accelerate away. But it didn't happen. We arrived on the helicopter landing site (HLS) in one piece. Even so, we couldn't let our guard drop. Given the location, it was a no-brainer that the IRA were close by. And it was no secret that their improvised mortars, fired from trailers or inside vans, had been doing some serious damage. Four years earlier they'd fired one into Crossmaglen Barracks, striking a landing Lynx. It hit the rear, chopped off the back end of the tail and forced a crash landing. Three were injured and an RUC (Royal Ulster Constabulary) officer had to be rescued after being trapped inside while the whole thing went up in flames.

So a quick stop on the HLS. We collected four and a search dog and I was braced to go up. Yet Dave's stare had by now become intense.

'Come on,' I said, turning to him, seconds ticking by. 'Out with it.'

'Nothing,' he said. And then, 'I have control.'

He'd taken over.

We lifted, the rear gunner swivelled the GPMG back in, closed the door and... whoosh. We bungee bounced upwards. The G-force was something else, burying me into my seat. It felt like everything inside my body was going to go outside. Heaven help anyone with piles. Even for Dave, this was really going for it.

At the required height, he launched into what's known as a 'bunt'. He shoved the cyclic forward, tilting us downwards fast, drawing a half circle in the sky. From positive G, we were now in negative G. From feeling heavy to weightless.

Was this what he called taking control?

'Look in the back,' he said.

I turned. The dog was literally floating three feet off the deck. It was about as baffled as a dog can be. It seemed to just sit there, in thin air, before coming down to land. Apparently, the handler had a fair idea what was about to happen but hadn't been able to get the dog fully secured in time. All four in the back were left on the verge of throwing up. It occurred to me that the AAC in Northern Ireland was not exactly going out of its way to provide a high-class service for passengers.

A later outing was with a man called Dave G, tasked to fly over Portadown and video a contentious Orange Order parade. These take place right through the summer in Northern Ireland, mostly band parades by mainly Protestant pro-UK unionists, which mainly

Catholic pro-Irish unity nationalists aren't mad about. There's so many parades that they call the summer the Marching Season. Demographic shifts mean that some traditional routes have become largely Catholic areas, so marches there are especially unwelcome. There was no finer example of this than the Drumcree parade along the nationalist Garvaghy Road in Portadown, in the north of Co. Armagh. There had been angry stand-offs and violence in recent years. We were expecting a busy day.

I established the hover and Dave tweaked the camera filters to get the clearest picture of scenes below. We were to track the parade until it cleared a particular point before returning to Bessbrook. Fifteen minutes in and there was an unusual rumbling feeling in the back of my seat. I put it down to wind conditions given we were pretty high. Five minutes later and the vibrations were getting worse. Then Dave said he was having a problem keeping the camera in position even though it was stabilised.

Something didn't make sense. We looked at each other. Dave checked temperatures and pressures. All seemed normal.

'Mate,' I said, 'that vibration is getting worse.'

He stowed the camera and called off the job.

'Could be an issue with the gearbox.'

'Shit.'

I turned towards Aldergrove, just fifteen minutes away. I stayed slow, kept the power minimal while Dave's eyes stayed fixed on the instruments. Still no information. But the vibration wasn't getting any better.

Do we ditch in a field? We talked it over quickly. Anywhere in mainland UK and that would be an easy decision, but not here. Yet we would if we had to. A forced landing and potential danger on the ground were better than a crash.

After what seemed like an eternity, I could see the outline of the airport. Dave let air traffic know we were inbound with an emergency issue. And then the gearbox temperature gauge began to rise. I dropped to 500 feet knowing that from there I could get the aircraft on the ground in seconds if necessary. Then a warning light. The gearbox temperature was soaring. The boundary line for the airport couldn't come quickly enough. I dropped into a slow dive, reducing the power further. At thirty feet I slowed some more and, without pausing, at about twenty knots, completed a run-on landing on grass as the skids dug in. An abrupt stop and we shut her down. By the time we opened the doors the emergency services were there.

It turned out that one of the planetary gearing teeth had started to fracture. We were lucky it hadn't disintegrated. The engineers reckoned we were ten minutes from disaster.

There were just a few days left of my tour. For my last duty I was put on standby because, as peace was bedding down, we were starting to see a reduction in tasks. Troop withdrawals were being discussed in high places, a quid pro quo for the IRA as its ceasefire was holding. Yet while the terrorist groups of the past might be taking a step backwards, intelligence was indicating new groups were seeking to step forwards. The most influential voices were talking peace, but there were those who wanted to keep on killing.

It was Saturday, 15 August 1998, and I was taking it easy. At about 3.30 p.m. I was called to the operations room and was told there had been a massive car bomb somewhere near Omagh. I raced over. More details by the time I arrived. A blast in the town centre. Multiple casualties. Several aircraft were being put on standby. They'd be needed to gather video evidence, to insert specialist police and bomb-disposal troops. It was the worst news.

The decrease in violence in Northern Ireland had been slow but sure. The power-sharing government envisaged by the Good Friday Agreement was coming to life and the IRA, via its political wing Sinn Féin, was still on board. A full and final peace, after three decades of brutal violence in Northern Ireland, really did seem possible. The Troubles had taken the lives of too many good soldiers, police officers and ordinary decent people – yet here it was again. It seemed to confirm that those dissident figures who didn't like the idea of peace still had access to the tools of war.

I was tasked with flying to Co. Tyrone that afternoon, to position directly overhead and gather video. It looked to me like a hole had been punched right in the heart of this ordinary, mid-sized town. Market Street had been torn up. There was debris everywhere, like the place was a rubbish tip. The bomb had flung masonry, wood, metal and glass everywhere. Worst of all, it had thrown people too. Cables were hanging down, water from busted pipes was gushing along the street, buildings and cars were smouldering. By the time I had arrived, the initial, gruesome clear-up had begun. Yet, from my bird's eye view of the carnage, police, medics, firefighters and soldiers were still working hard to make better what they could.

As a pilot, I've been able to do a lot of things, to make a difference, to change matters for better or for worse for people on the ground. I've been able to support others, to lead others, to warn people, to bring them to safety. But on that day I was unable to do anything but watch. In all, 29 people were killed and some 220 were injured. It was the bloodiest single incident of the Troubles, right at the moment when most thought the Troubles were coming to a close. Most of the IRA had moved on from the violence, but those few stragglers had stayed behind. They called themselves the Real IRA and, three days later, they admitted responsibility.

Tour over and it was back to Wattisham, the Suffolk home of 3 and 4 Regiment Army Air Corps. Straight back to flying in the local area, and to exercises on Salisbury Plain. At one point there was a flight to Duxford where we took a small number of ground crew out to the museum, and it turned out to be the best day in a while. Yet everything began to start feeling a little stagnant. When the opportunity came up for another tour in Northern Ireland, I couldn't get signed up fast enough.

Peace was still holding in 1999, despite the Omagh outrage. While I knew there was a dissident threat, I also knew it was limited and that the security services had a good grip of the situation. In fact, some of the paramilitary attention had turned inwards, towards what was known in those circles as housekeeping, where old scores were being settled. And there was the odd skirmish among factions, a bit of territorial muscle-flexing, the odd riot. Such relatively small internecine matters weren't making it into the national press given the big story was still in play, but they did suggest that the peace might not be as secure as was being claimed.

I'll be honest. There was no question in my mind as to what I was doing back there. Simply put, I wanted some more rapid ascents, some more rapid descents, some more throwing the aircraft around to avoid small-arms fire.

I was above Portadown on a video task when I was called to head to Newry. There had been a murder at the Barcroft Park Estate. Ten minutes later and we were approaching from the north with my eyes peeled for blue lights to help guide me to the right location. My co-pilot Phil was interrogating the map and I established an orbit in the overhead. Then we were given another location, Doran's Hill Road, a rural area just west of the city. It took a while before we spotted what looked like police cars and some tape around a crime scene. It wasn't until two days later that I learned the victim was called Eamon Collins. I knew the name. He had been in the IRA in the seventies and eighties before turning his back on it and co-authoring a memoir called *Killing Rage*. I'd read it soon after its publication in 1997. His murder, which may never be solved, had been pretty grim. It's thought he may have been knocked down on purpose before being beaten and stabbed. Ceasefire or not, it's hard to escape the idea that those behind it had, at the very least, IRA sympathies.

The rapid descents and climbs continued, as did the odd low overflight close to The Three Steps Inn. Also on my itinerary was, in the best of AAC traditions, a new habit of adding a little turbulence to flights after pickups. I enjoyed the possibilities, enjoyed explaining to shaken passengers that it was down to the rising heat from exhaust fumes from cars below and relished the confused looks.

Just as that second tour was ending, another murder. This time by loyalists in the Co. Armagh town of Lurgan. As we flew over it was obvious what had happened. An under-car IED. The roof and doors had been blown off a silver BMW. Her name was Rosemary Nelson, a prominent solicitor with IRA and anti-Drumcree parade clients. A group calling itself the Red Hand Defenders claimed responsibility.

As I left the province for the last time in uniform, I figured I'd learned a little about peace, learned that official peace and true peacefulness are not always the same thing.I could have had no idea how much I was soon to learn about war.

Chapter Three

'YOU'RE IN THE ARMY NOW.' UK AND GERMANY, 1980s/1990s

I COULDN'T WAIT TO join the army. I walked into the recruitment office and signed up on the day I left school. I was sixteen. There was no doubt in my mind. The military was the job for me.

My youth had been spent on bases. As any pad brat knows, you lose count of the number of times you change address and you make and lose friends at a rate unknown to most kids. Every couple of years it was time to pack up and move on once again. Another school to attend, another uniform to wear, new teachers to meet, new rules to learn, new accents to navigate. I suppose the army felt like home to me no matter where I was, the constant factor among all the moving around. What would I have done if I hadn't joined the army? I have no idea.

My parents had a Scouse twang to their speech but by the time I was secondary school age, mine was more of a mish-mash. I suppose it was a combination of so many influences that it became something of a neutral English accent. Neutral might have been considered useful in terms of being understood everywhere, but that wasn't how it worked when I lived for a while in the Midlands. I was the new boy with the funny voice and, as is the way of these things, the school bully turned his attention on me. I was thirteen and not exactly brimming with confidence when he picked up on the way I spoke. Within a few weeks his piss-taking took off and others began enjoying his routines. It wasn't physical bullying, but more a form of mental abuse that went on for a few days, then a few weeks, then months. The threat of violence was attached to it all. I had a grim dread that at any moment I was about to be hurt by this fella to the point that the fear became worse than the thing itself. I didn't tell anyone and I know now that was a mistake. I was sure I could deal with it myself, that it would fade away soon enough anyway. But I was wrong. He was in my class, not just my school, and he showed no sign of moving on. It only ever got worse.

I suffered with it for about a year before I snapped. I don't really know what happened. There had been no plan in place. But, after a long morning of taunting, red mist descended fast from nowhere. I exploded with rage, reached for him, shoved him across the desk and dived on top of him. Whatever had possessed me wasn't letting go. I started belting him in the face, punching as hard as I could – four, five, six or more times. And, as is often the way with bullies, he didn't have the guts to fight back. Or at least he didn't have the chance before the teacher dived in and separated us. Off I was marched to the headmaster's office for a reprimand. But I didn't care one bit. Something had changed somewhere inside me and I welcomed it. I held my head high after that. No one would bully me again.

When I walked into that recruitment office at sixteen, my heart was set on driving a tank. Part of that was probably because I liked the idea of packing a punch and heading straight towards the enemy. I remember having been spellbound while watching these mighty war vehicles manoeuvre around on a TV special. The comedian Jim

Davidson, who had his own show in the early eighties, had been out to visit 2 Royal Tank Regiment in Germany. They had just received the new Challenger tank and it was something to behold.

But it wasn't as if anyone was just going to hand me the keys. In fact, given my age, I couldn't technically even join the real British Army. Instead I was recruited into what was known as the Junior Leaders – training units for those under eighteen. It was going to be great in that I'd get trained and paid and, after a year, I'd be more than ready to be part of the Royal Armoured Corps (RAC). Except, they advised me, my start date was six months away.

So off I went into the civilian world to get a job. I was hired for some office work, to input financial data into a computer all day long. It doesn't sound thrilling but I can assure you it was more than thrilling. I was horny as a badger at that age and now suddenly surrounded by some plain-speaking mature women. I can't say I always keyed the right numbers into that computer, but I can say for sure I was never late for work. I knew I'd miss them all when my time was up and there was a lump in my throat when I said so on my last day. Weirdly enough, the office radio played 'You're in the Army Now' by Status Quo as I was getting ready to leave.

I and the other sprogs arrived at the RAC's Bovington Camp in Dorset in January 1987. We were lined up, a roll was taken, our kit was issued and we were shown to the eight-man rooms. And all that day I had a smile on my face. This was the place for me.

The troop – the armoured corps equivalent of an infantry platoon – would be tasked with a host of duties alongside training. One was to assist at the Farnborough Airshow, a major annual civilian and military aircraft exhibition in Hampshire, held each July. Booked to appear were the Blue Eagles, the Army Air Corps' display team. And as with the Challenger tank, I was mesmerised by their manoeuvres, yet this was more impressive given it was taking place in the sky. Those helicopters being thrown around like toys were ripping up the physics book. The crowd was yelling with excitement as the aircraft shot past and sailed up into the heavens.

I had to know more.

During a quiet moment, I made my way to the AAC's static display stand and approached one of the guys wearing a light-blue beret. After about twenty minutes of my questions and his answers, I came away with a whole new life plan. I had been told I was just the sort of lad they were looking for and, what's more, if I played it right I could be flying within a matter of weeks. I'd been so impressed by him personally and so taken by what he'd been saying that I didn't for a second assume he was talking shite, although it turned out he was. Nevertheless, I had never wanted to drive a tank as much as I now wanted to fly. When I got back to Bovington I sat down with the AAC major and stated my case. He agreed. The details of my recruitment were changed. My new plan was confirmed. On finishing up as a Junior Leader, I would enter the AAC. The initial idea was to serve three years. I ended up doing twenty-seven.

As for the year as a Junior Leader, I loved it. But that entry process is a thing of the past now. Back then we had Change Parades where, with a barked order, you had to run to your gleaming locker, radically restyle yourself and return for parade. Maybe you'd come back wearing a single boot, trousers and a helmet, maybe a sock, your pants and a jacket. The odder it was, the better. We had Mess Tin Order. where you had to run to that same locker and return wearing nothing but two strategically placed metal mess tins and a belt – and then march around on parade. It was bloody hilarious. We had to fold punishingly itchy blankets to make bed blocks, had to conduct torturous physical training in issue boots, got yelled at like prisoners and never even thought of complaining about it.

They pulled the plug on the Junior Leaders programme in the nineties. Along with it went much of what it was that made that year so effective for so many in terms of learning discipline, boosting self-confidence and team bonding. These days it's en suite rooms with quilts and no one shouts at anyone. Is that progress? Well, if every army on earth promises not to be mean in all future conflicts, everything will be just lovely.

Before my first posting as an AAC soldier could be confirmed, I had three things to do: Ground Crew Course, Signal Course, and I had to learn to drive. The latter turned out to be trickiest. The last car I'd driven was my dad's and that didn't end well. It had been parked in the garage and one day when he was out I decided to fire it up while in gear and shunted the thing into the wall, pranging a light and the number plate. I'd a lot to learn. And all the army had for me to learn in was a military truck. They would allow me three goes at passing the test.

First attempt saw me mounting a kerb and taking out a bin. Fail. I braked hard for no good reason the second time round. The instructor shot forward and whacked his face on the windscreen. I had, I would learn, broken his nose. Fail. So it all hinged on attempt number three. Make a bollocks of this one and I'd be looking at a career as an admin. clerk in some logistical regiment. It didn't actually go swimmingly but luckily the testing officer had bad eyesight and was partly deaf. He gave me the all-clear. I think they just wanted rid of me. I did wonder whether, having seen my driving, they ever discussed what chance I had of safely flying an aircraft.

Newly through the doors, we were given the option of being posted to Hong Kong, Canada or Germany. The word was that you could ask all you liked but basically you would be posted wherever the AAC wanted you. I asked for Hong Kong as a first preference, then Canada and, if that failed, I'd take Germany. So, Germany it was.

I was no stranger to Germany having already spent many years as both a pad brat and and spending time with my German aunt, who would insist on force-feeding me marzipan. Back in the late eighties most of the British Army was stationed in Germany. The AAC itself had a heavy presence with regiments and aircraft scattered among bases. I was posted to Detmold in the north, suddenly finding myself thrown into a culture of strong beer, currywurst and Asbach brandy at the tender age of seventeen. In fact, it was on my second night there that a few in the squadron dragged me along with them for a night out. We were, they said, going to the gyros centre. I had some German and knew what they were talking about. A gyros, pronounced 'gear ross', is basically a sort of kebab. I was a hungry lad and looking forward to it.

So with my belly rumbling, I found myself in a part of town where there were plenty of red lamps leading into a courtyard. There wasn't a gyros in sight. Instead there were scantily clad women in windows giving me the eye. I was pretty sure this was the red-light district, but had to check because I really was starving.

I looked around, then asked, 'Is this where the food is?'

After the others had stopped laughing, they explained the mix-up.

'Not gyros centre,' I was told, 'the eros centre.'

Germany really was an eye-opener for me. If we weren't in The Blue Beret Bar getting bladdered, we were on exercise. If we weren't being roared at, it was us doing the roaring. And it was certainly an education in the unexpected.

By way of example, I remember the day one of the corporals bellowed down the corridor, ordering us out. We all stood to attention at our doors wondering what the hell had happened. He ordered us all to one of the toilets where someone had dropped off a turd the size of a cat. Obviously they hadn't flushed it away. Imagine our horror as, one by one, we all passed by to inspect this enormous thing, the accusatory looks being fired between us. It was, in fairness, bloody impressive. There were a few surprised gasps and meaningful nods from the troops. But that wasn't the point.

Who created this bloody monster and never got rid of it?

The corporal sternly checked that we'd all had a good look before proudly announcing, 'I did that.'

The sense of relief mixed with admiration made me feel like applauding.

The daily routine was nothing to write home about. Much of it was guard duty on the camp's main gate, often doing the graveyard shift. A lot of it was exercises, typically sitting in the comms tent listening to a radio set. After a while it became monotonous. The idea that I'd be flying helicopters within a few weeks had never seemed more ridiculous. In the early days, as with every sprog, I wasn't even able to apply to become aircrew. I would need to crack on, serve my time as ground crew and work my way up. Literally.

So, while keeping my eyes open for ways to get ahead, I got on with earning my £12 a day (after tax) and, after a few months bought myself a quartz gold Ford Fiesta 1.3 Ghia. And, boy, did I love that car. Every weekend I'd be driving all over town, and on occasion even taking it on the autobahn into Belgium and on to the UK. It was a right-hand drive car so wasn't ideal when it came to overtaking on the Continent, but I was by now on a mission to become master of every machine that I could get my hands on ahead of flying.

By the way, the last filling station before leaving Germany, and the last place where we could stop off to use the army's discount fuel coupons, was in a village called Wankum. It may have one of the most photographed signs in the world.

My big chance to fly came during a pilot-selection opportunity in October 1990. I'd been ground crew for over two years by that stage and had been promoted to lance corporal quite quickly. Typically, the minimum pilot rank to begin application is lance corporal (recommended corporal) and corporal to start the course. I was a distance from that, but I couldn't resist giving it a go. As ground crew, I'd been refuelling, missile rearming and generally getting to know the various aircraft. I'd been enjoying it to a point, but frustration was starting to kick in. Being so close to these things was thrilling and not being allowed to do anything more than service them was torture. I was bursting to get going.

I had no idea if I knew enough to pass the test, nor whether they would even consider me given that I'd had no word on being recommended for promotion to corporal. I asked around and got some idea of what the selection tests involved, but good insight was scarce. My most notable academic talent was maths, but I wasn't exactly expecting them to have much interest in my long-division skills. It was a case of having the confidence to go for it, to get thrown in at the deep end and see if you can swim. The stories were almost scary. There was talk of one guy who had a civilian flying licence when he joined up yet found himself failing. And I was the guy who had failed my driving test twice.

What I had on my side was that fast promotion and an increasingly raw hunger to learn more, to do more. What was against me, among other things, was that I was a few years from becoming corporal.

I brought all my thoughts to my squadron boss.

'Apply,' he said.

'Really?'

'Yes,' he said. He reminded me that the selection process is long, that the course itself takes years. He said, with all that taken into account, the timing was good. He didn't have to tell me again.

It is worth knowing that the non-commissioned officer route to becoming a pilot was, and remains, unique to the army. The Royal Marines did have a similar system in place back then but they ditched it in favour of commissioned officer pilots only. That officer-only route puts a major obstacle in front of very many ordinary young men and women, like myself, who want to fly. But the army's NCO route is a way through. It provides an opportunity for the many who never did have, for example, private schooling and perhaps a degree in Classics from Oxford. In the AAC, it doesn't matter whether you did not spend your years in education wearing a top hat and sticking Meccano up your arse (or whatever goes on), because those who win through are those who have the dream and drive.

But the pilot's course was still a long way off. I had yet to get through the selection process. If I passed that, I'd have to tackle the flying grading phase. And it was only then that the end, or maybe the beginning, would come into view.

The initial stage of pilot selection came during a day at RAF Biggin Hill, best known for its role during the Battle of Britain. It had been one of the principal fighter bases protecting London and South-East England from attack by Luftwaffe bombers. Once there I was told I'd be sitting a series of tests that would judge my basic ability. One involved watching a succession of dots as they appeared at the top of a screen and began moving downwards. Every so often I was told to select a particular coloured dot. As time ticked along, the dots gathered speed and the colours changed faster. Another test saw me having to take stock of various aircraft instruments that popped up and then vanished from the screen. Another involved remotely manoeuvring a ball bearing to the centre of a glass-topped disc with the help of a rudimentary cyclic system. A multiple-choice question would follow each. What had been the aircraft's direction? What was its bank angle, speed or engine temperature? It went on for hours. When I was finally let go, I'd no idea how well or badly I'd done.

I went back to the waiting room. A handful of other guys were there, all of us having been through the same thing. None of us spoke.

A man appeared.

'Jones?'

'Sir.'

I followed him to an office. The door closed.

A clerk behind a desk looked up.

'You've passed,' he said. 'Just.'

Well, 'just' was good enough for me. I was chuffed to bits. However, I had only passed Phase One. Just.

Next up was a medical like nothing I'd known before. Everything was prodded and tested. After that, I was asked to hyperventilate, which wasn't something I'd ever done while sober. But my lungs worked, my heart was beating, I wasn't colour blind and didn't have TB or rabies. So things were looking good. I passed.

Next up, Phase Three – the interview.

By now I'd secured as much guidance as I could get and had swotted up on everything I could, but I still felt I was going into this thing blind. At least I knew I would ace the inevitable 'Why do you want to be a pilot?' question, and was fighting fit for the 'Where do you see yourself in five years?' inquiry.

Ready to give a good account of myself, I took my seat.

Nothing was said. An interviewing officer picked up a file labelled 'Disciplinary File.'

Bollocks, I thought.

I did not have a clean slate. There had been several reprimands and, although relatively minor, I probably had more than most. What would they think of, for example, me running a Land Rover into the back of a car at a junction? In my defence, that car had stopped suddenly. What about the fighting in the NAAFI bar? In mitigation, he was a knob. And insubordination to the Military Police? In fairness, they are knobs.

I fantasised for a moment that the selection board might congratulate me for the latter transgression, but no. Stern faces all round. We did not get into a merry chat about the NCO route or my groundcrew skills. Instead they said to come back in a year. My application was being deferred. In that year I must not add to the entries in the Disciplinary File.

And that was it. At least it wasn't a 'no' at Phase Three.

I'd be back in front of them in November 1990. I was damn sure I'd be giving them no reason to turn me down again.

The months ticked by and my nose was being kept as clean as a whistle. Indeed, if you had punched my clean nose I would not even have punched back. I spent every day with my mind on the goal, every day knowing that I was one day closer to getting back in that room.

In August, with three months to go, Iraq invaded and occupied Kuwait. It wasn't long before the USA, UK and allies were getting ready to unleash the dogs of war and get rid of Saddam Hussein, the Iraqi leader, once and for all. As a dictator ranted and world leaders posed around, as armies steeled themselves for 'Desert Storm', I cursed them all from my barracks bunk.

Pilot selection had been put on hold.

Chapter Four

THE BASRA ROAD, PERSIAN GULF 1990-1

AN ENORMOUS MILITARY build-up got under way in the Persian Gulf. Pretty soon it was clear that my squadron, 669, would become part of it. We were put on alert, told to prepare to deploy to Saudi Arabia. If the standoff continued, we'd go from there to Kuwait. And if we did go, we were told, they would bring in another squadron from another regiment. In the meantime, our squadron's personnel would be spread between other squadrons to bolster numbers.

And then it got real. In December 1990, for the first time in my life, I boarded an aircraft to fly towards an imminent war. Yet, while the posturing on TV screens became a nightly event around the globe, not a lot happened in my own little world. We were stationed at an old holiday complex, basically a mass of prefab single-storey three-bedroom houses in what felt like the far end of nowhere. I spent Christmas on an uninhabited beach looking at palm trees and daydreaming of flying and beer. Each day we prepared for the worst, checked our kit was in order and checked the respirators in case of gas attack. We were constantly ready to leap into one of the large deep dugouts in front of each property should a Scud missile came our way. Unfortunately, and importantly, none of them had a roof covering. So part of our duties involved rounding up bits of tree, old bed posts or biscuit-tin lids, whatever we could get to finish our shelter. In the end they weren't even waterproof, let alone bombproof.

By mid-January, everyone was bored.

Shock came when a Gazelle, on a skill-enhancing route recce patrol, crashed with injuries to the two men on board. Mirth followed when investigators developed recovered camera film showing Sooty and Sweep puppets on the crew members' hands. They had been flying low, holding them out of the cockpit window, waving at the traffic, darting between vehicles. The show ended when a wingover manoeuvre – a 180-degree turn via steep climb and drop – went tits up. The main rotor ended up stuck in the ground. Neither flew again.

On the 16th, word came that last-ditch talks with the Iraqis had failed. The air war would begin within hours. All of us checked our kit again, double-checked our shelters, got ready for whatever might happen. And, as war was launched via 'shock and awe', we waited.

It was a few days before we heard the first Scud alarm. Like a well-oiled machine, we dived into the dugouts and pulled on our suits and respirators. Up to that point we had only ever worn this kit for maybe an hour at most. But on that day we ended up sitting in those holes with the ramshackle lids for thirteen hours. In all that time we were in something equivalent to a child's den and, while such a thing cannot be breached by the bad guys in a child's mind, it certainly could in real-life war. We were vulnerable and helpless and, for a lot of the time, were scared shitless. And we had to wear those bloody respirators until the decision was taken to stand down.

With war under way, our duties changed. As ground crew we

were assigned to either the motor transport or signals sections. My job was signals. Our team had to maintain communications between ground-to-ground or ground-to-air assets. Specifically, in line with some of my training, I was tasked with driving one of the Sultan command-and-control tracked vehicles. These were invaluable in terms of supporting command posts at squadron locations or, if needed, serving as rebroadcast stations further out. It was like being the tank driver I had once wanted to be. Along with my commander Tim, this machine became our home for two months.

And now I was starting to enjoy myself. The comfort was limited, as were the grub and entertainment. And washing my bits while standing in a bowl of water wasn't great. But I relished operating as a small team engaged in what was important work. That said, the envy I felt as I looked skywards at pilots soaring up in search of Saddam's forces never dwindled.

The land war came and went fast. Most of us saw no action. The closest I came was when we examined bombed-out or abandoned Iraqi tanks and vehicles scattered around the place. I remember entering one T-55 tank, the smell of cheap aftershave heavy in the air as if some guys had just left for a night out. On the floor lay various personal possessions, including a bag containing a complete football strip and I wondered when its owner had last worn it, when he had hoped to wear it again. Those men had lived for a while in a tank, too. Who knows what became of them. It may well have been the last home they knew.

As things came to a close, a flight was scheduled to look over the six-lane main Kuwait–Iraq road, officially known as Highway 80 but better known as the 'Highway of Death'. US, UK, French and Canadian forces had bombarded it, blasting retreating Iraqi personnel from the air and ground. Close to 2,000 vehicles had been destroyed and unknown numbers died in one of the last acts of the war.

I asked if I could tag along and within hours was one of six passengers flying low in a Lynx over seemingly endless rolling sands. It was a vista I'd seen before only in movies. A dark patch, like some bleak stain on the tan landscape, appeared in the distance. The pilot slowed as we closed in. The rear doors were opened to give us an unrestricted view of the complete carnage below. Every eye was looking at miles of utter devastation stretching beyond the horizon. Burned-out cars, vans and military vehicles on their sides, some upside down, some in pieces, scattered like rubbish on this long, blackened junkyard of death. It was clear that fleeing Iraqi soldiers had grabbed anything on wheels they could get. I remember the oddity of a yellow American school bus in the midst of it all and reflecting on what story it could tell.

In September 1992, still waiting for the second shot at that Phase Three interview, I was sent off to British Army Training Unit Suffield (BATUS) in Alberta, Canada. This sprawling beauty of a place is seven times the size of Salisbury Plain Training Area and one fifth the size of Northern Ireland. It offers the British Army the ability to conduct the kind of exercises no UK base could accommodate.

Many of us had heard the stories about the freezing temperatures, the infamous Sin Bin Bar and the vast prairie where many hardy souls before us had been tested beyond their limits. I couldn't wait to get stuck in.

We were about forty to a room, grabbing beds close to each other as our little aircrew/ground crew clique formed among many other little cliques. Each day the aircrew disappeared to their briefing rooms and aircraft and the rest of us, the ground crew, collected our vehicles from the transport yard. My job was to support aircrew communications and refuel aircraft when needed.

The winter exercise, which was Number Seven in the BATUS calendar year, is colloquially known as Med Man 7. Temperatures on the prairie often dip below minus 20°C and we weren't many days into training before we learned exactly how that feels. I was lucky in that the signals section had a two-man tent and an always-on burner, but I was still sleeping in almost all the clothes in my bergen, including hat and gloves. One week in and the exercise was down by a third of its personnel. Two weeks in and only one third of those who started were still there. We were hearing of tank crews getting their hands frozen on to hatches they'd tried to open, of troops having to piss on them to get free. There was plenty to joke about, but no one was laughing.

At one stage we were told our ground-crew section was to be attached to an infantry company which was conducting a live-fire exercise. We grabbed our standard-issue self-loading rifles (SLRs) and made our way to the company in question. As lance corporal and therefore the senior in our group, I approached the first soldier I saw who didn't look as though he was in the process of dying from hypothermia

I told him who we were. He said, 'You're what? Who? I've no idea what you are on about. Sorry.'

No one had a clue who we were or what we were doing there. The lack of knowledge and short tempers continued to prevail. But after a while it was decided we could stay for the day. A problem emerged in that infantry units had converted to the new SA80 rifles while we were standing around with those SLRs. One important difference is that the SLR uses 7.62mm ammunition and the SA80 takes 5.56mm. More frayed tempers as everyone had to try and round up some 7.62.

In time, rounds were found and off we went on a jolly live-fire and manoeuvre package that involved trenches and doorways. I'd never done that before and it was, frankly, epic.

When we knocked off and went for grub, we were advised there was none. And, as we already knew, we had none in our kit. Luckily the kind-hearted sergeant in charge said he'd sort it. He came back ten minutes later with a small plastic bag.

'Sorry lads,' he said, 'this is all we have left.'

Inside were four boiled sweets, a slice of bread, two tea bags and a small hexamine cooker.

He said, 'It's shit, but it could be worse.'

'How's that?' someone asked.

A good question. We didn't get an answer.

I split the boiled sweets in two, cut the bread into eight and got four brews from each teabag.

With ice all over one of the Gazelle helicopters the next morning, a technician stepped up to help with a ball-peen hammer. He spent a while tapping at the ice on the aircraft, getting much of it off, before realising he had left little dents all over the fuselage. Another one of the original exercise group who did not return.

After those two weeks the overall commander cancelled the exercise. It had been the coldest winter in thirty years and would turn out to be the last Med Man 7 there was. It was just too bloody cold.

With time to spare, we headed out into the town of Medicine Hat to sample the joys of the infamous Sin Bin. This joint was dark as a bunker, grimy, smelly and packed with macho soldiers and locals dressed like lumberjacks. If you've seen *From Dusk till Dawn* you'll get the idea. I saw one guy being helped to his feet after being knocked out before being advised he had just been belted by one of the women there. I wasn't even sure I could tell which ones were the women. I stayed put for about an hour, breathing the stink and feeling the menace, before I'd had enough.

At the end, just before heading back to Germany, we had a squadron get-together along with the local AAC flight based in Canada. A few drinks in and I noticed one of the local flight lads having a go at one of our ground crew. By the time several of us went over to see what was going on, the thing had turned into a full-on punch up. Several of us dived in to break it up. And then a sharp pain on the back of my head. I turned to see one of the guys from the flight about to throw another punch my way.

I dived forward, shoved him into a door. It walloped open, both of us falling through with fists swinging. Inside, senior officers and their wives were enjoying a dinner. Now they were being joined by us two and more, the doorway spewing drunken yobs from one room into the next. We stopped fighting. They stopped eating. You could hear a pin drop. Apologies were made and we left. And then something else hit me – I had just stepped over the line once more. If this went on my disciplinary record, I might never fly.

The following day everyone involved was called into the boss's office one by one. I felt gutted, standing in front of him, fearing the worst. He looked me straight in the eye and said, 'Well done.'

'Sir?'

He said he knew I hadn't started the fight and that I'd acted to protect my peers. Phew! A close one.

Back in Germany and, finally, in November 1992, the delayed day arrived. If I passed the interview, I would move to Flying Grading in UK, the last phase before the pilot's course. I was pretty sure my conduct during the Gulf War would stand me in good stead. I said as much during the interview and they pretty much agreed. There had been no further mark-ups on my record and, at last, I passed. I was one step closer.

After that, the squadron kindly offered to take me in one of the Gazelles for the hundred miles to Hanover where I was to get my plane to the UK. The weather was pretty poor and the turbulence was more than I was used to in any military flight I'd been on so far. I had to tell the crew I was feeling ill and felt like throwing up. There was nothing to chuck into so, when the time came, I grabbed the only thing to hand, a dayglo engine cover from a side pocket, and hurled. Then hurled again. It was a brutal, embarrassing experience. Still, as long as it didn't happen again everything was all right.

Flying Grading was a two-week assessment at the Army Aviation Centre in Middle Wallop, Hampshire. Flying training was undertaken on the de Havilland Chipmunk, a two-seater, single-engine primary trainer aircraft designed, I was to learn, to make the trainee feel ill on every flight. There were twelve on the course, six NCOs and six officers. Pilot selection is open to any regiment so there were plenty of other cap badges around – Royal Engineers, Royal Artillery and infantry. Perhaps oddly enough, I was the only AAC there. I fell in with Matt from the Princess of Wales's Royal Regiment (PWRR), who imparted that if he failed grading he had already been advised that his career back with his battalion would be over. Basically, he'd be punished if his career change didn't go as planned.

On day one we were told we would be issued flying kit, suits and helmets and be briefed on how to put on a parachute. As we took our desks and looked over the forms and the coloured pens provided, the tone was set by the chief flying instructor (CFI).

'Good morning,' he said. 'It's nice to see so many people. Unfortunately, not all of you will make it through.'

He told us that in the week ahead we were to undertake thirteen flying hours and sit the dreaded interview at the end. He wished us all good luck, said 'Bye' and left. There was a pause because no one knew what to say or do. And then the door opened and the slightly bizarre sight of a line of what looked like Chelsea Pensioners shuffled in.

Some looks were exchanged, mostly between the students. They advised us they were to be our instructors and, as it became clear, they had more flying experience between them than we could imagine. These guys had flown Spitfires and Lightning jets, flown in both war and peace all over the place. What did we know compared to them? Nothing at all.

When it came to the introductions, we were told they were to be addressed as 'Mister'. My instructor was Mr Miller. He shook my hand with a firm squeeze while wearing one of those smiles that say you obviously have no idea what you've got yourself into. No time was wasted before I was walking out to the aircraft. It was more like a waddle than a walk, the parachute hanging down by my backside.

Each instructor demonstrated an external walk around the aircraft showing his student what must be checked before every flight. Latches, tyres, fuel contents, more. I climbed into the very basic-looking front cockpit, which was also cramped as hell, and I'm not a big guy. Mr Miller told me about the harness, the flying controls, the instruments and that as the instructor he would be immediately behind and we would talk to each other through the comms system.

Flight One was primarily a demonstration sortie, but I was expected to hold the controls in my cockpit so I could feel what inputs he was making during each phase.

Everything was hunky-dory apart from the fact that, before we had even taxied down the runway, I was hot, sweaty, claustrophobic. For as we had begun to move, it struck me that I was too small to have any idea what was going on out front. The Chipmunk, with its small rear wheel, points its nose skywards when on the ground. I could barely see over the engine cowling. As we rolled along, my instructor told me about that rear wheel, that it was a castor and therefore easy to manoeuvre off a straight course. If we wanted to go left, he said, brake left and the wheel would turn us. And the same for turning right.

I was trying to hold it together as we lined up on the grass runway, my skin getting clammy, stomach fizzing. He ran through various checks and then asked if I was ready. I wasn't but didn't tell him that. With a small splutter the engine power increased and the noise ramped up to a scream. I won't say we shot off the end of the airfield but more likely helped by the curvature of the earth. I was glad to discover that, as the tail of the aircraft lifted and put us on the horizontal, I could see over the nose for the first time.

The early idea was to learn how to fly a circuit, a predetermined lap of the airfield. It's about ensuring you keep the aircraft at the required height and speed and that you begin building the habit of conducting checks. Mr Miller went methodically through each stage, telling me that next time round he'd be expecting me to do it all myself. The hour flew by. I'd been feeling good despite that ropey start. I'd picked up a lot. But in the last few minutes, once again the unwelcome airsickness hit me. And once again, I kept it to myself.

Mr Miller landed sweetly with a dainty single bounce, which is way harder than it looks, and we rolled to a stop. At his request, I taxied us back to demonstrate I'd been paying attention, and once again I was looking out at sky. Somehow or other, although feeling as queasy as could be, I managed to park us up with only a couple of hard-braking events.

I told myself, 'It's a one-off, Steve. Just another one-off. You won't feel ill again.'

The thing about flying, I've come to know, is that anyone can be taught to do it. As long as you get enough hours in the air, it will fall into place. But army courses have set time frames. If you fall behind the curve you won't make it. I knew from the outset that I didn't have time to be sick.

Every sortie that followed introduced a new exercise, and things became more intense. Steep turns, loops, circuits, landings, rolling take-offs – the learning came thick and fast. When I was heading straight and level, I had no problem. But when we got into the aerobatics, my stomach wanted to empty. At one point Mr Miller commented on how green I looked – and he was only seeing me from behind. The more testing the flying became, the worse my sickness got. It came to a head when we had to cut a sortie short by ten minutes. I needed to get out.

Mr Miller had my back. He was calm and confident at all times, never flustered, never suggested I had no hope of getting through this when I could think nothing else. He said he had seen it all before. There were certain manoeuvres that set certain people off and that's all there was to it, he told me.

By the time I got to sortie number seven, with six hours under my belt, my instructor changed in line with common practice. By this stage the bravado was kicking in among the students with some of them acting like they were Chuck Yeager, the American flying ace credited with being the first pilot to exceed the speed of sound. I overheard one young officer bragging after apparently being told he was so good he would 'easily get through'. No such thing had been said to me or Matt. Neither of us had a clue how we were doing.

The new man was Mr Gunn, a kind and quiet gent who took extra time to go through everything. I liked him partly because, at about five foot seven, he was as short as I am. I knew he'd understand the issue with looking over the engine cowling.

Our first sortie went badly. I came crawling home, nauseous, ready to lie down and rethink it all. I sat on my own in one of the briefing rooms and collected my thoughts. If I threw in the towel, my flying career ended right away. If I kept going, I was going to have to go through hell every day. Something had to give.

Mr Gunn took a seat beside me. He knew something was up. I told him my sob story. He took it all in, nodded, stood up and walked out of the room. A couple of minutes later he walked back in and thrust a couple of grey bands at me.

'Wristbands,' he said.

'Wristbands?'

'Wear one when you're flying. They've helped many before you.'

I thanked him and said I'd give it a go. The next day, wristband firmly attached, I flew like I'd never flown before. The illness had gone, the smile was back on my face and I watched the world slip and slide around me as my stomach stayed calm. It was an amazing transformation. Right after that I offered Mr Miller one of the sincerest thank-yous I will ever give in my life.

We cracked on. The last sortie, with a third and final instructor, covered everything learned across the two weeks. I did my best, landed with only a few bounces, shut it all down and waddled back to class, hoping hard. We would all learn our fate the next day from the CFI.

That evening all us NCOs went to the bar for a beer. I kept my thoughts about it all to myself. I didn't sleep much, got up early and braced myself for what was coming. One by one, we were called from the classroom. I was called last. I waited outside the CFI's door. A fellow student walked out. He shook his head. He'd failed. Shit.

My name came next. I stood to attention, turned left and marched up to the large desk where the CFI sat.

'Corporal Jones,' he said.

And paused.

My heart was bashing around like it wanted to escape. I hoped he would get a move on in case I passed out on the floor.

'You are,' he said, 'a little small.'

I knew that.

And then he paused again.

My mind went haywire. Yes, a little small. Yes, I've had a few airsickness issues. Yes, I'm perhaps a bit introspective, a bad singer, a terrible artist – tell me something I don't know. But have I passed?

'But...'

But what? Out with it!

'I'm pleased to say you have passed.'

I may have fainted because I have no memory of leaving that room, nor any of getting back to the accommodation. Quite a few of the group, including Matt, had already packed up and left by the time I showed up. He and nine others out of the twelve had failed, including the guy who thought he was Chuck Yeager. I was the only NCO to get through. In a month's time, I'd begin training as an army pilot.

Chapter Five

HOW TO FLY: MIDDLE WALLOP, 1992–3

I GOT MARRIED. I'D been in a German nightclub when I met a local girl and the chat went well. We dated for almost a year before I learned I'd be going to the Gulf. Six weeks before deployment, we got hitched. My wife was twenty-one, I was twenty and suddenly stepfather to little Kelly, eighteen months old. Neither of us had much to put in our new home. The bathroom stool was our TV stand and my mother-in-law kindly gifted us a sofa.

We had been living in married quarters in Detmold for a few months when my pilot training was confirmed. Army protocol for married couples dictated that any course longer than nine months, and beyond your home base, would mean having to give up your digs and move. My course was going to take at least a year.

It was the tail end of 1992. We had only a few weeks to pack up, clean up, book the removals, get the new house organised and move out, and all over the Christmas period, too.

What lay ahead in 1993 would be a year which I hoped might be the making of me. It was daunting. I was the youngest NCO to get onto the army pilots' course, but I told myself not to let that faze me.

There were five NCOs and seven officers on my course, all due to learn the three main flying phases – Basic Fixed Wing, Basic Rotary Wing and Advanced Rotary Wing.

It kicked off, as almost all army courses do, with a group photograph, some physical training and a mile-and-a-half timed run just to make sure you know who's in charge.

There was plenty of kit to get, which inevitably meant spending time at the store. As any soldier will tell you, no one is quite sure who works there, what they do, or whether they do or do not live in the dark and unknown recesses of the place. Once again, I was made to feel as if the flying gloves, the suits, the helmet and all the rest of the gear I needed were on loan from their own personal stash. 'Stores are for storing,' I was told once by one of these strange keepers of the kit. I think I'd asked something cheeky like, 'Would you be able to issue me with that any time today?'

So the Basic Fixed Wing end of things would take eight weeks and involve thirty flying hours. The sortie profiles would be similar to those I already knew from grading but would also incorporate instrument flying, low-level navigation and map reading.

Luckily, Mr Gunn was to be my first instructor, the man who handed me the wristbands that saved my career. I thanked him again, told him they had become as important to me as my helmet, and that I wouldn't leave the ground without either.

The first few sorties were a consolidation of everything I knew, nothing steep in the way of a learning curve. Around sortie seven, each pilot was in line to go solo – but that depended on the pilot. The better you were, the earlier you went. Think of it like school football, where no one wants to be the last person picked for the team. In both subtle and not-so-subtle ways, the pressure to do well was climbing.

One of those early sorties hammered home to me the sacred

aviation saying, 'Aviate, Navigate, Communicate'. It's the order in which to manage matters while in the sky, something to bear in mind when all hell is breaking loose. We were exploring engine failures at the time with Mr Gunn demonstrating what I needed to do. He operated the Chipmunk beautifully, touched down gently, lifted off sweetly and landed once more where he was supposed to, all while under a theoretical engine failure.

My 'touch and go' was up next. There would be a no-notice call of 'engine failure – go' at some point in the minutes ahead. The plan would be to choose a clear landing sight, ideally flying into wind and prepare for an emergency landing. My instructor behind me made the call having obviously already identified a good landing area ahead. I didn't see things the way he did. I found myself aiming for a field thick with bushes and trees. And I was running out of height.

I didn't want to make the call but knew I had to.

'Going around,' I said, applying full power, aborting the whole thing, climbing the aircraft up to 500 feet.

And from my co-pilot, a very calm, 'I have control'.

I could feel his input on the flying controls.

'That was poor, Steve,' he said later. 'Aviate first.'

I'd become so engrossed in configuring the aircraft for landing that I had failed to look out and fly it. Aviate, Navigate, Communicate. Flying the plane comes first. Always.

I wasn't first to go solo, but I wasn't last. And I didn't see it coming. We had just landed when word came from the back, 'Keep the engine running. One circuit and I'll see you back here.'

He undid his harness, pulled back the canopy and got out. I was alone for the first time in an aircraft, controls at my fingertips, engine running.

As my heart took to punching me from the inside, my words to myself were stern:

'Steve, do not bollocks this up.'

All I had to do was take off, fly a circuit, land and not crash. And it was like being with my alter ego in there. I found myself talking away, keeping myself calm.

'Okay Steve, apply power. Keep the nose straight, pull the stick back a little.'

I was packed with nerves and worries and fears of all kinds but then something lovely happened. As I turned downwind and felt that little Chippy find its place in the sky, all those concerns slipped away and my heart rate slowed. I was flying, I was alone and the master of my fate.

That's not to say I didn't double-check everything, that I wasn't worried I was in the middle of making some monumental mistake. But no, I seemed to have got everything right.

Then, on final approach, I clocked what else was going on. Four other students were also flying solo and, as peripheral vision revealed, all of us were lining up for finals at the same time.

'Okay Steve, mate. Do not look left or right.'

Despite a surge of anxiety, I touched down with just a small bounce (for a change). Right next to me another one came down at the same time, bouncing hard and getting airborne again to the point it was wiser for him to keep flying instead of trying to land again.

Mr Gunn climbed aboard, strapped back in and asked me to taxi back to the dispersal.

'How was it?'

'Enjoyable,' I said, quietly chuffed to bits.

Next up was Navigation, using a map to follow a pre-planned route. The key to navigation was to ensure required route headings and timings were continually monitored by assessing wind speed and its relative direction. We had no satnav or other electronic way of working out where we were going, so it was vital to mark reference features and potential hazards, like masts or pylons, correctly. It took me a few goes to get comfortable and get things right in terms of working out wind speeds, but I got the gist.

Then on to instrument flying, which means flying solely with reference to aircraft instruments, something made only harder by the aircraft's windscreen and side screens being whitewashed so you couldn't see through them. That was a test of nerve and something which, I suppose, helped develop the bond between man and machine. But at the same time the white-out effect had me feeling claustrophobic and, once again, a bit ill. Thankfully, I got better as each sortie went on, partly due to random rain showers which put enough streaks in the windows to allow me to see what was going on outside.

Twenty-five hours in and we were all due to be let loose alone once again. This time we wouldn't just be doing the circuit but heading off on Solo Navigation. It was a big step. There had been many incidents where students had got lost and needed air traffic control intervention to bring them back. Some strayed so far off course they had to call on London radar services. Indeed, one of the men about to take the same course, whom I was to meet later on, would wind up going so far he ended up in space. To be fair, though, his name was Tim Peake and he had by then become an astronaut.

So on my final leg I saw things I wasn't expecting to see. The terrain didn't look right. Where had that river come from? None of it was making sense. Ah, balls. I was lost.

'Keep calm, Steve.'

I called air traffic control using a term set aside for those who really know where they are but are practising being lost in case they ever really do get lost.

'Training fix, training fix. This is Army Air 146, training fix. I'm unsure of my position and request directions for heading back to the airfield.'

A long pause. I suspected they knew very well I really was lost.

The answer was almost sarcastic, 'Army Air 146. If you immediately turn right ninety degrees, call finals for the runway and you will be okay.'

Say what? I had somehow meandered back inside the circuit and was right beside the runway.

The Final Handling Test, which closed this phase of the course, would be taken by Mr Hogg. He was an aerobatics wizard and enjoyed demonstrating the loop when time permitted. Towards the end of the test, which was going well, I asked if he might want to show off the loop to a grateful student who had not experienced many before.

'I have control,' he said.

G-force. And lots of it. Earth turned to sky and sky to earth. It felt like my arse was coming out of my mouth. And then it felt like I was going to throw up again.

'Thank you,' I said. My cunning plan had worked. After his demonstration, Mr Hogg hadn't time to test me on anything else.

I'm glad to say that all twelve passed.

Next up was Basic Rotary which meant, for the first time, I'd finally learn to fly a helicopter. Before moving on, I wanted to thank Mr Gunn again. Without his patience, and that wristband tip, I don't think I'd have got through. I was very sad to hear that some years later he was involved in a terrible accident that resulted in the death of a fellow instructor named Pat Bushby. His and Pat's Chipmunks collided upon landing at Middle Wallop. No pilot, regardless of experience, is ever more than a moment from tragedy.

Basic Rotary meant around 170 hours in the Aérospatiale Gazelle, better known as the 'Chicken leg' because that's what it looks like. It's a single-engine French five-seater commonly used for reconnaissance and light attack duties. Being the diligent type, I'd nipped over to the hangar the day before to get a good look at one of them, to get inside it, to get a sense of the harness and seat.

We're talking about a large Perspex cockpit with a tightly packed instrument cluster in the middle to allow maximum vision outside. Compared to the Chippy, this cockpit was vast. I knew that, once airborne, the view from above, side by side with a co-pilot, would be incredible.

I got on board as my next instructor, Bob Weston, after a walk around, did the same. With a flick of a couple of switches, the turbine engine came to life. That Astazou engine has a distinctive high-pitched whine during start and when at flight idle, to the extent that there's an aircrew put-down that goes, 'You whine like an Astazou.' Now I understood why.

Our plastic bubble shook as the volume increased, as the rotor above our heads gathered speed and smudged out. When the blades hit full speed, the aircraft stabilised. It was like a little adventure all of its own and I was loving it. Bob ran through the checks but I'm not sure I took it all in. He gave the thumbs up, allowing the waiting ground crew to come under the rotor disc for a final walk round. And then a dream began to come true. Bob taught me how to fly a helicopter.

There are three controls: yaw (or anti-torque) pedals, the collective and the cyclic.

Yaw pedals: yaw is the movement of an aircraft about its vertical axis – essentially, from side to side. The yaw pedals are the means of controlling the nose of the aircraft left or right, deviating while on a straight course. The two pedals at your feet take account of that. It's all about Newton's law of action and reaction – the helicopter fuselage wants to turn in the opposite direction to the main rotor blades on top. This torque, or turning power, must be controlled before flight is possible. So the tail rotor, controlled through the yaw pedals, allows the pilot to command direction. The pedals increase or reduce tail rotor thrust, so the nose yaws in the desired direction.

The collective: on your left-hand side (in the majority of helicopters), roughly parallel with your thigh when sitting.

This lever controls the pitch angle of the main rotor blades. When you raise it, blades collectively (hence collective) angle up, increasing lift. On take-off, when the lift generated by the rotor exceeds the weight of the aircraft, the aircraft climbs. Increasing or decreasing the lift means you're either climbing or descending.

The cyclic: in front of the seat, between the pilot's legs, rising up from the floor. This stick controls the rotor disc. Moving the cyclic forward tilts the disc (all the blades when rotating), moving the aircraft forward; moving it back does likewise to move the aircraft backwards. Tilting it left or right means the helicopter will roll into a turn in the desired direction (roll is movement around an aircraft's longitudinal axis). The cyclic helps control the pitch of the helicopter (movement around its lateral axis) resulting in climbing or descending flight. In a hover, it is key to controlling movement forward, back, and laterally. And during forward flight, inputs into the cyclic cause flight-path changes.

It's tricky to get to grips with each of the main controls and to operate all three at once feels at first like riding a unicycle downhill backwards while wiring a plug. But, of course, Bob had mastered it all long ago. He climbed the Gazelle into a perfect hover just a few inches off the ground. And when he descended it was like sitting gently down on a collection of cushions. It was masterful.

I'd have to work hard to make it all seem so easy. And that's what I did for all of the hour-long sorties ahead. My checks, my take-offs, my landings, my hovering, my circuits.

I'd call, 'Okay, clear left and right?'

Bob would look around, confirm, 'Clear.'

I'd pull the starter switch up and the engine instruments would flicker into life, the whine from the turbine would begin and the blades would turn. My eyes would fall to the temperature gauges, the fuel and oil levels display, the pressure gauges, the voltmeter. Once the engine was at operating speed and the aircraft stable, it was on to the next set of checks.

Bob's philosophy was explanation, demonstration, imitation. First, he would explain what he was doing, then demonstrate through action, then get me to imitate his actions. He started by letting me loose on one of the controls, then when reasonably happy, two of them, eventually – when he felt brave enough – allowing me to control all three.

My first few takes-offs and landings were a little bonkers. Coming to terms with the power in my hands, and with knowing the difference that even the smallest adjustment can make, took time. Initially I found myself all too easily overcontrolling, rapidly launching the aircraft into the air then descending like a lead weight, forcing my heart to spend a lot of time in my mouth.

'This time,' he'd tell me, 'slow it down, feel the aircraft, no rush.'

Once I got the hang of not climbing like a dingbat, I mastered holding the aircraft steady and not swinging backwards and forwards like something from a fairground ride. And in time I got the hang of arriving rather than crash landing. And all with the reassuring support of Bob who, every now and then, would gently take control from his seat alongside me.

And then it was repeat. Take off, hover, land, repeat. Take off, hover, land, repeat. All around me other helicopters were doing the same. Climb, attempt to hover, descend. And, naturally enough, now and then I'd catch sight of someone losing it with a rapid nose-up then a dive as if briefly out of control, all the while trying to stay within the borders of Hampshire. My giggles were short-lived because sometimes it was me.

Huge amounts of time between sorties were spent on 'hangar flying', where students revise checklists, terminology and everything else with stationary aircraft. And in the classroom, we were getting stuck into meteorology, navigation, performance, rules and regulations.

Ten sorties in and, on landing, Bob removed his harness and said, 'Right, Steve. One circuit and I'll see you back here.'

'Okay then,' I said to myself. 'It's now or never'

It was scary stuff. Checks complete, engine whining, blades at full pelt and everything ready for flight – yet I was all alone in that thing, my head bursting with bits and pieces of information that I had to corral into a rational order. Everything seemed noisier than before, the cockpit more vulnerable than before, more fragile.

I looked at the empty seat beside me, looked outside and said, 'Right, mate, seriously. Time to man up.'

I realised seven instructors were standing to the side and watching my every move, including my solo conversations, as well as those of a handful of other students about to do the same thing.

My hands now hot and sweaty, gripping hard on the controls and I could feel my overdramatic heartbeat in my toes. In that massive moment I forgot absolutely everything, then remembered all the wrong stuff. My brain was racing, crashing, racing again. I was about to fly a flippin' helicopter on my own. The whole thing suddenly seemed insane.

And then I did what Bob kept telling me to do. I took a deep breath and relaxed. I had to do this.

'Relax. Steve, relax.'

I slowly increased the power and calmly climbed to a stable hover.

I went through the after take-off checks fast to keep up the momentum. As I pushed the cyclic forward, the aircraft began to accelerate. I applied more yaw pedals to ensure I maintained the same heading while raising the collective to climb. At 500ft, I made a right turn, increased speed and, as required, set out to fly straight and level at 100 knots in the right direction. Other aircraft were doing the same and it was a job trying to ignore them. Another right turn, then another and then on to finals.

With all calls completed, I just had to get the aircraft somewhere near where my instructor would be waiting. I'd need to find that fine balance between reducing height and reducing speed. Overdo it and you'll come in too shallow or too slow. I arrived in the hover too high having arrested my descent by too much. But finally, I touched down with a small bump. I'd done better and I'd done worse. This time, however, I'd flown a helicopter alone, and for that brief moment I felt on top of the world.

Things moved on to Advanced Transitions, which saw us having to take on board different departure and arrival profiles. We'd have to respond to an imagined reduction in engine power, such as when operating at high-density altitudes where the air is thinner so the engine has to work harder. Or operate as if the aircraft was heavily loaded with passengers or freight and so more power would be required to get airborne than was available. The instructor would indicate how much power there was by giving a fictitious maximum figure. Students then had to figure out how to take off, fly and land without busting this limit. It forced us to recall and apply everything we had learned both from the books and in the cockpit.

Twelve and a half hours after that first solo flight, it was time for the mid-phase check, or the Intermediate Handling Test (IHT). Without passing this sortie there would be no final phase. Luckily enough, my instructor for this was Ian Shoobridge, the flying instructor from my previous squadron. I'd talked to him a few times about aircrew selection, and it had been he who ensured I didn't lose heart after being deferred at the time of my initial interview. Even so, I knew him well enough to know there would be no easy pass with Ian overseeing this test.

He told me the test would start with me demonstrating a circuit. That was it. He was saying no more. Fair enough. Before we walked to the aircraft, he grilled me on some general aviation knowledge including meteorology.

'So,' he said, 'can you tell me what is meant by scattered cloud?'

I had no problem with this. In meteorology, flying conditions are estimated in terms of how many eighths, or oktas, of the sky are clouded. Sky clear = zero oktas; few = one or two oktas; scattered

= three or four oktas; broken = five to seven oktas; overcast = eight oktas.

From that alone, the pilot can then review a reasonably sound weather report to help determine the amount of cloud. The correct answer to give Ian was 'Three to four oktas.'

Unfortunately, I somehow managed not to recall that this was how it was done. I don't think my brain was working right.

Bullish as I could be, I invited Ian to look at the sky.

'Okay,' I said. 'Scattered cloud.'

'Yes,' he said, a little curious.

Pointing upwards, I said, 'Imagine you have one bit of cloud there to the left, another one there in the middle and another one on the right. Okay? That cloud is scattered.'

I was sure I had got that right. I brought my arm down. I looked at him and he looked at me.

'Right,' he nodded. His look was saying it all as we continued towards the Gazelle. And what it said was 'tosser'. I can only hope he thought I was taking the piss.

The ninety minutes that followed were hectic. I was totally drained when I shut down the aircraft.

'How do you think that went?' he asked.

By this point in my career I'd learned how useful this question can be. Indeed, years later when I would be on the other side of the table as an instructor, I was a fan of asking it myself. It's a great question because nine times out of ten the student will stitch themselves up with their answer. They'll offer a full debrief, outline what went wrong in each exercise and say what they should have done. This is gold dust for an instructor who might not have caught all of what has just been outlined. It adds value to the process of determining grade. The trick in answering, as I had been advised, was to be positive about everything and say as little as possible.

Funnily enough, it had been Ian himself who advised me of this tactical response back at the squadron. I think he remembered doing so just that after I delivered him the shortest debrief, I'd ever given. He certainly couldn't mark me down for not applying knowledge. Indeed, his only real suggestion was that I should slow down when operating in the cockpit.

I'm sorry to say that ten years later Ian was killed alongside two engineers. He had been conducting a maintenance test flight not far from Thruxton Airfield when, due to a mechanical failure, the aircraft crashed. He was the nicest, most professional guy and a gifted pilot. I can't imagine an aircraft being in safer hands than his.

All students passed the IHT, which was a great result. From there we moved to Engine Off Landings, Night Flying, Confined Areas, Instrument Flying and Low-Level Map Reading.

Engine Offs, carried out at Netheravon on Salisbury Plain, can only be described as madness. The idea is to position the aircraft in anticipation for turning the engine off, aim for a landing area and basically hope for the best.

It was Bob who brought me to the point where we would shut the engine down, 1,500ft above and just before the airfield boundary.

His words were, 'Practise engine failure – go.'

And then reaching up to the roof, he retarded the engine throttle.

Silence.

Here comes gravity.

Oh God.

We went, naturally enough, into immediate freefall. We needed to counteract that by entering autorotation. An autorotative descent is a power-off manoeuvre in which the engine is disengaged from the main rotor disk. The rotor blades are driven solely by the upward flow of air. The key is judging when to apply the relevant flying control. Firstly, the cyclic must be pulled back to slow the aircraft. As the speed reduces, the rate of descent must then be controlled by the use of collective. At the right height and speed, simultaneous forward cyclic helps level the aircraft while a straight flight path is maintained with the yaw pedals. All being well, your plunging chunk of metal should now be straight enough and at a manageable landing speed. Then it's time to use whatever built-up kinetic energy remains in the rotor system to help land the thing. If that meant you pulled the collective lever all the way under your armpit then so be it.

'Practise engine failure – go!'

My mind was going like the clappers. And so was the helicopter. I lowered the collective. But I knew right away it wasn't down far enough and so wasn't in true autorotation in which zero power is applied.

'All the way down,' said Bob, his commanding calmness ironically indicating that he had his concerns.

I did as I was told. And Christ, we were hurtling towards the ground at hundreds of feet per minute. The once small world below us suddenly got bigger.

What the hell am I supposed to do again?

'Watch your speed,' he said.

Speed was the key, too fast you could overshoot your landing point, too slow you could drop short. It was a fine balance as you're closing in on the earth. The rule is around eighty knots to start, then assess. But it's a fine target to strike when your brain is speeding through nightmare scenarios and you're shitting yourself hollow.

Yet the helicopter pilot emerging from somewhere within me began telling me that all was okay, that I was in control, that my position was good.

The big issue approaching, along with the ground, was when to start the flare – pitching the nose up and helping transfer forward motion energy into the main rotor, spinning it faster and helping achieve that smooth landing. Helicopters are designed to be able to do all this but, trust me, it takes a while to get the hang of it. Thankfully Bob had the hang of this kind of thing.

'Five hundred feet,' he said. 'Four hundred feet. Three hundred feet. Okay, start your flare.'

I gently pulled back on the cyclic to slow down this whole crazy event. Right away I felt him pull back more on the same control.

'Level,' he said.

I needed to pull up on the collective to arrest the rate of descent, then push forward on the cyclic. But where was I going? The flare meant the landing zone had vanished from view.

Christ. Was I really in control of this? Instinct said to pull up on the collective and reduce the impact coming our way. But Bob wasn't having that. As I tried to move it, his hand stayed firm. He had judged that we should descend and slow for a little longer. I had judged that the skids were about to come through the floor. Had he lost his mind?

And he wrenched up the collective. It was just in time for the aircraft to, amazingly, land easily and run forwards on the skids before stopping. If he'd left it a moment longer, I'd have insisted on doing the same, maybe even pulled the collective myself, maybe shouted at him that he was a maniac who was going to kill us both.

He said, calm as you like, 'What did you think of that?'

'Fantastic,' I gasped, arse clenched.

From that point on, I had to be ready at all times for those words. 'Practice engine failure – go!'

Night flying was also daunting, yet it turned out to be something beautiful, as well as something that would go on to become second nature to me in Afghanistan when flying the Apache. In those early days, seeing the splashes of lights on the ground below, the lines of the buildings, towns and traffic, the flashing indicators and streetlamps, was a surreal and strangely calming experience. I say 'strangely' because there's no reason why it should have been calming at all.

Every daytime reference used to judge height and speed had been snatched away and reliance on instruments had become paramount. But that's what it was for me – a balm for my once-panicked rookie pilot mind.

Included in the toolkit for night flying was the landing light used to assist with lighting the surrounding area below and around the aircraft. It was vital for the ground references it offered in terms of holding a stable hover, and important too when manoeuvring to ensure no interference with other aircraft. But that powerful beam, when it strikes what's below, can bounce back up onto the aircraft and illuminate the bottom of the barely visible blades above the pilot's head. I found that to be a mesmerising sight, to look up and see that unreal, other-worldly spectacle backgrounded by a night sky. Everything at night seems slower, higher, somehow deeper, as if it has all taken on a different way of being. From above, in that Perspex cavern, the darkness ahead looks like infinity. And to see flashing lights all around the black sky, to be only just able to make out the ghostly silhouettes of aircraft attached to them, filled me with a kind of joyful wonder. Few people ever have the privilege of getting to witness all of that and I felt fortunate back then, and still do now, to be one of them.

I turned to Bob on that first sortie, after he'd asked me to return, and said only, 'Just loving it.'

He answered, 'I can tell.'

It was as though I was at peace with myself, in control of everything. It was almost as though I didn't want to fly during the day any more.

Low-level map reading had a much less calming effect. We would be operating at 500ft before gradually working down to just a couple of hundred. I was used to flying at 2,000ft. Everything was going to look different and hazards, be they wires, pylons, structures of who knows what, would appear fast.

'Okay, large wood straight ahead five hundred metres, go left.

Fifty metres beyond the wood expect a thirty-foot set of electrical wires running right to left,' and so on.

It got fast and furious for both pilot and map reader. It was like having to unlearn all that stuff about staying relaxed. Low level doesn't give you a chance to relax.

We were wrapping up one session when, with Bob at the controls, I briefed him about a railway bridge ahead.

'Should be straight ahead coming up,' I said.

No bridge.

'Should be no more than 200 metres away,' I told him.

No sign.

I'd figured we would be at it within eight minutes, but eight minutes came and went.

'Bob,' I said, 'I'm not happy.'

'What do you want me to do?' he said.

'Just slow down and orbit here please.'

I needed to examine the map again. I was sure I had been doing this right.

'Where's the bridge, Steve?'

'I don't know.'

He cleared his throat, invited me to 'look left five hundred metres'.

There was never a more obvious railway bridge. Bob knew these routes like the back of his hand and had clocked it miles back. My less experienced eyes missed it because there was high ground, because I'd been expecting it to be surrounded by trees, because I had been more aware of the map than the ground. The trees on the map had been cut down in the real world. Another lesson learned. The map, as one philosopher once said, is not the territory.

I didn't sleep that night. I felt, at this critical point, I was missing obvious things, enjoying the wrong things, failing to adapt fully. I was too fast sometimes, too slow at others. I lay there angry with myself, unable to escape the grim sense that I might not be good enough, rounded enough to get through.

I studied my next map like my life depended on it. I moved away from other students, found a quiet room to learn everything about every obstruction. It was only then that I realised I'd failed to see a river and some wires on my first inspection. I cursed myself and studied that map again and again.

'Okay, Bob,' I said when airborne, 'heading one-sixty, height two hundred feet. Time for this leg is seven minutes thirty seconds, fuel is sufficient, instruments are good and radio call is complete.'

Off we went.

'Okay, twelve o'clock, five hundred metres village, come left, 300 metres start to parallel small wires. At the end of the wires is a small road turn right thirty degrees, speed is good, time is good.'

All going well.

On the final leg I looked ahead and spotted the pylon wires I was expecting to see. I announced them and as we closed in, Bob climbed to avoid. All going well.

But no.

Something was wrong. The map said there was a small lake beyond the wires – but there was no small lake. Had I missed a lake? How could I have missed a lake? Not sure. Shit. I'd done something wrong. Badly wrong. I looked everywhere. No lake.

Back in the crew room and my worried head was once more hanging over that map, my eyes checking and double checking. How had I made this error? How had I missed that lake? It was killing me. And then I noticed something. The 'lake' was stuck to the map. It had never been there. Someone had cut a lake out of another map and glued it to mine.

And that was the kind of maddening shit that went on between students. I'll admit it took me a few moments to see the funny side. Mind you, I did laugh hard at the guy who'd had a small village inserted onto his map. Funniest of all were the handful of students whose maps had been 'cocked' – a strategically located cock and balls drawn somewhere on them.

Six months in. Forty-four hours fixed wing, sixty-three hours rotary. I couldn't wait for the rest.

Chapter Six

WINGS, 1993

MOVING TO THE Advanced Rotary Wing phase meant moving to 670 Squadron, which manages the operational conversion of the pilots' course. The exercises ahead would hammer home what we'd already learned and add in a whole lot more. They would include formation flying, directing artillery engagements from the hover, mountain flying, and culminate with each of us planning, briefing and leading missions.

I'd heard some horror stories from the others about their instructors and knew I'd been lucky so far with Mr Gunn and Bob. Even-tempered, understanding souls seemed to bring out the best in me and I crossed my fingers that my third instructor would be just that. I now know that finger-crossing doesn't work.

John M had plenty of knowhow but not a shred of patience. He was a member of the Blue Eagles, the AAC's flying display team, part of the crews behind those breathtaking aerobatics that had changed the course of my life. Maybe such activities had him thinking he was a cut above, but to my mind that was the wrong attitude for an instructor.

So the exercises came and went, this time with John's raised voice, off-putting body language and sarcastic comments. My confidence took a knock. Luckily, after the mid-course check, there was another change of instructor. And despite John's best efforts to make me feel shit, I passed. I wasn't interested in the grade or the feedback, I just needed to know that the next guy would have some grace.

Gary H was a whole world of fresh air, a man with a bone-dry sense of humour, an easy charisma and plenty of patience. When we talked about his background, I learned this was a man who had completed thirteen engine-off landings on the thirteenth day of the month in a Gazelle (with the tail number XZ666). By the end of that story alone, I liked and respected him in equal measure.

Our first sortie was formation flying, joined by an aircraft flown by another student. We would manoeuvre around the sky practising as a pair, formatting on each other. I messed up with a couple of the calls and, immediately after, Gary rightly took the piss out of me. That made me laugh and, more importantly, made me want to do it better next time around.

Our twelve-month course had subsumed the previously separate aircraft commanders' course, so towards the end we were to take on command-flying scenarios, moving from the right- to the left-hand seat. The instructor would act as the pilot while we commanded each of the sorties, tactically directing the wing aircraft, map reading and leading with the radio comms.

It was my first left-seat trip. Although sitting just a couple of feet over on the other side of the cockpit, I found the Gazelle felt like a different aircraft. Before, I would reach for switches and buttons with my left hand, now I was having to use my right. It was only a small adjustment, but I'd just got used to locating them with my left; also I now found myself having to shift around in my seat to see past the pilot to my right, especially when manoeuvring in turns.

It was during the first sortie that Gary asked me to conduct a downwind quick stop (QS) from the left-hand seat, and it was like doing it for the first time. A QS or 'rapid deceleration' is a coordinated manoeuvre undertaken when a rapid decrease in forward airspeed is required, bringing the helicopter to the hover. There are two types: an into-wind QS, where you commence and finish into the wind, and a downwind, where you commence downwind and finish into the wind. Gary wanted to see a downwind QS. All parameters including speed, angle of bank and heights need to be tightly controlled throughout, and all need to factor in the ever-changing aerodynamics. I selected a clear area, worked out my downwind heading, spotted a hedge line to use as a marker and, brain crackling with all the things I had to take on board, commenced the run-in. I dived to the start height and accelerated to the required speed.

The setup felt uncomfortable, however, and I wasn't at the parameters I required. Yet I wanted to get on with it and so made the exercise entry call.

'Quick stop quick stop – go!'

I began to flare the aircraft using cyclic, pitching the nose up while lowering the collective in an attempt to avoid the aircraft climbing. I lowered the collective more to stop the ascent, only to realise that I'd wandered left off my required heading. I began to overcompensate, turning right. The turbulence was stronger than I had anticipated, unexpectedly strong for this manoeuvre.

A final application of forward cyclic and collective power brought the aircraft into a stable hover. The helicopter's responses were so sharp that I was now thinking it wasn't turbulence but that I was somehow over-controlling from the left-hand seat. It was as though all my hard-won muscle memory was out of sync.

'Okay, Steve,' Gary said, and I knew what was coming, 'I have control.'

'Okay,' I said, annoyed with myself.

'What exercise did I ask you to do?'

Why was he asking that?

'A downwind QS.'

And right then it hit me like a boot in the nuts. I had ended up downwind but was supposed to start downwind, turn and finish into wind. No wonder I was experiencing excessive turbulence and vibration in the hover.

'Ahhh,' I yelled, 'knob!'

Gary laughed. I'd been blaming the turbulence, the seat location, telling myself that I'd be doing great if it wasn't for every other factor but myself. And there was, justifiably, a high price – a fail. My first red grade. I had to refly the sortie.

'A simple mistake,' he said. But we both knew I wasn't about to be picked to become Britain's next astronaut. That night, as had become my habit, I cursed myself a thousand times and lay down for a restless night with one thing on my mind. Next day I did what I had been asked to do.

Air observation post sorties boil down to looking for artillery, something that our predecessors in the First World War had conducted from biplanes and captive balloons. This was one part of the course which really felt like training for conflict. We started off on simulators, getting to know various artillery guns while practising relevant terminology used in adjusting them to the target. After that, it was the real thing. We learned to communicate initial fire to establish fall of shot, take the map reference, adjust accordingly, fire again.

Before the Final Handling Test came the closing showdown – Operation Woodlark. Off we went to Fremington Army Camp on the north Devon coast. Most of the sorties would be over open countryside, a sprawling area with two large valleys and woods, with the high ground of Dartmoor to the south and Exmoor to the north-east. Our task was to operate those agile Gazelles tactically as a single aircraft and as part of an aviation recce patrol (ARP). Airborne fieldcraft, handling and captaincy were up for inspection.

The first tactical exercise (TACEX) sortie was about getting to know the area, flying with Gary at my side. This included wires awareness, on how best to cross them during low-level flying. And without having them identified to us, I don't think that anyone on the course would have seen them from their aircraft.

Each day's flying programme came from Command Ground Training Wing (CGTW), so before anything else we had to bring the maps out and get planning. After that, we went off in three or four waves – sets of Gazelle pairs – with each of us being given the chance to lead a mission as time went on.

When it was my turn as mission commander, I sat down two hours ahead of take-off to prepare, to write up orders and bring in my No. 2, in the second aircraft, to conduct the map recce. One hour later, I gathered the team and delivered my orders to my wingman crew, Gary and the instructors and other members of the training wing. Along the way I had my No. 2 interject here and there to flag up information, hazards, and other relevant points. That worked as a breather for me, allowing me to step back for a few moments and get my next set of thoughts together. At the end, silence. Zero questions. I was either crystal clear with my plan or, much worse, the instructors were keeping schtum because they'd spotted a flaw in the plan and wanted it to play out.

Off we went, swooping low to avoid exposure once beyond the airfield boundary. I was left-hand seat, map-reading the patrol to the target, communicating with air traffic and my wingman, observing everything going on around us. I had to reign my wingman in once or twice when the lateral distance, or side space between aircraft, grew a little too wide. And among all that, Magic checked in, too, this typically being the callsign of an early-warning mobile asset, usually an airborne warning and control system (AWACS), piping up to advise of potential danger. In this case Magic was another Gazelle flown by exercise staff. And on this occasion its job was to play the red herring, to make my job more complicated.

At the forming-up point, we began making our way cautiously to the final target, bounding ahead, stage by stage, taking stock of everything. The task was to get eyes on a particular road junction by a particular time, report what we found, bring back as much information as possible.

I used the ground observation aid (GOA), a magnification sighting system built into the cockpit to scan the terrain from 3 kilometres out. I needed to make sure it was clear of hazards and/or enemy. I did the best I could but the clock was ticking – we were already pushing our luck in terms of making the deadline.

We needed bigger bounds forward. I chose to split the two aircraft, to give No. 2 free reign to move ahead given we were likely holding them back. I just had to hope we wouldn't bound into each other as we both hunted that junction. It didn't matter which one of us found it. My eyes stayed hard on the GOA. I locked all my attention on to the goal of the mission – but still I couldn't locate it. I couldn't even see any roads at all.

Five minutes to go and high ground ahead. If we climbed, we would skyline – expose the aircraft to the fictitious enemy. I had Gary turn, head back to a river junction I had spotted, to try another direction.

Three minutes to go.

'Gary,' I said, glued to the magnified view, suddenly confident I had this sussed now. 'Just push up to the small tree line in the twelve o'clock, fifty metres.'

I was sure we were just out from the junction yet moving to the trees would keep us out of harm's way. As we arrived, I directed Gary to turn, to face where we needed to be. And again I scanned ahead, left to right, changing magnification throughout.

Damn it.

'Anything from Number 2?' I asked.

'Not yet.'

Two minutes.

A truck came into view up ahead. It was of no interest. I scanned further to – wait! Where there's a truck, there's a road. I panned back. An army Bedford. On the side, 347 – our course number.

'Found it,' I said, calling it in to No. 2. They had eyes on the same static vehicle.

Not much more than a minute now to take on board everything of significance about the territory. That done, we both pulled away, slipped back into formation and headed for base.

My debrief went well enough. The staff had been concerned that my map recce hadn't been in-depth enough and felt my timings would not work. My decision to split the pair had been a gamble but it had worked. I was marked down for this but a sortie pass was a pass.

All that was left between me and the army flying badge, or 'wings', was the final handling test (FHT). And despite the knot in my stomach, I couldn't wait to get it done. I was introduced to Sean, a major known to many as 'Badge Man' because he wore every Velcro patch he could get on his flying suit. The exam took seventy-five minutes but felt like twenty. I did as well as I could. Afterwards, I fell into a chair in the briefing room to await my fate. Sean and Gary arrived without a word.

Sean sat down opposite me, poker face, looking down. He looked back up, smiled, said, 'Well done, you passed.'

And in that moment, and in every moment since, I have been able to call myself an army pilot.

Sean shook my hand and left. I was on the edge of losing it, couldn't even look Gary straight in the eye as he gripped my sweaty mitt. I'd never worked so hard for so long in my life. I'd been referred back for being too young at the outset, spent the early days flying on the verge of vomiting and, worst of all, had been locked in a struggle with my own sense of self-worth. Some days I wanted to quit, some days I wanted to take on the world. What a journey. But now I had 215 hours of flight under my belt, and all but 44 of them were in a helicopter.

All who began the course had passed, all of us attending the Wings Parade at the Museum of Army Aviation at Middle Wallop. Family and friends looked on as each of us came to attention and marched forward to the awarding officer, General Sir Michael Rose. He had been the CO of 22 SAS during the 1980 Iranian Embassy siege in London – one of the few men who can truly say he was there on the day. I went on to win the award for the most improved student.

With Christmas just ahead, we all went our separate ways. And it's strange because even though the AAC is a relatively small corps, there were those among the twelve of us on that course whom I would never see again. I can only hope all are safe, well and proud of making the grade in those Gazelles all those years ago.

Chapter Seven

LEARNING THE LYNX, 1994

THE GAZELLE SNEAKS deftly forward, peeps around corners, quietly helps extend the army's intelligence reach. While it gets easily buffeted around in wind, it also offers a smooth ride when conditions are right. Those classic, swift, round-faced machines were considered invaluable during the Cold War, always deep reconnaissance-ready in an era when hordes of Soviet tanks might appear over the next hill. The Gazelle would be there to spot and observe them, to remain in place, observing, or duck away fast and report back.

And it was then that the front-line squadrons would have brought the other key rotor asset into play, the Lynx. These ruggedly handsome, sharp-nosed devils would do the anti-tank business. They would rush in and engage armoured vehicles with their tube-launched, optically sighted, wire-guided missile system – which, to save us all time, gets subbed down to TOW. Highly manoeuvrable and physically sturdier than the Gazelle, the arrival of the heavyweight Lynx in theatre indicates that business will get done.

Yet the surprisingly spry, British-built Lynx has very much proven itself to be a multi-tasker. A twin-engine helicopter, it has also earned its stripes for troop transport and casualty evacuation. All in all, it's exceptionally agile and, in the right hands, truly versatile when it comes to aerobatics and pace. In 1986 it was a modified Lynx, registered G-LYNX, which broke the world helicopter speed record by hitting just over 400 kph, or 249 mph.

No big surprise then that, in line with most helicopter pilots, I wanted to fly one. Luckily enough, the British Army agreed that I should and put me on the next available course.

Given that the Lynx has two engines, there was first a new suite of processes to learn when it came to malfunctions. In the Gazelle, if everything goes tits up, you launch into that arse-clenching autorotation strategy. Not so with the Lynx. It can fly on one engine, although there are so many internal and external variables and vagaries that it almost makes autorotation sound straightforward.

The Lynx course, unlike that with the Gazelle, involved concurrent simulator flights. And these simulators were as close to the real thing as you can get. When there's an engine fire or gearbox fail, or when the tail rotor goes kaput, you are too busy panicking to remember that you are safely inside a hydraulic box inside a building. There are rumours, by the way, that it is possible to shit oneself with terror in a Lynx simulator...

The first thing I had to learn on this course was my place. Army life has both a formal rank structure and an informal pecking order. Far more preferable to work your way up both of those than just one of them. And part of doing that is acknowledging the big picture, finding peace with where you stand. It saves a lot of time. So, as the freshest and youngest recruit on the course, I was the Brew Bitch. It sounds worse than it was. I was basically making the tea. I reminded myself often that this was only a stepping stone, a temporary position on my way to having the tea made for me. And, anyway, I agreed with myself that I make great tea.

Whatever else was going on in my life, and in the world at large, took a back seat. Ahead of sorties, I'd use every moment I could to hangar fly, to practise the relevant checks again and again. My new instructor was 'Budgie' Ashurst, a thoroughly decent, chilled-out sort of man. In fact, such is the small world of helicopter aviation, he and I would fly together again twenty-five years later, this time from the same air ambulance base.

The course demanded thirty hours in the air and the same in the simulator. Circuits, advanced transitions, night flying, instrument flying, autorotations – all the stuff we covered in the pilot's course, just in a different aircraft. Yet this time around it never felt as daunting, never as confusing or concerning. I put that down to the fact that my wings were in the bag. It felt like the pressure was off.

After initial instructions, I flew with another student, the dry-witted Pete M, whose claim to fame, about which he was not at all happy, was that he both looked and sounded like Homer Simpson. Pete captained our first sortie, and off we went to Salisbury Plain for some general handling before swapping over controls for him to do the flying. It struck me afterwards that most of that time had been spent in ripping the piss out of each other, much of it *Simpsons* based. I had become yet more comfortable while in the air.

The course passed with no real issues and before I knew it the FHT was knocking on the door. This time my FHT instructor was an ex-Boscombe Down test pilot named Colin D. After about forty-five minutes I piped up to say that I'd only completed a handful of wingovers in my time, and asked him if he wouldn't mind demonstrating one to me. The reader will now see a trend building here: if in doubt, use up time on a check ride by getting the instructor to demonstrate something they enjoy. He took control and spent ten minutes flying that helicopter around like we were in a dogfight with Iron Man. Now my turn. 'Go for it,' he said, handing over control.

We're talking about initiating a steep climb, then turning the almost vertical aircraft, diving back down and levelling out. The wingover is a high-energy manoeuvre, vital when a fast 180-degree turn is needed but when you can't afford to slow or lose altitude. They're what a Lynx pilot, and the Lynx itself, love to do. It is vitally important, however, to get the speed right, the angles right, the heights right, or else lots of things can go wrong and you might meet terra firma head on.

Height – 300 feet or higher, to allow a little room for error. Speed – 120 knots, to counter the major cyclic input that will slow the machine. Position – downwind, to end up heading into wind. I was ready.

'Wingover wingover – go!'

A hard pull back on the cyclic sending the nose upwards – thirty, forty, forty-five degrees, dashing towards the heavens, G-force pinning me into my seat. At 60 knots, push the cyclic sideways, rolling to a 60-degree, now 90-degree angle of bank. Stretch the neck, look sideways and into the turn balancing the yaw pedals to control the turn, to avoid skidding. Twisting to face the ground, ramp up the speed, level out, return to original height and speed. When it comes to packing a few seconds with drama, not much compares with a wingover. And in those tiny, weighty moments, I was that young lad looking up once again, that junior leader who held his breath as he watched those Lynx wingovers, and came up with a career plan on the spot.

After that, off to Larkhill Ranges on Salisbury Plain for more fun – this time, live firing. Lynx can carry eight TOW missiles that are loaded into booms on each side of the aircraft, each boom housing four tubes. Max range – 3,750 metres, considered to be plenty at the time.

I'd had many hours on the simulator's TOW trainer, a basic setup using crosshairs and a very sensitive joystick. And when I say basic, I'm being polite. We were training to fire missiles yet the target this wonky piece of kit presented would randomly stop after getting in the crosshairs. Invariably missiles would overshoot. I've dug a lot of fictional holes in simulated ground with that thing.

But this was no simulation today.

We touched down at Larkhill for the range-safety brief as ground crew began loading the aircraft with 1.7m, 22kg missiles. Eighteen months before and I was the one doing that same job, yet now I was about to fire my first live guided missile. I watched appreciatively as they opened the rear of the launchers, slid the weapons inside, twisted them to ensure the firing lug was gripped to the firing mechanism at the top. The tube was closed, secured and the arming levels on the TOW booms were locked down. All eight missiles were good to go.

We took off, came into the hover, crept forward to the observation point. The left and right arcs, or limits, were tightly defined for safety reasons. I dropped the sight, adjusted my seat and put my eyes on the magnification sighting system, the foldaway piece of kit operated from the left-hand seat.

I scanned left, took stock of a clump of trees defining the boundary. I scanned right, noted the same thing. Parameters understood, I needed my target.

I scanned the rough bearing, zooming in and out while in search of an old Chieftain tank hulk oriented east to west around 2km away.

'Identified.'

'Clear to engage.'

Crosshairs on target. Joystick steady in right hand. Weapons pre-engagement checks. Then the final switch – from SAFE to LIVE.

Click.

A trigger pull.

A shudder inside the aircraft.

Thump.

The right-hand seat pilot observed. We both needed to know that the thing had launched, that it hadn't fired yet stayed in the tube.

'Missile away.'

Still holding that sensitive joystick now, crosshairs on the centre mass of the tank. Just a tweak could knock it off course. Don't fart, sneeze, cough. Don't shake. Don't lose track. Don't think about anything else. And don't miss.

The missile swung into the centre of my sights, charging onwards, exhaust plume trailing behind. The thumps of my heart now hard enough to make my hands jerk.

Imminent strike.

No.

What?

That exhaust plume had vanished. A clear picture now in front of me. No explosion. Nothing.

'Rogue.'

A one-word incoming message confirming the missile had gone wild, slipped out of my control, torn off in another direction. A terrifying technical error.

We pulled away, needed to get on to ground and make the aircraft safe as urgent enquiries kicked off. Range staff had watched as the missile, out of the blue, began a vertical climb, then a spiral dive before striking land far from the target. Thankfully it had not strayed beyond the safety arcs.

Someone said, 'Your first missile?'

I nodded.

They laughed.

'I know,' I said, trying to see the funny side.

It was hard to take. I'd be hearing about this for weeks. The bastard thing had developed a fault and crashed of its own accord. As I shook my head, worse news. It would be recorded in my logbook as a miss.

'But... ' I said.

'Steve – it's a miss.'

Nothing I could do. And then I had to do it again. Second time around and that old tank finally got a booting. But it wasn't the ending I had hoped for.

Test passed and this all-new Lynx-qualified pilot was to be posted back to 669 Squadron in Germany, my old squadron from eighteen months before. I had left it as a ground crewman. I was coming back as a pilot.

I was all done with making the tea.

Chapter Eight

RETURN TO GERMANY, 1994 – 1995

FAREWELL TO BLIGHTY once more and off to the Hackadal in Detmold, a sprawling concrete flats complex that looked like it had been designed by a Soviet sadist. On the upside, many of my old colleagues were still knocking around, which made settling back into aircrew life that bit easier.

After a few more training sorties, I received my first formal task as an Army Air Corps pilot. I had to collect the Deputy Supreme Allied Commander Europe, or DSACEUR, from his barracks and fly him to Belgium where he was leading a large military briefing. I was advised that he was a very important man and acted like it too. He didn't like to be late for anything. To ensure no issues, we would take two Lynx – one for the man himself flown by Mike Barnes and Joe M and a second, to be flown by myself and Phil P, for his entourage. If one became unserviceable, we should still be able to get him where he needed to be on time.

With a fair-weather forecast, we landed at his base and formed up outside the aircraft to welcome him aboard. He appeared exactly five minutes before scheduled departure time.

It should have ticked along like clockwork from there, but after just a few minutes the air visibility was fading. The forecast had been inaccurate.

'It's getting worse,' said Phil.

He opened comms on our own frequency with Mike, captaining the lead aircraft.

'We're slowing,' said Mike, agreeing it would be foolish to go on as planned.

I followed suit, ensuring the same longitudinal distance between helicopters. But minutes after that we found ourselves flying into thick fog, visibility vanishing fast. I drew closer to the lead and we both dropped to just 100 feet so we could at least see ground features. Mike called for both aircraft to switch on landing lamps before deciding to abort.

I slowed and hovered while he turned, disappearing from view as his aircraft arced around, waiting for him to pass by in the opposite direction. Just us and nothing for a moment before the dark front of the Lynx appeared through the ghostly, soupy air. It was obvious now that the return journey would be no safer than heading on the initial destination.

Mike updated. 'It's no good,' he said, slowly passing, 'we need to get down.'

'Roger.'

The forecast had missed this altogether. It was an extraordinary development, a good reminder that the vagaries of weather can trump any pilot's plans.

'Okay,' Mike said. 'I saw a large open quarry a little distance back. Follow me.'

I turned, followed and, slowly, carefully, both Lynx set down on an unscheduled landing on level ground among blasted rock. Phil turned to me, said, 'This could get interesting. The very important person is not known for his patience. He's sacked people on the spot before.'

The general's face was like thunder as he disembarked from the rear of the lead aircraft. As the aircraft captains, Mike and Phil got out to speak with him. I watched, wondering if our man was about to hand out some P45s, unsure about whether my flying career was to be the shortest in army aviation history.

A brief exchange and Phil returned.

'We out of a job then?'

'No,' he chuckled. 'Must be in a good mood today.'

Two taxis pulled up at the entrance twenty minutes later, whisked the VIP and his team off to travel the rest of the way. We spent a while waiting for the fog to lift before returning to base.

A couple of months later, in April, it was announced that the Army Air Corps was to receive a guidon, or colours, in recognition of its role on the modern battlefield. Or, to say it more appropriately, Her Majesty the Queen had graciously advised that she would be pleased to authorise the grant of a guidon to the Army Air Corps, and the emblazoning of honours on it. It would be presented by our Colonel-in-Chief, Prince Charles, during a large ceremony back at Middle Wallop.

Planning began right away, and it sounded like a good day out. Parade troops were to be dropped off by Lynx flying in formation. It wasn't until we arrived at Middle Wallop the week before that we realised the scale of it all. About forty Lynx were called in from every end of the corps, lined up in rows across the grass airfield. Crews, air traffic and coordination staff met in a jam-packed room for a rehearsal brief. Aircraft, loaded with troops, would be repositioned on the day to one of the large sports fields beyond the camp. On call, each would fly a low-level route running into the parade location on the airfield. Easier said than done. We had to organise timings, formation flying, and coordinate with troops getting on and off aircraft. If just one helicopter, even just one person, made a bollocks of their job then the whole thing could go pear-shaped.

During rehearsal, this time I would be flying with Mike Barnes, one of the squadron's senior pilots. I liked the man, appreciated how he had taken me under his wing on my return to Germany. He said I should do the hands-on flying, advising it was all good experience.

The Lynx were split into sections of five, all in a row. All actions were to be coordinated and so a nominated section pilot would illuminate strobe lights, the brightest beacons on an aircraft, which warn other aircraft of its presence. He would call 'Rotor brake, rotor brake – go!' blades would spin and, at the command 'Go!' the section would take off, transition forward, turn right, fly the fifteen-minute route, land, take off, return. Right behind his section another, and another. No hovering at any point, just a smooth conveyor belt of British Army pilots showing what they could do, a precision, seamless spectacle – it would all look bloody impressive. If it worked.

In the first practice, the fifth Lynx in Section Two stayed in the hover while the rest of them moved forward. He was probably doing checks while stationary when he should have been doing them while moving. It was the air equivalent of daydreaming in your car when the lights have turned green. He had to rush to catch up.

At the call 'Five Section lift, lift - go!' I was off. I climbed into the hover and transitioned to line up with the guy in front and the one who would be on my right in the formation. As we turned, I could see the multiple white strobe lights of the many aircraft miles ahead.

Then – 'Whoa!'

The aircraft in front abruptly slowed as if it had slammed its brakes on. I pulled back hard on the cyclic. And this was going to be the issue. It took just one aircraft somewhere ahead to do something unexpected and the ripple effect could be immense.

The instructions were pouring in over the radio.

'Landing lamp, landing lamp – go!'

'Land land – go!'

'Lift lift go.'

It became clear that there were way more aircraft in the air ahead than there should have been, that one whole section had buggered up its timings. I slowed, along with the aircraft on my right. But he slowed more. So I slowed more to keep us level.

'Bloody hell,' Mike said, 'we'll be hovering if this doesn't get moving.'

Eventually we landed, pretended troops were disembarking and, on 'Lift lift – go!' we were off again. The guy beside me lifted slower. I had to hover to wait for him to reach me. We reset back to our start points and received a message over the air to do the whole thing again. The CFI was unhappy with just about everything.

With initial blunders out of the way, the blame game banter began, insults hurled, piss taken. As we did it all again, more insults, more jibes, more taunts about everything from sexual preference to the alleged night-time activities of various people's mums. Plenty of laughter. It was all good fun. But the CFI didn't see it that way. He was raging.

His voice clear over the radio: 'The next person to comment will be in trouble.'

The chatter fell away fast. But for the churn of dozens of rotors, a tense silence took hold.

It was never going to last.

A crackle on the radio.

'Last one to the bar is a homo.'

The guidon parade was the ultimate flying experience, especially for a very junior pilot for whom everything was made easy by having the cool and collected Mike watch over me throughout. Sadly, Mike would die of cancer several years later. He is sorely missed.

The next year involved bouncing around between exercises, sharpening skills and honing anti-tank drills. A good deal of that involved flying at night in a pair, activities central to the Lynx's duties. Each time one or more variables would be altered, often in line with developments around the world. Responses to the changing nature, tactics or locations of any possible enemy were always borne in mind. But no one could have had any idea what lay ahead.

The Gulf War had ended back in 1991 but the outworkings were being carefully tracked as tensions in the wider region remained high. By 1996, in the aftermath of Soviet Russia's 1989 disengagement from Afghanistan, Taliban militant Islamists had gained the upper hand over local rivals and seized power. Their message, with support from powerful elements in Pakistan to the south and east, was one of uncompromising adherence to Sharia Law. As it swept ruthlessly from region to region, it took the people right back to the seventh century. Girls were banned from being educated; women banned from working. The new regime dished out barbaric discipline via stoning, whipping and public executions; it burned down farms and homes owned by those who disobeyed; it chopped off limbs; massacred civilians; blocked UN food supplies as punishment for hungry communities. The Taliban, who practise an ultra-conservative Sunni interpretation of Islam, behind these measures were delighted to be riding roughshod over the population, convinced that this shitshow was their destiny. And as their grip grew stronger, so did their resolve to continue.

A certain gentleman called Osama bin Laden, from a rich Saudi Arabian family, was making his presence known in the region around the same time. He thought all this was great, had strong ties to Afghanistan and was living there for the second time around in 1996. Years earlier he had first arrived to help fund the anti-Russian mujahideen resistance. And now he was building and recruiting his Taliban-supporting al-Qaeda faction and becoming increasingly chuffed that the future for millions was looking austere, grim, hellish. But while we were broadly aware that the situation over there was deteriorating at the time, it was playing no significant part in our lives.

I was enrolled on to a night-vison goggles (NVG) Category 2 (CAT2) course. This involved flying low-level as a close pair using the eyewear. It was high-stakes stuff. By that point I'd used NVG on the pilot's course and for a few hours in the Gazelle, but nothing more. In fact, most of my time in darkness had been reversionary night flying (RNF), in which no enhancement device is worn, and sense has to be made of contrasting points and patterns of light and dark by eyesight alone. NVG was a different ball game.

It must be said, it's fantastic technology. It works by capturing and amplifying whatever light is available and converting near-infrared light to visible light, a process known as image intensification. The darkness is stripped away and the image appears in a slightly ghostly luminous green. It's a happy coincidence that green is the best colour for the job since the human eye is most sensitive to green light.

These binocular-style goggles are attached to the front of the helmet, with their battery pack to the back. Both parts are heavy, getting on for over 3kg, so they offset each other quite well. That said, after an hour it feels as though your neck is suffering whiplash. And, also on the negative side, your depth perception is compromised as well, because NVG can make things seem farther away than they are. It's important to keep moving your head to look around outside the cockpit, to get as full a picture as you can, to remind yourself that awareness in the air is about not just one thing, but everything.

Departing the airfield was normally reversionary night flying because the intense airfield light would be too strong for NVG, like having a torch shone in your face. Once clear, aircraft lighting is switched to NVG mode, the goggles are flipped down and that's where they stay. It is a strange thing indeed to lift your goggles and see nothing but the inky black silhouette of the control suite, then flip them back down and watch it light up like a flying pinball machine.

The first part of learning NVG was typically all about formatting on the lead aircraft, about matching his moves. We'd swap over after a few minutes, one leading the other and vice versa, each tightly controlling heading, distance and speed.

With that completed, we would split and drop down to take on the low-level route one after the other. Beside me, I'd see the NVG-compatible light kick in, telling me the aircraft commander was reading the map. He'd provide the commentary of what to expect next.

'Wires fifty metres, height thirty feet.'

When I saw them, I'd call them, quickly climbing to clear them before descending back to fifteen or twenty feet.

We'd swap controls after about twenty minutes. My turn to read the map, his turn to fly. At the halfway point both aircraft would come to a hover. I'd pull ahead and take on the lead role. The duty is more onerous for the lead, since he's the guy who can never play less than his A game when it comes to lookout.

For a lot of my time night flying with NVG, I was comfortable with my speed. I wasn't hanging about but at the same time, in the latter stages of the course, I had to push a little harder. My timings were coming in slow. I took on the challenge, but it was a case moving beyond my comfort zone.

Bit by bit, faster and faster.

I remember, as lead aircraft, becoming fixated with obstacles, things that I knew were ahead. I wanted to ID them fast, to call them early. But there was one thing I kept forgetting.

'Keep your head moving, Steve,' the commander told me. And told me again. And again.

Sliding through that green-lit tunnel at night was almost like being hypnotised, but the longer I let it tell the story the greater the danger. Yet my brain was telling me to stay focused, that it was getting the hang of this, that I should avoid interfering with or shaking up the picture of what lay ahead. At one point I became fearful that if I moved my head the entire balance of the aircraft would be impacted, that I would move off route. When put together, the mental and physical dance we were playing out was exhausting. And still I had to go faster.

'Keep your head moving, Steve.'

'Yes sir.'

Hovering and spot turns (turning while hovering) at night are a whole new ball game from performing them in daytime. It's all about moving only your head in the direction of turn to ensure no obstructions, then yawing the aircraft round to align with your new head position. There were other exercises too, all things I had managed during daylight and was having to relearn for the night. Little did I know that the experience I was gaining would pay dividends when I flew the Apache, that events would see me routinely operating low-level at night in a hostile environment.

At around the same time, we learned that our regiment, along with 3 Regiment, were moving from Germany to Wattisham (aka 'what a shame') in Suffolk, in line with the ongoing gradual drawdown of British forces. The base and all the quarters in the Hackadal would also be part of the handback. For a time, our presence in Germany had become awkward. In broad terms, the Germans felt it was time for the British, based there from the end of the Second World War throughout the Cold War, to go. Additionally, the emerging green politicians had gained a lot of press by frequently hammering the military over gas-guzzling vehicles and equipment. Society was changing, too, with many migrants appearing on German streets. The Hackadal, after being handed back to the local authority, was to become a housing complex for the new arrivals. Before they moved in, all the kitchens and bathrooms were to be replaced. But, in classic army style, we still had pointlessly to scrub everything clean beyond belief before we departed. When we went, we left our hosts with shiny sinks and floors, but unfortunately took 2,000 decent jobs from local people.

I'd been in Germany for seven years, arriving as a single air trooper on just above the minimum wage and leaving as a married corporal pilot. And, most significantly of all, I was beginning the next phase of my life as father to my own little girl, named Robyn.

Chapter Nine

EMERGENCY IN BRUNEI, 1996

L IKE I SAID, Wattisham – what a shame.

I was a highly trained pilot, itching to put my skills to use, to do what I could for my country anywhere in the world. And all my country wanted me to do was stay in Suffolk and not bother the locals.

There had been, we knew, quite a few complaints about aircraft, especially helicopters. We were moving on to turf the RAF had vacated and it seemed that we were a little noisier, a little less refined than the previous chaps.

My little family set up home in Woodbridge, about twenty miles from the airbase. It was a fine little town but we never felt entirely welcome. My wife and I tried to work out why, without success, but it was noticeable, especially while we were out shopping, or, in the local dialect, 'sharrrpin'.

Two months in and I was keeping my eye out for army pilot vacancies. An interesting one came up in 7 Flight AAC, Brunei. It was short notice, required a pilot trained up on the Bell 212, yet had the ring of adventure. I talked it over with my wife. We agreed I should go for it.

I got myself on the Bell 212 conversion course at Middle Wallop. Compared with the Lynx, this two-bladed medium helicopter, with pedigree dating back to the Vietnam War, was a whole new kind of craft. It could carry two crew and fourteen passengers and what it lacked in speed it made up in muscle. It was fit to lift an external load of around 2,000 kg – ideal for operating in jungle conditions, perfect for winching materials and troops in and out of high canopies. One key difference in the cockpit was that those big blades and rotor head were nowhere near as responsive as the Lynx and I would soon find myself pulling at the controls like a steam-engine driver.

Since Brunei's independence in 1984, British forces have been stationed there at the request of the Sultan, based in Seria, about forty miles west of the capital, Bandar Seri Begawan. A resident Gurkha battalion operates as the British Army's acclimatised Far East reserve. And having a foothold in the South-East Asian nation, with that equatorial climate, offers first-class opportunities for jungle-warfare training. Which explains why it's home to the army's Jungle Warfare Training School. 7 flight AAC provides key support to the training effort, and was on hand if needed elsewhere in Brunei.

I dreaded the eighteen-hour flight out with my family, fearing eight-month-old Robyn would yell the whole way. But she was pretty much as good as gold the whole way, making me think that, one, the early airsickness must have skipped a generation and, two, that she was happy to be moving away from Suffolk. The contents of our new home were in storage so, on arrival, we really did hope there would be an item or two of furniture in our quarters. And there was – an item or two. It took weeks to straighten all that out.

Then, just a few days in, while still battling jetlag, melting in the heat and being driven bonkers by the night-time buzzing and clicking of cicadas, a mighty, almost biblical storm unleashed itself over the military estate. We would have woken to see the two inches of water it inserted into our home, but the cicadas had ensured we were already awake so we got to watch it happen live.

The unit, 7 Flight AAC, was made up of about thirty personnel and two Bell 212s. On our first meeting, resident qualified helicopter instructor (QHI) Bash asked when I'd last flown the Bell. It had been a few months, I told him, since I completed the conversion course. He said he'd been in-country for about four weeks and was still figuring things out, still acclimatising.

We boarded the aircraft, stayed put on the dispersal, pulled on the helmets and went through the systems, the doors and windows open as sweat poured from us. With the engine started it was a blessed relief to have the rotors turning, our own industrial-strength fan.

Once airborne, we flew over the main camp as Bash showed me the sports fields and parade ground where we'd collect troops. Then further inland to the green zone, beyond the clear defining line where the real jungle begins. The vegetation was suddenly so dense, so complete and seemingly endless. The maps were marked with numbers representing landing sites (LS). Bash said any task – supplies, water, people, drop-offs and/or pickups – would simply list the numbers in order. Most of the sites were small clearings where trees had been cut and levelled, and there wasn't much room for manoeuvre in any of them. I was told that, on the rare occasions when a casualty needed to be winched out and there was no landing site near by, a few sharp blades and a Gurkha or two meant that one would shortly appear.

Brunei hosts courses year-round, none more gruelling than Exercise ATAP Hurdle, the jungle phase of SAS selection. I'd gone through a week in the jungle during survival training and I can say with confidence it was like Hell squared. The humidity, the endless sweating, the endless whirr of insects and the unstoppable bites, the ink-black of the nights that bring a whole new assortment of critters and squeaks and screeches – and all that's while in your hammock. SAS candidates are there for weeks, navigating, patrolling, fighting, surviving round the clock. I was told to expect to be called out often for casevacs (casualty evacuations), given the mad merry-go-round of broken bones, infected bites, flesh wounds, heat exhaustion and all the rest of it. Still, this time around I was the guy in the helicopter and not the hammock so I couldn't wait to get stuck in.

Although we were on constant standby, there were daily visits to the Panaga Club, Brunei Shell Petroleum's leisure facility midway between Kuala Belait and Seria. The pool was hugely popular, which at first seemed strange given the miles of picture-postcard coastline not far away. Yet the beaches were all but empty. Problem was that the moment you showed up, horseflies would come at you like a plague of vampires, landing all over your head and limbs as you ran for the water or for home.

Social events were in the Sergeants' Mess or in one of the several restaurants up town. Brunei is a Muslim country but you can request and drink 'special tea'(aka beer) with a meal, or even bring along something of your own if it's in a closed container. And there wasn't much else to do. It's a small nation with a small capital offering not a great deal in the way of shopping. I remember the day that we headed off for Jerudong Park, a £1bn amusement centre that had launched just a year or two before. Unfortunately, it was shit. Some of the rides had never even opened and those that did were in bad shape. I feared a little for the sanity of my wife, who had no chance of getting any kind of job, and worried even more about little Robyn and my stepdaughter Kelly, who were having to deal with dramatic environmental changes.

An official visit to Brunei from Prince Charles was memorable. As the AAC's Colonel-in-Chief he inspected the flight lines and afterwards we took him sightseeing. We had to scrub and paint everything including the grass before his arrival because even Far Eastern jungle does not escape the British military's obsession with spotlessness. I was part of the crew that brought him for an overflight of the capital, Bandar Seria Begawan, and then on into the wild. As a small boy some twenty years earlier, I'd met his wife Diana. But now, in 1996, that marriage was very publicly over, so naturally I didn't mention the encounter. But I would go on to hear from His Royal Highness – now His Majesty – in times to come, and I'd get to know his younger son, too. That, however, is for another chapter.

Brunei marked the first time I worked alongside the Gurkhas, the soldiers with that most deserved reputation of being both unfailingly professional and ferociously courageous. Much the same is said of the SAS and, after working with training staff in the casevac and resupply operations out there, I started to wonder whether applying for selection might be the way to fire things up a little in my career. I'd relished the fight to get my wings, but things had grown a little flat since then.

I looked into it, found out what was needed. Over the next eighteen months in Brunei I ran and swam myself from being a reasonably fit bloke into someone who would not be out of place in the Special Forces. The fact that I was air and not infantry, I was sure, would count against me, but it wasn't enough to stop me giving it a go.

Along the way, thanks to one of the training team, I managed to bag a visit to SAS home ground in Hereford at its regimental HQ, Stirling Lines. Seeing the 'Who Dares Wins' motto after passing through the camp gates was like a shot in the arm. I was twenty-seven. It was now or never. And off went my brain again, spinning around, exploring every angle, raising all the doubts it could find. It was telling me that I was a married man with young children, asking if I was really seeking to take on something that would undoubtedly eat up all my time, strength, energy. Everything whirled around in my mind for a week, until I forced myself to make a decision. The answer was no. I was a helicopter pilot and proud of it, a father and proud of it. I had a career, a marriage and a daughter and stepdaughter to nurture and protect. I did what I knew in my heart to be the right thing and stepped away.

In those two years in Brunei, I was called out many times, day and night, for casevacs but, more often, for VWs, or voluntary withdrawals, to fetch back someone who had called it a day. These were straightforward sorties, usually taking around an hour. On various calls I was with Mark D, who had arrived in Brunei at around the same time as I had. There was one occasion where the landing point was familiar, one often used by SAS cadre staff. Mark flew and I directed him in as safety pilot, opening my side door ang getting out as we landed. A little distance away, I saw SAS staff and one deflated-looking guy sitting on his bergen. No prizes for guessing which the VW was.

I directed him to the rear doors and as he climbed in, I went to lift his bergen. Jesus wept, it was heavy! – 90 kg or more. I manhandled the thing into the aircraft, got back in, secured my harness and as we set off, that familiar smell. The poor guy had been crawling through the jungle in the same kit for weeks and was giving off the peculiarly putrid stink of old sweat, dirt, blood and piss. I didn't like to say anything about it and opened the window. The man had enough on his mind.

Heading back, a call from base.

I turned to Mark, shouted it out, 'Emergency casevac.'

It was 10km away. We'd need to get on it fast. The casualty had been bitten by something and was in a bad way. That was all we knew. The nearest landing site to the casualty's grid reference was 3km.

I asked it, loud above the din of the engine, 'Can you get the casualty to the landing site? Over.'

There was no hope of that, they said. And could we get a move on?

A quick unplanned site would have to be cut. We'd need to

winch the man up on a stretcher, and then winch up the medic tending him. Plus we still had our VW in the back. It could be useful having him to assist, but I was genuinely concerned that I'd retch if I got close to him.

In the overhead at the location, but we could see nothing. We orbited a couple of times, eyes hard on the canopy below, and still nothing. And just as I was wondering if there had been some kind of balls-up along the way, trees began to fall. One second they were standing straight, the next they just seemed to lie down.

'This is our area,' I yelled.

One hour's fuel left. With the job here, transit to the hospital and back to base, we'd be cutting it fine. We needed to get the winch down and up twice inside thirty minutes or we're up Shit Creek. And they were still cutting the trees. And they still had to go get the casualty when we dropped the stretcher to them.

More appearing now beneath the thinning canopy, troops working hard to clear the area. The gap they created was around 15x15 feet, tight but maybe just enough to do the work. A good steady hover would be required to ensure we, and the casualty, came straight up after dropping low. Mark did the necessary as I unstrapped and climbed in the back. The exhausted VW looked at me in knackered bewilderment.

'We have a casevac,' I yelled. 'I may need your help.'

He smiled, gave me a thumbs up.

I pointed at his kit, gestured for him to clear it away. I'd need to be evacuated myself if I had to lift that bloody bergen again. I detached the winch hook and checked it over. I put on the waist harness, secured it to the floor and slid open the door.

Nothing could have prepared me for it.

The hot air that hit me was a foul cloud of aviation fuel, a complete mouthful of engine flavour that would probably have made me retch not that long ago. Looking down, it struck me how high we were, that even at 150 feet it was like standing on the edge of a tower block. Held only by a waist harness, my brain starting racing, urging me not to fall, to step back, to get away from this. It was noise I didn't need.

The stretcher was a foldaway, compressed into a small carry case attached to the hook. I hit the down button on the hand controller and filled in the blanks for Mark.

'Come left five, right three.'

The stretcher reached the ground. We had fifteen minutes before we had to go.

And then it started to rain. Just little skinny drops at first, then fat, heavy blobs, all over the windscreen, over the guys below who had dashed off with the stretcher. The jungle canopy began to look restless, the aircraft slipping a little to the side. This wasn't just rain, there was wind too. Mark's difficult job had just got harder.

Minutes were passing like seconds. And still nothing doing.

A shout from inside, 'What's going on, Steve.'

Mark's tone changing, the pressure was mounting.

'Still waiting.'

'Ten minutes,' he barked. 'Then I have to go.'

'I know,' I shouted back.

Come on, come on. One emergency is enough for now. Hurry the hell up, guys.

'Eight minutes.'

Yep.

Nothing.

'Seven minutes.'

I know.

'Six minutes.'

Understood.

Movement below. Four men from the heavy undergrowth, each holding the corner of a stretcher.

'Yes!'

A fifth man running for the winch, grabbing the hook,

connecting it to the stretcher, lifting it just off the ground. He waved up at me. But as soon as they let go, the stretcher started to spin. It was maybe hooked on badly, maybe the wind all around was forcing it, maybe it was the downdraught from the rotors, or maybe a combo of all three.

I either had to get the casualty up at high speed, while spinning, or put him back down. Putting him back on the ground meant we'd have to leave without him. And he might die.

But we were dangerously low on fuel. Single engine failure could be imminent. If that happened, we'd lose the power to hover, have to dive and move out – while we had a casualty attached to the aircraft. I'd either have to cut the winch to avoid it getting entangled in the trees or, if the casualty was above them, just hope we'd stay high enough to keep him from getting tangled up.

'Five minutes, Steve.'

'I know,' I shouted back. And I started to winch the spinning casualty up.

The aircraft was twitching, getting shoved around in the worsening wind. The spinning was bad but not so bad that I felt I had to abort. I kept my finger hard on the up button, the winch light confirming our casevac was coming. The patient cleared the tree line, coming up now nice and smooth. With 3 feet to go I reached out, grabbed the stretcher and, together with the VW, pulled the casualty into the back. It had taken one minute.

And now we had to do it again.

One look at the casualty told me he was conscious but very, very unwell. He smiled and I smiled back. I unclipped the hook, sent it back down with a man harness. We could not have left without the medic on board.

'Four minutes, Steve.'

The second winching was quicker. He just needed to throw the harness on. It started well. But wind hit, the aircraft lurched left. We all braced.

'Sorry,' Mark called. 'Wind's buffeting'

'No problem.'

'Three minutes.'

'Okay.'

The small movements above, amplified below. The ascending medic had narrowly missed going into the trees.

'Two minutes, Steve. I'm really struggling here. Make it quick.'

I had the winch controller in hand, the medic safe so far. We were going to make it. And then the winch light went off and the medic's progress halted.

'Mark,' I called. 'Bloody winch failure.'

Just the wind shouldering us around, just the sound of the churning engine, the pulsing blades.

I looked back down, the medic looking up. I needed a solution fast. The guy was still below the tree line. No way we could move with him there. But we had to move or we were done for.

'One minute.'

'Mark,' I called. 'Climb vertically – and fast.'

Not a second wasted. He pulled at the collective. The aircraft shot up, the door open, the rain pelting.

'Keep going,' I called. 'Almost clear.'

Second later and the medic was above the tree line, his face startled. He wasn't the only one wondering why the winch had stopped. And if I couldn't get it going again, he'd be hanging there all the way to the hospital.

I thought right then about teaching troops to heli-abseil, about flying with them attached to a rope before gently touching down in a safe area. But those guys had been expecting it. This stranded medic hadn't a clue what was going on.

The controller handset had let me down badly. I gave it a hard smack more out of frustration than anything else. The green light illuminated.

'Jesus,' I said. 'What?'

The smack had fixed it. Our medic was moving upwards again. Mark was at 30 knots by the time we were pulling him in the door. There wasn't anyone on that aircraft who didn't deserve a long, cold drink that night.

I flew just shy of six hundred hours as both crewman and pilot in Brunei. Yet the situation worked against me in the sense that I was able only to stack up a handful of command hours, and I'd need many more of those to become an aircraft commander. When I got back to Wattisham, I focused on doing just that. One year later and it was done.

In that time, in those aircraft, in that sky, with all I had already done and all I had yet to do, it occurred to me that I would have been mad to give up on it. I already had the greatest job.

The author with an SLR at the back of the Sultan command-and-control vehicle, Iraq, 1991...

and (*centre*) with the rest of the signals section.

An AAC Gazelle in the desert, Iraq 1991.

The 'Highway of Death' – the Basra Road, Iraq 1991.

Young and green – the author practice-firing a GPMG in Iraq, 1991.

Spoof certificate awarded to the author on passing the Lynx conversion course.

This is to certify that

Cpl S Jones
attended

81 LYNX CONVERSION

and despite his Instructor's efforts managed to bluff his way successfully through the course.

Date....04/03/94....Signed....................................Instructor

Left: The author preparing for a sortie in the Lynx.

Below: The author with a Lynx 7 in Germany – not good flying weather.

The author in a Lynx ready to deploy troops on exercise in Germany.

'Playing soldiers', Germany; the author is at right, with, behind him, a Lynx 7 with skid undercarriage.

Nap-of-the-earth flying in a Lynx – flying low and fast to reduce the risk of ground attack.

The author in a group photograph with Prince Charles when he visited the AAC in Brunei, 1996.

The author's certificate for passing the RAF's combat survival course, February 2000.

ROYAL AIR FORCE
AIRCREW COMBAT SURVIVAL COURSE

This is to certify that

.... Sgt Jones ....

*has successfully completed the Royal Air Force School of Combat Survival and Rescue, Aircrew Combat Survival Course No....54...........
having received training in Evasion Planning, Combat Survival, Personnel Recovery and undergone practical Conduct after Capture training.*

Dated 7 Feb 00   Signed B Baxter

Officer Commanding

Royal Air Force
School of Combat Survival and Rescue
St Mawgan

Lynx AH9 with wheeled undercarriage, Bosnia 2001.

The author in the cockpit of a Lynx, Bosnia 2001.

Above: The author (left) with a Lynx 9, Sarajevo, Bosnia, 2001.

Left: Badges in the author's den at home, including the one he made reading 'Not egotistical – just great'.

The crashed Lynx from which the author rescued the two crew, Oman, 2001

The telegram from Prince Charles that the author thought was a wind-up . . .

STAFF SERGEANT
STEVEN JONES AAC
1 REGIMENT ARMY AIR CORPS
BFPO47

HAVING HEARD THE SPLENDID NEWS OF YOUR AWARD OF THE QUEEN'S
COMMENDATION FOR BRAVERY, I WANTED TO SEND MY WARMEST
CONGRATULATIONS. WELL DONE.
          CHARLES
          COLONEL IN CHIEF

THE QUEEN'S COMMENDATION FOR BRAVERY

By The Queen's Order the name of

Staff Sergeant Steven Jones
Army Air Corps

was published in the London Gazette on

Friday, 19th April 2002

as Commended for Bravery.

I am charged to record Her Majesty's high appreciation.

Secretary of State for Defence

. . . but it was followed by the actual certificate.

Chapter Ten

'I'LL DO SOME DIGGING.' BOSNIA, 2001

MY MARRIAGE WAS suffering. I'd been working long hours, had been off serving in Northern Ireland, training in Romania and other places, and my home life was getting messed up. My heart was with my family, yet it was in everything I was doing in my working life, too. When it came to striking a balance, I wasn't getting it right. And, given the demands of my career, I wasn't sure I ever could. After ten years of marriage, we agreed to call it a day. I moved out, rented a flat, ensured I would see Robyn and Kelly as often as I could. I blamed myself, and only myself, for all of it. It can't have been easy for the three of them.

I told myself afterwards I'd do all I could to keep busy, to get as much experience as possible. When a NATO-led Bosnia and Herzegovina tour came up in 2001, I went for it. Getting away would be good for me, helping to ensure I didn't slide deeper into the rut, keeping my mind sharp. And what better place for that than a war zone?

The British Army deployed to Bosnia in 1992, tasked at first with protecting aid convoys then staying on for peacekeeping duties.

The thirty-eight nations of NATO's Implementation Force (IFOR) had by 2001 managed to separate and contain the three ethnic factions, Bosnian, Croat and Serb, which had been battling hard for years over issues springing from the breakup of the former Yugoslavia. After IFOR came the Stabilisation Force (SFOR), its mission to help keep things on an even keel and allow rebuilding. UK troops were, at that time, based primarily at an old metal factory at Banja Luka (BL) and 120 miles to the south-east in the capital, Sarajevo. That city had borne the brunt of brutal war, under attack by Serbs from 5 April 1992 to 29 February 1996 – the longest siege of a capital in the history of modern conflict.

I arrived with a fellow squadron pilot and friend, Trevor T, to find large parts of the airport in ruins. We were driven straight to NATO HQ at Camp Butmir on the outskirts of Sarajevo. The city was putting on a brave face, but the signs of poverty, of war and of the region's bleak Communist past combined to create a tragic atmosphere, imbuing the drab buildings and streets with a sense of hopeless desperation.

Camp Butmir contrasted sharply. A sprawling base, bursting with life, energy and accents from all over the world. Turkish forces were on the gates, Irish military police were running internal security, Americans were running administration in the HQ. Each unit was housed in two-storey prefab blocks, and competition was fierce between all sides to see who could host the best barbecues and the loudest parties. The British detachment had just moved up from Split in Croatia to support SFOR's Deputy Commander Operations, General Sir Richard Dannatt (now Lord Dannatt). He was well regarded and, as a man who went on to speak his mind about improved pay and conditions for troops, became only more popular with the rank and file.

The UK Helicopter Force was comprised of two Lynx Mk9 and some thirty personnel. As in Northern Ireland, we would fly as a crew of three, including the rear door gunner, given our mandate allowed us the right to self-defence. In terms of duties, much of it came down to moving General Dannatt and staff around. Flight Operations was housed in two stacked Portakabins shipped up from the British base in Split. They were already knackered. We provided our own security while sleeping on cheap sofas and watching videos. It was on one of those very cheap sofas that I received the first ever call to my first ever mobile phone and I was thrilled to answer it. Sadly, it was a wrong number and cost me fifteen quid to accept the call.

My first sortie was in the Lynx Mk9, whereas I'd previously flown only the Mk7. So now I had an upgraded gearbox and a wheeled undercarriage instead of skids, meaning that the aircraft could be taxied on the ground. First sights from the air included the bombed-out Sarajevo newspaper building left to serve as a potent reminder of what had taken place. Then north-west to the Banja Luka metal factory, a base for American, British, Canadian, Czech and Dutch forces since 1995.

Other sorties came and went, with aircrew often receiving scant detail of what lay ahead until we were well on our way. One task was to head to Tuzla, about seventy-five miles east of BL, and I set off with Bertie C, a down-to-earth Royal Marine officer who, when not naked arm wrestling, spent his time insisting that the two pips on his shoulder made him the army equivalent of a captain. Everyone else spent their time avoiding naked arm wrestling and reminding him that lieutenants make the tea.

We were met at BL by a man with no insignia on his fatigues, taken to an operations building and briefed. We were to take six individuals to a grid location in the Tuzla area, drop them, return to BL and await further tasking. That was it. Back in the aircraft, six guys in plain clothes boarded, gave the thumbs up and away we went. I'd been around enough special forces in my time to know who our passengers – or pax – had been. Forty minutes later we landed by a main road. A white truck pulled up, they jumped out and, twenty seconds after touching down, they were away. Three hours later, we were tasked to collect the six and get back to BL.

'Bertie,' I said, refuelling in BL. 'You think you can find out anything?'

'I'll do some digging.'

He did. They were SAS on the hunt for former president and forever war criminal Slobodan Milošević. Intelligence had suggested he was in the Tuzla area.

Luckily for him, he couldn't be located on the day. But some six weeks later, on 1 April that same year, 2001, he was arrested after a thirty-six-hour armed standoff between his bodyguards and police at his villa in Belgrade.

That tumultuous, ongoing story of the whole region is one of Europe's most significant and most heartbreaking. I learned a lot from tours into Sarajevo, from a visit to where, on 28 July 1914, Archduke Ferdinand of Austria-Hungary was assassinated, putting in motion a chain of events culminating in the First World War. I saw Markale Market, where, much more recently, sixty-eight civilians had perished in a single bombing. Nor should I forget Black Beard's Market where, in more upbeat days, I availed myself of its bloody amazing and seriously cheap array of pirate DVDs. That said, I soon learned that most had been filmed in cinemas, so that figures kept blocking out the screen as cinema-goers stood up and headed for the toilets.

In late February 2002, as my tour was coming to an end, some bad news from back home – a Lynx crash. We gathered in the ops room, speaking in hushed voices, all needing to know more. Our best information wasn't from official sources, but from the Professional Pilots Rumour Network (PPRuNe). A crash landing onto the airfield at Leeming, Yorkshire. It was infuriating to see other military personnel and pilots logging on to offer their thoughts, to judge and castigate crew decisions before anyone even knew for sure what had happened. The real cause was no one's fault.

The Lynx was returning to Leeming with tail-rotor control problems. The mechanisms had failed completely ahead of landing. Thankfully the crew walked away.

I returned to Germany as I had left, alongside Trevor. He had been there at the start, when a downbeat man's marriage had just fallen apart, and he was there at the end when the same guy had a little more insight into just how bad life can get. And he was there all the way through as a good colleague and a great mate. Cheers Trevor.

And as for Sarajevo, I remember my heart lifting in March 2012 when I read how that extraordinary, re-emerging city had been voted one of the world's best places to visit. It's a strange irony that no one keeps peace better than men who know war.

Back in 2002, in October, I was appointed flight commander for an exercise in Eastern Europe. The destination was a small Romanian Army camp close to the Carpathians, a 930-mile densely forested mountain range packed with lynx, bears and wolves. Mountain flying, day and night, was on the agenda for Exercise Green Carpathian. Sounded good to me.

Three aircraft set off from Gutersloh for the 1,000-mile trip via Bratislava in Slovakia, then Budapest in Hungary and on to Bucharest's Henri Coandă International Airport.

We reached Budapest with no issues before poor weather hit and we had to delay. I was accountable for all expenses and resisted the crews' encouragement to have us all stay at the nearby five-star hotel. Instead, I found a decent three-star that would be a tad easier to justify. The weather remained hostile for the next two days, yet pressure mounted for us to move on. The ground party was already at the base, my boss kept calling for updates and, on day three, with just a little improvement in the weather, I made the decision to forge ahead.

The area we arrived at was raw with the kind of grinding poverty that leaves you counting your blessings. The place was home to many destitute people living as best they could in ramshackle dwellings with almost nothing. Indigent Roma families in horse-drawn vardo caravans were a common sight alongside the broken roads. It all seemed lawless, cheerless, hopeless. Within the camp we were split between three blocks – all of which had seen better days – while the aircraft were parked on a nearby sports field. The local troops did offer to guard the helicopters when not in use, but we insisted we'd do it ourselves.

After one flight briefing, one of the British corporals asked us to go to the operations room. On arrival we met several stern-faced Romanian officers and our own medical officer. Something was up. A flying helmet had been stolen from one of the blocks. But given that, as we were informed, the culprit had been identified and the equipment recovered, we weren't sure what we were all doing there.

Someone asked, 'Okay. And what's the issue?'

In patchy English, a Romanian officer gravely advised that under army regulations the thief must be disciplined. We were directed to look outside at a sickly pale and clearly terrified young soldier being ushered to the middle of the sports field by a guard. He was, it became obvious, about to be whipped.

'Whipped!?' someone called out, all of us shocked by this barbaric development.

The officer advised that the go-ahead for the whipping must come from the victim, and as it turned out to be my helmet, I was the so-called victim and so the decision would rest on my shoulders.

'No way,' was my response.

The flying helmet was likely worth a few years' wages to that lad. Of course, he deserved sanction. But, at the same time, this was 2002, not bloody 1702. To the dismay of the guard, this vicious public spectacle was called off and the soldier led away.

On the return journey to Germany, bad weather delayed us in Budapest again. This time the only accommodation going really was the five-star hotel. We didn't know until we checked in that the lobbies of local high-end hotels were, as standard, well-stocked with working girls. And they weren't exactly shy about letting guests know what was on offer. While that was, I suppose, an enhanced form of room service, I did advise aircrew that I already had enough on my plate trying to justify the five-star digs.

Career wise, from then on, in my newly single status, I sought to bank as many qualifications and skills as possible. It seemed to be a good use of my time. One course that followed, Wire-Guided Technology, took me and my mate Pete L to the Defence Academy in what was still the Royal Military College of Science site at Shrivenham in south-west Oxfordshire. The truth was the pair of us enjoyed a few courses here and there, both sharing a specific interest in useful studies that had no exam at the end. Shrivenham was fertile ground for this and our combined attendances were beginning to build up points that could ultimately add up to the equivalent of a science degree.

We were the only two army on the Wire-Guided Technology course and the only two who did not have a degree. But then, this wouldn't exactly be rocket science, right? Wrong. This was actually rocket science. Pretty much everyone else there had some form of education in rocket technology or design. It was like *Dumb and Dumber*. All we knew in this area was what we had learned from our TOW missile experience. On the plus side, however, we were the only students on the course who had actually fired live munitions. That fact went down well with the majority of the others, who had spent most of their careers in laboratories.

Fridays featured a late lecture with the academy laying on wine and cheese beforehand. Not one to refuse free goodies, I did get a little merry at times, as did Pete. It was in this merry state that I recall witnessing a PhD student taking a phone call during a lesson. He lifted his mobile, reached across to the window alongside him, opened it and dived out. A truly bizarre thing to see.

Luckily, we were on the ground floor. Pete and I looked at each other in shock. And the lecture just carried on as normal. I still can't work it out.

On another occasion, with booze on board, Pete and I chose to exit the academy grounds by climbing the fence instead of walking to the gate. On the way down, Pete snagged his new North Face jacket, practically tearing it in two. We wandered on towards the pub, him in silence and me laughing my nuts off. By that stage a number of AAC officers on other courses at Shrivenham had joined us and it was in that very pub that we found ourselves having to explain why we had arrived half-cut and with one of us in half a jacket.

I remember Tim Peake was there at the time, someone I first came across during pilot selection back at Middle Wallop. No doubt he was impressed with me and Pete for upholding the best of AAC traditions. A couple of years later, in 2011, Tim and I met up while I was instructing on the Apache. He said at the time he was hoping to secure a place on an upcoming space mission, which indeed he did, being launched at the Interntional Space Station in in December 2015. I'd like to have talked more with him but was called away to fly a sortie. That was unfortunate because I had a couple of wind-ups in mind. . .

Chapter Eleven

HOW TO SURVIVE.
CORNWALL, 2001

THE FIRST TIME I saw a man in a woollen onesie, a belt and a hat was at the outset of survival training. It was very likely the last time too. The poor guy, who was RAF crew, hadn't brought all his bags to the training camp in Cornwall. But, in the best traditions of military resilience, he used his initiative and presented on day one in an item usually worn underneath a sea survival suit. If the young airman could survive the piss-taking he got from that, he'd survive anything.

As someone who enjoys the work of Ray Mears and Bear Grylls, I volunteered for the course in 2001. Passing it would mean I'd become squadron Survival Rescue Officer (SRO), responsible for survival training. It was held at RAF St Mawgan, near Newquay in Cornwall, home to the Defence Survive Training Organisation (DSTO) which teaches Evade, Resist, Extract (SERE). We were warned it would get intensive.

In the first week the twelve students covered the various survival principles, including single and multiple crew dinghy drills. On Monday morning of the second week, we were in the pool conducting wet drills, inflating the personal life vest and swimming from one end of the pool to the other. On our backs was an awkward pillow-sized, single man dinghy pack. We inflated the thing at the end, but only when we had reached the limit of how far we could swim.

The dinghies are, in theory, small enough to be worn while flying but they push you forward quite a bit because of their size. Pulling the beaded cord removes a pin which breaks the seal on the built-in gas bottle causing the thing to fill up fast. Conveniently, every time we did the drill, one would fail to inflate, the gas valve having been sabotaged by trainers. This happened to me a lot. Have you ever tried to pump 3,000 breaths into a dinghy while knackered beyond belief from swimming? Don't.

Then you clamber aboard, get the canopy up, ensure the locater beacon is active, dry the canopy floor and take an anti-sickness pill. And that's when the instructor swims out, capsizes your dinghy and tells you to repeat. Except this time he assigns a random injury.

For example: 'Your arm's injured. You can only use one from now on.'

From there, we were doing the same thing except instead of the pool, we headed out to sea in fast boats. In the depths of winter, one by one we leapt, for some reason as stylishly and dramatically as we could, from the boat to inflate our dinghies. I went in with a back flip that didn't work as planned. It was like being slapped with a slab of concrete. When I got my breath back while in the icy embrace of the Atlantic, the dinghy failed to inflate. Just a matter of another 3,000 breaths, climbing aboard and doing those drills. After hours that felt like days, the helicopter arrived and winched us all aboard.

I read somewhere around that time that some shipwreck survivors had spent weeks and even months in one of those dinky dinghies. The trick, I remember noting in case the worst happened, was basically to eat anything that passes, from seaweed to turtles.

And also to down a shot of your own urine now and then. At one point I became so overwhelmed by the training that I felt I could sympathise with the rare breed who had been through that. Yet in reality I had only been in the thing for an hour. And I didn't get any plaudits, just an itchy arse for failing to empty out all the sea water.

More theory involved the four Principles of Survival – Protection, Location, Water, Food. This saw us dispatched to the wilds with nothing more than an aircrew survival tin – some flint, a striker, Tampax, boiled sweets, fishing line and hooks, wire snares, small waterproof sheet, heliograph and other bits and bobs. We were told to get everything done as fast as possible.

First thing was to build a shelter. I spotted some felled trees lying near a small stone wall. I collected branches, bound them together and laid them against the wall at an angle. I insulated the roof with leaves and ferns and made a bed inside with the same material. Protection: tick.

The next stage was devising something to make others aware of your presence when required. I built a raised structure that I could set alight. The tripod frame was fashioned from strips of tree bark with an inside shelf that I was sure would stay dry if it rained. I packed dry grass and tinder in there and stacked up other wood to keep the fire going, then covered my creation with a small plastic sheet. I made sure some of the firewood was damp, knowing that would make it smoke heavily and, ideally, alert a rescue aircraft. Darkness falling, I chose to call it a day. Location: tick.

A cold night but I did get a little sleep, learning the next day that some were still building their shelter into the early hours. That morning, I went in search of a stream, found one and managed to collect, filter and store some water. Water: tick.

In terms of grub, it might take days to chase down and catch any kind of animal, so I got on with buildings traps and setting fishing lines. Food: tick.

I called in the instructors after that. They bombarded me with questions then asked to see my location beacon alight. I proudly pulled the plastic sheet from over the tinder and began striking away at the flint, trying to light the dry grass. I tried a few times with no luck. Sparks aplenty, but no flame. In a moment of genius, I pulled out the bone-dry tampon knowing I had no other use for it. The thing caught light quickly and from there I used it to light the dry grass and tinder. The beacon did its job. I and seven others passed that part of the course. Four failed, one an RAF officer who believed that wrapping his feet in tin foil and clingfilm for seven days to avoid getting wet feet was a good idea.

From there, things moved up a gear to Conduct After Capture (CAC). CAC training includes Resistance to Interrogation (R2I), in which trainees experience hooding, sleep deprivation, time disorientation, deprivation of warmth, water and food. Delivered in strictly controlled conditions, the idea is that if you're nabbed by hostile forces who don't abide by the Geneva Convention, you'll have some idea of what to expect. The training has three levels, A, B and C, with C being highest. It's the one that those on the Prone To Capture (PTC) list need to undergo. That includes Special Forces, who face being caught inside enemy territory, and aircrew, who face being downed from above it.

We were split into pairs and, before being dropped at various locations, told to rendezvous with an agent to receive further instructions. As we made our way, a hunter force was dispatched to track us down. On learning that the hunter force were members of the RAF Regiment I felt, as any soldier would, a lot safer, and considered wearing a hi-viz jester's outfit to help them out. Nonetheless, capture was inevitable. Interrogation was part of the process. We just needed to put some effort into the evasion.

I was fortunate to be paired with Gary L, a familiar face and part of the same squadron. On day one we had about thirteen miles to do to make it to the first point, an isolated gate on a dirt track.

We used the map to plot a route through lumpy terrain, taking it one hour at a time then stopping to take stock. At sunset, we had about two miles to go. We held for a while after dark to let our eyes adjust then headed for the wood line that ran in the direction of where we needed to be. There was some flashing of torches some distance away, but nothing too close to suggest they were onto us. Still, we went as stealthily as we could and made it to the gate. And waited. And waited some more.

Two hours later, a car driving up the track. As it approached, it turned its lights off, then stopped. That was our cue. We emerged from the bushes, approached, got a cup of hot soup each and the location of the next RV point was passed to us. We headed back into the murky wilderness.

We had one day to finish the next leg, a yomp of eighteen miles. We reckoned we would keep going, get there first, then take it in turns to get some kip. More flashes of distant torches telling us the hunter force was out there, suggesting they had intercepted others, but still they were far from us. Even so, it was only a matter of time before we were funnelled into an area of their choosing and captured.

We made the second point, got the grid ref and checked out how far to go for the third leg. It was about twenty miles. As we took that all in and looked at the terrain ahead, both sets of eyes fell on a large complex about 500 metres away.

'That looks like a hotel to me,' I said.

'It certainly does.'

Maybe, just maybe, someone there might be able to offer us a bit of help, possibly even a lift, perhaps something to eat. We cautiously stole over, quickly spotting a bar and restaurant area. Through the window we could see a young couple having a drink, deep in conversation.

Tap tap tap.

They looked around, unsure what they had just heard, and went back to their conversation.

Tap tap tap.

The man looked over again. This time he saw us. I waved, pointed towards the side door. He looked baffled. So did she. He came towards the side door, his puzzled face saying he really wasn't sure about this at all. He pulled it carefully open, his eyebrows dipped in a frown.

'Mate,' I said, 'so sorry.'

As he looked over two filthy, knackered soldiers, I gave him the briefest of briefings.

'Any chance you could give us a lift a few miles up the road?'

I'm pretty sure he liked the idea of what we had just asked, almost as if he had been selected to take part in a classified operation.

'No problem,' he said. 'I'll get the keys.'

The heating in that car was glorious as we made our way towards the final rendezvous (RV). The young man asked a lot of questions and we gave very sparse responses, telling him there were parts of what we were doing that must remain secret. Forty minutes later, we thanked him very sincerely for his help and disappeared once again into the cloak of night.

'We have adapted to our situation,' we told each other, laughing and not feeling in any way guilty.

'We have used our initiative,' we continued, reminding ourselves that we had walked twenty miles less than the others.

The following morning, after a couple of hours' shuteye, all groups met with the training staff. We joined the others in devouring a Mars Bar and heard how some pairs had been caught before being returned into the exercise to keep going. We said we had avoided capture, although we managed to leave out the bit about the car.

From there, each pair was loaded into a Land Rover and driven to another exercise area. Minutes later, the vehicles were attacked by simulated enemy. CAC had begun.

Yelling was coming from outside. I braced myself. The door was wrenched open, guns pointing, hands grabbing. This truly did have the feel of the real thing. We were blindfolded, hands bound behind our backs with plastic ties. One sense down, we were driven away at speed, the vehicle bouncing hard on bumpy road. Sharp right turn, hard left, bump, right, right, left, left, bounce, thump – it was impossible to keep up with it.

Sudden stop. Dragged out, heads pushed down, walked somewhere, shoved to the ground.

'KNEES! Get on your fucking knees!'

I'd no idea if Gary was with me. Couldn't picture the location, had no clue how many people were around me.

Suddenly a baby crying. My brain, already in overdrive, now filling with some primeval urge to help the child. But I knew too it was all part of the show, all designed to disorient me. It seemed to be working.

The infant's wails morphed into a fuzzy scream that became a full-on punishing white noise like a high pitched hissing. Now running water, a tap pouring somewhere, maybe a burst pipe close by. Then the baby again, then the white noise, then the water. I caught myself worrying about how much water was being wasted and remembered it wasn't real. Or was that bit real? Was it good that I was questioning myself?

After a while I managed to adapt, to tune out to an extent and assure myself that everything was okay, to think of that Mars Bar and that guy giving us a lift, to dwell on happier things. And, as I orientated, I became sure that Gary was right beside me.

My thumbs were grabbed and pulled, forcing me to stand. I was dragged to another place, pushed back onto my knees. More of the same. Then thumbs seized again, moved, forced back down again. And then –

'Stand up.'

I stood. My blindfold was removed. As I blinked my way out of blurred vision, I saw a large man right in front of me. His eyes were locked on mine.

'I am the umpire,' he said. 'Who am I?'

'The umpire.'

'If you need to get out or want to withdraw, call for me. Okay?'

'Okay.'

The blindfold went back on again, my thumbs were grabbed once more and away I went, led from I didn't know where to I don't know where.

Blindfold off again.

Two big guys, both screaming at me – insults, abuse, obscenities point blank into my face. It was hard not to respond, hard to avoid their eyes, to feel their breath and spittle and remain unmoved. But it was mind over matter now, logic over fear. I told myself that my personal space was not my own, that it would not be my own for twenty-four hours.

I could do this.

The questions came fast. What was I doing there? Who was I with? What did I want?

But I could only respond with the basics – name, rank, number, date of birth. The only other permissible answer is, 'I cannot answer that question, sir / ma'am.' Beyond that, do the basics your captors ask, but do not agree to undertake any unreasonable tasks.

And it went on and on, the screams, the insults, the yells into the face, right into the ear. I thought of eating, of sleeping, of flying, of the way cities look so beautiful from above, of the way the stars sparkle.

'What are you fucking doing here?'

'Who are you with?'

'What do you want?'

And on it went.

It stopped after who knows how many minutes. A woman entered, her body language suggesting right away that she was going to be pleasant, the good cop to the bad cops I'd just met. They were wearing me down, seeing if I would give in, seeing if I might now talk to the nice lady after the two guys had done their best to scare me shitless. And if not, they had plenty of time. I knew the shouty men would be back.

'Take off your clothes. All of them.'

I did as instructed. It was very cold.

She searched my kit, asked me a lot of questions then handed me some overalls and a set of blacked out goggles. She called the guards and I was dragged from that room, thumbs first, and further into the depths of the building.

In the next room I was put in the first of many stress positions. I had to lean into the wall with only my fingertips touching it. Any time I would try and move to help ease the discomfort, I was aggressively repositioned. Then into another stress position. Then another. It felt like it was going on for hours. I really was beginning to hate these bastards, although I knew that too was part of the psychological shredding. I knew I couldn't slip into that pattern of thinking because that was just what they wanted.

Grabbed and dragged to my first interrogation. Good cop, bad cop. One would bawl and shout and threaten, the other was relaxed, acting as if he was my mate. Those threats were bloody awful – heavy, hard and seemed very serious. I was consciously starting to think were they real? Should I just give in? Now back to white noise, back to the stress positions.

I knew this hell would go on for twenty-four hours, but I'd no idea how long I'd been there. It was when I was taken to the toilet for the first time that I saw a sliver of daylight from one side. When I was taken later, there was no daylight. It was the only reference I had.

Goggles again before they pulled me back out, sat me down, took them off again. I was in front of a man dressed like a vicar. He spoke softly, asked how I was? He said he was on my side, that he wanted to help, that he could explain things to my captors.

It is worth saying here that I wished he was for real, that I wanted to tell myself he was legit. I knew deep down that he was part of the show, but he was very good at it. By that stage, with no idea how much more of this I would have to face, I really could have done with a break and he really did seem to be the guy who could provide it. But I knew it was weakness, that my brain and body had been worn down, and that I could not give in.

So I began to tell him a story about getting lost in the area, about having no interest in what was going on here. I'd been over it many times in my head and, as I put it into words for the first time, I was rewarded with a snack and a brew, which the briefing had said I should accept if offered. And then, after saying little but offering some form of excuse, I went back to saying nothing. So it was back into the stress position, back to the white noise.

At this point, oddly, I was feeling okay. I knew I'd been close to the edge but at the same time, in clearer moments, I could remind myself of all that was going on. I told myself that it was cold in there because they were controlling the heating, that they were purposely inducing a chill to make me – all of us – shiver, but nothing more. Even more bizarrely, it was during those intensive twenty-four hours that I learned to stop myself shivering by simply recognising it and telling myself to stop. Amid all the madness, I was chuffed about exerting some useful mind control of my own.

Back for another interrogation, for another change of direction. This time a scenario was put to me, one with which I agreed but could not respond to as they wished. I was sorely tempted just to do what they wanted, to do what I wanted – but I wasn't giving in. Back into the stress position.

Shouting from a room next door. Furniture being thrown around. It was an unspoken threat to me, a clue as to what was coming next. Or was it? Was that for real or part of the show? I commanded my mind to repeat to me over and over: mind games, just mind games, only mind games.

The room was getting warm, getting hot now. The lighting

was dimmed. I was told to sit on a chair and the moment I did so my eyes quickly closed. I could have drifted off in an instant. I blinked hard, forced myself awake. My head dipped again. Back up again. Back down again, like a nodding dog.

And a guy starts asking a question. The same question. Repeating it over and over and over. Then my own voice, speaking out, as if I hadn't even thought of it before I said it.

I said, from nowhere, 'Does this man ever shut up?'

They ignored me. Then the same question, more and more. And a switch – a new question. And now back to the old one. Over and over.

BANG!

His hands slamming on the table.

'Thank you very much,' he said.

Why was he thanking me? Had I spoken in my sleep? I was unsure. Did I or didn't I? This was what they wanted, to sow doubt in my mind.

The door swung open, bashing against the wall. Hauled off to a cold room, into the noise. It was here that I started to ask how long I could hold on for, whether I really could see this through. Had it been eight hours? Twenty hours? I hadn't any notion. Hungry, angry, irritable beyond anything I'd ever been before.

And I was asking myself, 'Who gives a shit if I fail? Who really cares but me if I pass this? Is it worth passing it? What am I doing here? Why am I doing this?'

The questions were getting louder in my head, seeming more and more reasonable as time went on.

Now a man sitting in front of me telling jokes. He was there for ages, cracking away, drawing things on paper, funny little diagrams and conundrums. I couldn't work it out. Never mind what I was doing there, what the hell was he doing there? Did they want me to ask myself if I was imagining this? Or, come to think of it, was I imagining this?

But, Christ, was he irritating.

To be fair, some of the jokes were quite funny, though I don't remember laughing.

More stress positions, more noise, then pulled into a room with a table and two chairs. As a man calmly began asking questions, the door burst open and a huge guy dashed in, slammed a cosh hard on the table. He yelled at me, stared at me like he was going to kill me. I was startled, shocked, terrified. I was certain I was going to get belted by this man even though I knew I wasn't going to get belted by this man.

The calm guy directed my attention to a piece of paper, said I should sign it.

'I cannot answer that question, sir.'

He asked me to fold up a piece of paper into something that resembled a rollie cigarette. I decided that this was not an unreasonable request. I rolled the paper. He asked me to fold another. I agreed. He said to insert each into an ear. I did. They both laughed. They asked me to roll up two more, which I did. I was to put these in my mouth and let them hang down like teeth. I agreed. There were more of them in the room now, appearing from somewhere, all to get a look at me doing whatever it was.

Then they asked me to pose as a rabbit. I adopted a rabbit pose. They laughed their nuts off. Then asked me to waddle around the room like a 'gay rabbit'. I did so. The raucous laughter was almost shaking the walls. Then it stopped. I was blindfolded and dragged out, told to sit.

A while later, I was told to stand. The blindfold was removed. The umpire was standing in front of me.

'I am the umpire,' he said, 'the exercise is over.'

My reaction was a complex confusion of joy and distress. I felt overwhelmed, free, exhausted, ecstatic.

It turned out that, of the eight who went through those twenty-four hours, I had the longest single interrogation, just one minute short of two hours. And, I was advised, my rabbit debut had been recorded, although I have never seen the tape. I can only hope that no one ever does.

And now, with just a follow-up course in teaching the survival lessons I'd learned, I was the Survival Rescue Officer (SRO) for the Squadron.

I took things a step further the following year by signing up for the RAF Winter Survival course at Oberammergau in the Bavarian Alps. German mountain troops assisted in snow survival and skiing instruction, including langlauf skiing – which is basically skiing cross-country under your own steam, rather than downhill. The challenges and distances grew to the point that, between digging shelters and carrying a 'casualty' for several gruelling kilometres, we found ourselves in a kind of wintry hell. Relief came in the form of a fairly ferocious drinking session, complete with party games, ahead of the final, awful, three-day test.

German troops from the Alpine Division were to act as the hunter force so I reckoned we were likely to get caught several times. I was paired with J from the RAF Regiment and luckily he and I hit it off right away. Dropped off at our start point, we immediately moved into the cover of a nearby snowy wood line to gain our bearings and form a plan. The rendezvous point was some 20 kilometres away which, with snow at times up to our waists and bergens on our backs, it would us take all day to reach. Despite the temperature, our exertions had us sweating hard as we battled onwards. Looking like boil-in-the-bag beetroots we eventually met our agent, before trying to get a couple of hours' rest. A blizzard put paid to that as the pair of us, caught out by the speed of its arrival, huddled by a tree in sleeping bags as snow piled up.

Night marching followed, exhaustedly ploughing on to the next rendezvous point, the frequent crackling of twigs and rustling of leaves ramping up our paranoia that capture was imminent. That paranoia proved well-informed when shadows came alive and came belting out from among trees while barking orders. Bergen on, looking like some kind of knackered turtle, I made a run for it but, inevitably, two hunters had me face down in the snow in no time. We were put on the back of a truck and taken for interrogation before being ferried to a new position, one that would add 5 kilometres to the route. Capture had been, I was sure, unavoidable yet J had taken it badly, as if disappointed they had got us.

The final day, with almost zero sleep, was one I'll never forget. We were making our way across a hill, both dead beat, our weary muscles driving forward by sheer will alone, when the hunters jumped us again. I stood my ground when I saw them coming from nowhere, all kitted out with camouflage gear and night-vision aids. I just didn't have the energy to run and instead waited for the rugby tackle.

Again we were taken to a camp, questioned, loaded back on the truck with two of the hunter force accompanying, and back out onto the road towards the next drop-off.

I was just settling down, trying not to think of the continuing nightmare ahead, when J stood up. We were motoring along at about 50kph at the time yet he had taken to his feet. Without warning, he ran to the back of the truck and dived head first through the canvas flap.

Had I just imagined that?

The two guards looked at me and I looked at them.

My fist banged the rear of the cabin. The other two joined in, hammering hard, needing the truck to brake immediately.

We got it to reverse a distance before, almost too late, we spotted J lying in the middle of the road. He was not conscious, his breathing shallow, blood seeping from one ear. It looked to me like a head injury. And here we were deep in the middle of nowhere, in the middle of winter.

One guard bolted off to find help. The other and myself wrapped

J in sleeping bags, being careful not to move him. We kept talking to him, hoping hard that he was not going to die there. Ten agonising minutes went by before a car came into view and the guard with me waved it down. We were very lucky that an off-duty nurse was driving, lucky too that the other guard had managed to call for an ambulance. It arrived around forty minutes later.

I followed J to the hospital, keen to alert medics to the potentially dangerous emergency flares he was carrying. They had cut his clothes away and were trying to work out his injuries, eventually diagnosing a swelling on the brain. J would need later treatment at a specialist hospital, they told me, but he would survive.

I'm sorry to say I never saw him again. I'd like to have asked what possessed him to leap head first from a moving vehicle. Perhaps the lack of sleep and overall conditions had clouded his judgement. Or maybe it was his disappointment at being captured that had convinced him to attempt some kind of daring escape. I'll probably never know. What I do know was that other groups had been caught as many as four and even five times, so there was no shame at all in how he and I performed.

I hope J was able to make a full recovery, whatever it was that went on with him that day.

Chapter Twelve

CRASH. SEPTEMBER, 2001

'**A** PLANE'S HIT the Twin Towers.'

Some guy said it. He stuck his head through the door of the tent, made the announcement, ran off.

'What did he say?'

I shrugged. Had another sip of tea. It couldn't be serious.

Tuesday afternoon in the Omani desert, 11 September 2001. Commotion outside. Curious, we exited the tent. Something was up. People were dashing towards the operations centre, a large marquee tent a couple of hundred metres away.

'What the... ?'

The place was packed, people crowded around the large TV screen in the centre. I couldn't see it at first.

'What's happened?

'A plane's hit the Twin Towers in New York.'

I pushed my way through, got sight of the screen. An airliner slamming into one of the skyscrapers. An enormous plume of black smoke already coming from the first tower. Gasps all around.

Someone said, 'That's the second one.'

No one spoke.

Someone else said, 'That's terrorism.'

I don't think there was anyone there who didn't have a sense that, one way or another, this would impact on us. Within days, as the nationalities and motives of the terrorists became clear, US President George W. Bush was hinting at war in the Middle East. We were already out there.

More than 22,500 British Army personnel had shipped to Oman for Saif Sareea II, or Swift Sword II – an exercise involving the largest deployment of UK forces since the Gulf War. We had with us 6,500 vehicles, 21 naval vessels, 49 fixed-wing aircraft and 44 helicopters. The point was to test the UK's expeditionary warfare strategy and, chiefly, the mettle of the new tri-service Joint Rapid Reaction Force (JRRF).

After 9/11, without any official announcements, the tempo and tone of the exercise changed. Everything became more serious, everyone becoming more determined. Somewhere along the command chain, people knew more. One week after the attack, in a change of plan, we were deployed into the middle of the Omani desert.

I'd signed up for Swift Sword II in July. A request had arrived for a detachment of four pilots to join 4 Regiment AAC from Wattisham on a large joint-services, three-month exercise. Our new home was Thumbrait Airbase, just north of the major coastal town of Salalah. And, man, it was hot, hovering between 38 and 42 degrees Celsius. Our accommodation amounted to camp cots inside an old green canvas twelve-man tent. No air-conditioning, so it was like a kiln in there. The only way to get any slight control of the temperature was to keep the flaps open all day. The payback was that little, and not-so-little, squalls randomly flung sand into the tent throughout the day. To get the stuff off, along with the rest of the grime and sweat, we would take often searing solar showers, the water sun-baked in a black rubber bag with a tube and shower head attachment. After that, it would be back into the desert fatigues, which were way too thick, and the heavy sweating would begin again.

We were being asked for our feedback on such things along the way, asked whether improvements could be made to the kit. Of primary interest to the army were the all-new desert boots that had been issued to all troops. They looked the part, but I'm not kidding when I say they started to melt within a few minutes after beginning a walk. I clearly remember the fury on the sergeant major's face as he ripped both disintegrating boots from his feet, flung them into a dry ditch and marched back in his socks to make his feelings known.

The flying, though, was epic, not least because landing Lynx on desert was a whole new nerve-racking adventure. You need to get down quick because you're always seconds from total brown-out. And those mini sandstorms we were whipping up were taking their toll, the abrasive sand causing immense damage to our (very expensive) rotor blades. To spare them, usage of each blade was slashed from hundreds to tens of hours. From blades to boots, the British Army was learning a lot about modern desert warfare. The timing for that could not have been more fortuitous.

In early September, before 9/11, my fellow Lynx pilot Baz was tasked with conducting an escape-and-evasion training day, including crashed-aircraft procedure. Little did we know how relevant this was to become. One early morning several Lynx were tasked with conducting separate route reconnaissance sorties for future flights. We were to make note of any observations, mark them up on the map, brief other crews. Andy B would pilot my Lynx while I was aircraft commander.

On that morning I watched the other aircraft take off, watched as the Lynx became a silhouette inside a brown bubble before it crashed down, bounced back up and crashed again, before it began breaking apart as I stood, terrified, glued to the spot just metres away. Bursting with adrenalin yet paralysed by fear, I'd no idea what to do, no time to do it. Without thinking, my eyes closed, my hands went over my ears and I turned. I put my back to it all, left it to fate.

And everything stopped.

Not even the sound of the desert any more.

Was I dead? I didn't think so.

I turned, trying to see through the haze of smoke and sand. There was a shape in front of my eyes, flames a few metres further along. The Lynx had somehow rotated 180 degrees and come to a rest on its side. It was so close that part of its tail was beneath our rotor disc but now it was facing in the opposite direction. It was literally right in front of me and it was on fire.

'Fuck me that was close.'

But no one else was talking.

I don't remember any conscious thought, but there must have been one or two. For in a second, I was scrambling up the twisted underside of the aircraft, already aware of how and where to get access, aiming to get down into the cockpit, my voice in my ears going, 'Crash crash crash!'

At the top – which had been the side a minute earlier – just the mangled remnants of the cockpit door, most of it ripped away and flung into the desert.

I braced myself, looked into the dark interior. One crew member was in a crumpled heap at the bottom, his face cut and bleeding. I wiped my eyes, sand in them, sand everywhere. The guy had been shot out of his seat and was now on top of the other crew member.

'Get out now!'

Again, I don't remember thinking about it, just recall shouting it, trying to get his attention. The engine fire, with plenty of fuel to burn, was not going to put itself out and, semi-conscious or not, these guys needed to know it. This thing was all set to go up like a 5-tonne firework. But there was precious little in terms of movement inside the cockpit. I leaned in with one arm and, holding tight to the outer frame with the other hand, got a grip on the first man. He was almost awake, almost understanding the situation, almost able to help himself, but not quite. I pulled him upwards and out. I leaned in again. The other man was likewise just half aware, half there. I grabbed hold of him, pulled him out too. I can only say that these were actions of instinct because they had to be. If I'd thought it through, I'd have told myself that a small-build 5-foot 7-inch guy would never have been able to pull two larger men out of there with one arm.

'Crash crash crash!'

As they got their legs working, found a foothold and climbed off that crashed Lynx, my pilot Andy appeared through the dust like some kind of mirage. And thank Christ for that. I grabbed both stumbling crew, directed them towards Andy and all three headed back to the operations and accommodation area.

I turned my attention to the flames on the other side of the aircraft. I slipped down the outer fuselage, dashed around, took stock of the blaze, the flames really taking grip now. And, like a man who had lost his mind, I ran back around, climbed back up into the banjaxed aircraft and dipped back into that dim and crumpled cockpit in search of the fire extinguisher. It wasn't where it should be, but nothing else was either. Luckily I found it quickly, climbed back down and ran around once more to kill the fire. I aimed it and nothing happened. I tried again, nothing happened. I could only assume the thing had been damaged. And I was becoming sure I was about to get a little damaged myself.

I was just about to call it a day and run for my life when I remembered. I flipped the extinguisher upside down. How could I have forgotten that? Gas pumped out, covered the flames and I forgave myself for my absent-mindedness. It had been a busy few minutes.

Voices now, people arriving at the scene. At that point I was ushered away and the area was cordoned off. This was now an accident scene. Everything there was evidence and needed to be protected.

I learned later that a technician who was 200 metres away at the time leapt out of bed after mishearing 'Crash crash crash!' for 'Gas gas gas!' He pulled on his respirator while running around in his pants urging everyone else to do the same.

The four of us in the accident were flown to a local hospital. Andy and I hadn't a scratch and the other crew had minor injuries and bruising. Quite a morning. And it was not yet 7 a.m. I took the rest of the day off.

The following morning the CO arrived in my tent bearing a brew. He said there would be an investigation and that the first step was for me, while taking whatever time I needed, to answer his questions. He listened carefully to every word and, after about an hour, thanked me for my 'unselfish actions' and 'sheer bravery'. I smiled. I didn't know what else to do.

In the coming few days, as all the squadron returned to the base, I was getting my hand shaken a lot, getting quite a few pats on the back, a fair number of meaningful nods. I understood why, but it was a little uncomfortable at times.

After a while my mate Pete L and I decided to go for a wander. He knew I needed a break. I told him, 'I just want things to get back to normal.' He said that might take a while.

Someone said, 'Steve?'

I turned. The two aircrew I had pulled from the Lynx. I hadn't seen them since we were at the hospital two days before. Andy, the RAF exchange officer, shook my hand and said 'Thank you.'

'Any time.'

John, the pilot, didn't speak. He manfully squeezed my shoulder instead. No words needed.

The banter, which had been on hold for a couple of days,

recommenced. The piss-taking directed my way centred on my operation of the fire extinguisher. I was, I was told, an 'arsonist's dream'. It was good to hear that stuff. It meant we were moving on.

By the time I was due to appear in front of the investigation board, I was at ease with it all but still unsure what lay ahead. A team had flown out from the UK to examine the scene, inspect the wreckage, and interview all involved. When called on, I sat down in front of a presiding officer, a major, and three other figures. For the next three hours I went over every particular in minute detail. I was shown a huge array of aerial and ground photos of the scene to help me to explain it all.

It was during those hours that the enormity of it all sank in. The aircraft had come to rest underneath the rotor blades of my aircraft. Parts of it were strewn all over the place. I could see how and where I had climbed the crashed aircraft, see where the fires had been. The metal carnage – pieces of gearbox, bits of blades, lumps of fuselage – was everywhere. Parts were found in the technicians' accommodation 200 metres away, and pieces of aircraft metal were discovered under camp cots. Chunks of aircraft had come hurtling within inches of me, and ripped steel had ended up under my Lynx. Yet miraculously, I, Andy and even our aircraft had remained entirely unscathed.

I slept deeply later that day, my mind heavy with the new discoveries, with the unwieldy facts of what had taken place, with the strangely unnerving truth that I had survived only by chance. I remember hearing fast blades chopping the air, a helicopter getting closer, the deafening noise and its invisible source heading right at me. I woke – startled, looking around in the half light. All the others were fast asleep. I'd had my first flashback. But the first of how many? I had no idea. But I know now. And thankfully that first flashback was also the last.

While awake in the heat, I thought about it all again, more than I wanted to. I couldn't get it out of my head. I thought of those gut-driven, crazed, illogical minutes. I reflected on how it had been the cold, crisp logic of the fact-gathering investigation that had spelled out just how insane it had all been.

I began to feel a burning sensation somewhere near my stomach. Within a couple of weeks of giving evidence, everything I was swallowing was causing me pain. I had to step away, to spend time at the military field hospital. An endoscopy confirmed what I'd feared – a stomach ulcer. It seemed clear that the stress was wearing me down, burning me up. I was grounded from flying, told that dealing with a burst ulcer in the sky isn't high on anyone's must-do list. I understood, but it sent me on a downer. And to top it off, the military advised they would medevac me back to the UK for treatment and then to Germany for ground duties while I was on the mend. Needless to say I wanted none of that, but had to take it all.

The C-130, heading for Blighty, was packed with soldiers with all sorts of injuries- broken bones, skin burns, serious flesh wounds. In the middle of it, I sat there like a malingerer looking to bunk off. I kept schtum about the nature of my problem.

After a while I spotted one of our pilots at the far corner, tucked away behind cargo stacked along the centre of the freight deck.

'Hi Gary,' I said.

'Oh, hi Steve.'

'What are you going back for?'

'Well,' he said, a little sheepish, 'I have piles.'

It was the first time I'd laughed in a day or two. And I just let it all out.

'Oh Jesus, that's funny,' I said.

Six months later and there's something unexpected in my mailbox. A telegram. Who the hell sends a telegram?

I wasn't sure about this at all. In the military there is a constant need to be on your guard for elaborate wind-ups, for rogue practical jokes, for things that get lined up with the sole purpose of making you look like a dick.

The telegram said it was from Prince Charles, the Prince of Wales, Colonel-in-Chief of the Army Air Corps. This had got to be a piss-take. Why would he write to me? Yes, I met him when I was a little boy, but it's not like we'd kept in touch. And yes, I flew him around in Brunei when he visited that time, but it's not like we became pen pals.

My boss had an office near by. I went over to seek his opinion.

'What do you reckon to this?' I said.

'A telegram, Steve? Who sends a telegram these days?'

'My question exactly. Says it's from Prince Charles.'

'Prince Charles? Saying what?'

'"Having heard the splendid news of your award of the Queen's Commendation for Bravery. I wanted to send my warmest congratulations. Well done. Charles. Colonel-in-Chief."'

'Yes mate,' he said. 'That's legit.'

Chapter Thirteen

ENTER THE APACHE, 2004

I WAS IN BRUNEI when I first heard that the AAC wanted an attack helicopter replacement for the Lynx. There were three in the running – the Denel Rooivalk, the AH-1W SuperCobra and the AH-64A Apache. The latter first entered service with the US military back in 1985. It had proved itself with flying colours during the Gulf War of 1991 and it didn't take long for it to win over the Ministry of Defence (MOD). The Apache was winning every fight it entered.

The UK looked first at getting one hundred or so of the A model. But the more capable D model, with its fire-control radar, was just coming on to the military hardware market. The UK went for that instead, splashing out the same intended sum on sixty-seven of them. The total acquisition, completed in 2004, came to £4.1bn.

Amid all this, quite a few helicopter pilots were trying to find out more. Rumours flew suggesting that the aircraft would be crewed only by officers, that the criteria line would be beyond most AAC pilots – and it was all bollocks. In the end it came down to pilots having a good track record, rightly so.

The UK instructors, having finished conversion training in the US, were designing a course for Brits. This was going to take time. And the training itself would take months.

Volunteers were selected, including yours truly, and told we would become part of 9 Regiment AAC based at Dishforth in North Yorkshire. At the time the regiment operated the Lynx, and those aircraft would be relocated to Wattisham to make way for the new machines. The initial conversion to type (CTT) training would take place at Middle Wallop, squadron by squadron. I was with 664 Squadron, the second course to go through Apache training after our sister squadron, 656. As the AAC recognised that more flying instructors were needed, some of our squadron were asked to delay to CTT course three. I didn't mind volunteering for that, feeling that I could get useful feedback from the lads who went before me.

But sooner or later I would have to part from both Germany and the girls. My ex-wife and I had joint custody of Robyn, allowing me to get a small married quarter in Dishforth so that she and Kelly would be able to visit. My start date for the course was now August, 2004. I was looking forward to it although, as a father, those final months in Germany had been darkened by a terrible incident.

It had happened in June the year before when, along with colleagues Pete L and Rob A, I had been asked to attend the annual RASS (Rhine Army Summer Show), a military fair and general family fun event which included a helium balloon ride. We arrived via Lynx at Rheindahlen, the British Army's German HQ, set up our Army Air Corps stand and chatted with visitors in glorious sunshine. It took us by surprise when the weather turned, the sky dimming and wind picking up fast. We sheltered in the Lynx as it got worse – thunder, lightning, hailstones, tents blowing over, chairs getting flung around. There was visible chaos as gales pounded in at close to 100mph.

An urgent message came for us to get to the operations tent.

There was unconfirmed word a child had been caught up in the tethering rope of the Royal Artillery balloon, which had torn free of its moorings and been blown away. We raced back to the aircraft, rose into the now fading winds to search from above. For an hour it seemed as though no news was good news, that no sign of tragedy meant no tragedy. Then we were issued directions to a scene of concern some distance from the base. In a field there we saw a silver balloon stretched out. It had struck a power line and crash-landed after a journey of forty-three miles. Soon afterwards, the body of a little girl was discovered near by. She was five years old, the daughter of a British serviceman and his German wife. The accident report concluded that seven tethering ropes had been torn from their anchors in the powerful, freak storm, and that one had wrapped itself around her arm. It was said the child may well have been conscious as she was pulled away and carried so far, and that it was likely to have been the impact with the ground that killed her. She must have been frightened beyond belief.

Another family's unfathomable pain had me spending a while longer with my children, saw me taking more time to consider just how precious they are, made me consider just how unbearable losing a child must be. I left for England with firm plans to see them soon.

Advance information advised that the Apache I was now due to meet was packed with revolutionary features, not least the flight symbology system that displayed data right into your eye. The idea of being among the very first Brits to experience this highest-tech cutting-edge new fighting machine was thrilling – though it would be a struggle to keep up with the course. But I knew I'd give it all I had.

And so, training began at Middle Wallop. On arrival, the Apaches had been given their own high-security area inside the already secure camp, giving a sense of their value. These walls within walls were high, electrified and punctuated with Threat of Death notices.

Behind them were parked eight Apache Longbow gunships for which 673 (Training) Squadron had the keys. Their role was to convert Army pilots on to the new aircraft. CTT would involve the hands-on raw flying skills – mountain flying, instrument flying and learning to operate the Apache by day and night. And then, for conversion to role (CTR), we'd be back at Dishforth learning to fight the aircraft in an operational context with live firing and environmental training. But only if we made it that far.

The officer commanding (OC) was Nick W. His opening words were: 'Anyone who is not prepared to use the aircraft to shoot and kill the enemy, then this is not for you.' I didn't have a problem with that. Besides, I was thinking of the more immediate future, of getting up close and personal to an Apache.

Off to the classrooms to study our nation's newest war machine. It was, for a flying soldier, like learning poetry. I was caught up with the words, the potential, with the ideas brought together to form what the Americans had dubbed, not so poetically, the Flying Tank. From armoured glass to bulletproof seats to multiple, colossal weapons systems, so much about this stub-winged, iconic bird of prey had been designed around fighting capability and survivability.

One key distinction, we were learning, was that of the seating positions. Instead of the conventional side-by-side cockpit, the two crew were one behind the other, pilot in the back, co-pilot/gunner ahead of him. Comms would be via intercom supplemented by a small mirror positioned in the front seat. Useful during the day for seeing what the pilot beyond the armoured glass behind was doing but useless at night.

We studied some more and began simulated sorties, learning our imminent new immediate environment, getting a sense of what goes where, and there was a lot to learn. After that, we moved to the day phase in which we'd finally get to fly. It involved thirteen daylight sorties culminating in an end of phase intermediate handling test (IHT). It would be heavy going and, if you didn't make the grade, it would be goodbye Apache.

On the morning of 12 October 2004, I set off to board an Apache for the first time. I'd barely slept from excitement. I will never forget the first time I walked into the hangar and got up close and personal with this extraordinary new aircraft. It was over in the corner and giving off no shine at all from the lights above. It was like a bulky, rugged shadow, enormous yet almost discreet in its understated appearance. I'd had the privilege in the past of flying some beautiful machines and this new, dark addition was not going into that bracket. Because this thing, like a brooding Grim Reaper from a brutal, alien future, was very, very ugly indeed. And it was the combination of all the above that made her absolutely jaw dropping.

Rich Y, my instructor, was a font of all knowledge. He pointed out the 30mm chain gun mounted beneath the fuselage. He showed me the sensors, explained how they can be slaved to the pilot's right eye via a helmet-mounted monocle that displays flight symbology and thermal imagery. When the pilot's head turns, the sensors will follow. We looked at the nose where the TADS (target acquisition and designation system) and PNVS (pilots' night-vision system – pronounced 'pinviss') dominate. The TADS, the larger bucket turret, holds the stabilised electro-optical sensors, a laser rangefinder and laser target designator. When slaved to head movements, its images are projected onto the crew's helmet-mounted optical sight. PNVS, meanwhile, contains an infrared (IR) camera, again slaved to the pilot's monocle and rotatable +/− 90 degrees in azimuth and +20/− 45 degrees in elevation. PNVS has a high rate of movement (120 degrees per second) so can match the pilot's head movements. Between them, TADS and PNVS are the eyes of the aircraft.

Next, the Longbow dome, installed over the main rotor and looking not dissimilar to a large round block of cheese. This is home to the FCR (fire-control radar) target-acquisition system.

The elevated position allows detection and missile engagement of targets even if the helicopter itself is concealed by an obstacle.

'Handy,' I said, or something like it.

Handrails and steps up to the rear cockpit. The aircraft felt sturdy, as if this very agile thing was in fact immovable, like an elegantly forged block of iron. I was going to the top, all 15 feet of it, and when there I could look along the full 50-foot length of the Apache. I opened the weighty cockpit door and, climbing aboard, almost fell into the seating position. Rich was right behind, sitting down just outside the cockpit. It was clear there was more room in here than there would be in the front, but not much. The rear cockpit – clean, friendly, ergonomically efficient – was dominated by two MPDs (multi-purpose displays). No more lumpy, clunky switches. I had quite literally just stepped into the era of the digital cockpit.

Buttons all over the cyclic and collective controls, just as in the simulations. I knew that in time I would do all I could to learn them and their purpose by feel alone. It helped that each was of a different shape in the way that, for example, an Xbox controller might be. Then a quick explanation from Rich of everything before the fitting of the monocle which would display flight information including speed, height, torque and sensor-in-use.

Show over, familiarisation walk-round completed, it was now off to our allocated aircraft. She was sitting poised and ready on the dispersal as we approached. As soon as I saw that beast I knew my name was all over her. Rich climbed into the front, or CPG (co-pilot/gunner's) seat. He signalled for me to turn the batteries on and the silent aircraft came alive. Twin screens lit up and advised that internal checks were under way. Intercoms on, I took my time to ensure my monocle was set correctly. For some reason my head was hurting under my helmet, a sharp pain right on the top of my forehead. I wasn't about to let it get in the way of this day.

I started the APU (auxiliary power unit), firing up more systems without the need to start an engine, to make further checks. And it was all exactly as we had practised in the simulator. All checks were completed slowly and methodically. And once at flight idle, Rich took control to demonstrate the ground taxi. As we rolled off, I could almost feel my heart being stolen away.

The Apache is a top-heavy aircraft and therefore requires finesse when cornering on the ground. Too much cyclic and it will lean in and, if too little, there's a possibility it will lean out. Neither is good. There's a fine balance to strike. Yet it's light to the touch, turning gracefully when required to do so. I followed Rich's inputs on the controls from the rear, ensuring everything he was doing made sense to me.

Once clear of the dispersal, a full-bodied thwapping as the aircraft lifted into a steady hover. We slowly air taxied to one of the perimeter roads where Rich set her back down nice and gently.

'You have control,' he said.

Everything at my fingertips was now awaiting instruction. Someone had just put me in charge of a £35 million aircraft. The pressure at the top of my head was getting worse yet, at the same time, I was feeling invincible. For the next half-hour I ground taxied her back and forwards and even chanced a pirouette. I loved it, and Rich, offering encouragement, could tell.

The second sortie was with Scotty, whose favourite phrase was 'It's all noddy', usually said while drinking cola. We went through the controls, the autopilot, the low-level environment systems. But that sharp pain was back at the top of my forehead. Was this like the airsickness I used to suffer? Was this a new illness threatening to derail my career once more? Back in the ops room, I broke the news to Scotty.

'It just gets more painful the longer I'm in the Apache,' I said, certain now I was having some kind of bizarre reaction to the aircraft.

He took my helmet, looked inside. Part of the liner had folded back creating a pressure point.

'That's the problem,' he said, and handed it back.

'Just that?'

'It's all noddy.'

'Righto.'

Back into the simulator to go over, as with every sortie, what I had just been exposed to. Fly, sim, fly, sim – and on it went.

The next sorties would cover climbing, descending and sloping ground. The sloping ground teachings are needed in the event of landing on uneven surface. There is potential for the aircraft to roll over given the Apache's top-heavy weight distribution. Even at an angle of just 10 degrees from the vertical it can feel as though the aircraft might fall. If close to the limit, the landing must be aborted.

Then circuits, getting all the checks sorted, flying with precise balance at the allotted speed and height. The monocle was key here, providing cueing dots indicating a particular reference point and guiding you there.

Into advanced transition sorties, instructed by Shaun Wyatt, a familiar face, an AAC legend and, as mentioned earlier, recipient of a DFC for his work in Northern Ireland during the Troubles. Only three DFCs and one DFM (Distinguished Flying Medal) were ever awarded for service in Northern Ireland during the Troubles. I got the hang of the new set-up quite quickly because Shaun was everything I had expected – patient, thorough, incredibly talented.

By now, and by choice, my free time was at a minimum. I was giving up weekends to rest, to read, to prepare. This new aircraft was already under my skin and missing my shot at this stage would have cut deep. Sadly, my mate Rob G was having a harder time. He was being pulled between seeing his daughter and dealing with his ex-wife, and with a head full of complications there was little space for the complete and calm focus required for the course. Many a time I remember hearing the metal waste bin getting kicked down the corridor, knowing that Rob was about to appear at my door, knowing there had been another unpleasant phone call, that another bad situation had arisen.

Running take-offs and landings were up next, with Rich demonstrating both. When called on, I pushed the cyclic forward to get the aircraft rolling, raised the collective allowing the rear wheel to leave the HALS (hardened aircraft landing strip), held the Apache on a level plane, used the pedals to keep it on the centreline. And just as I was running out of HALS, the helicopter belting along, I raised the collective launching us towards the heavens. Then into take-off checks, turning downwind to begin circuits of specified parameters, then pre-landing checks, finals turn and into the running landing.

From there, we were on to autorotations and practice forced landings (PFLs). As described in Chapter Five, autorotation covers the actions required to establish the aircraft in a descent without power to the rotors. In contrast, a PFL takes the autorotation to the next level, requiring the ability to manoeuvre the aircraft in anticipation of a practised landing, this includes conducting immediate actions, landing-field selection and turning into the wind.

The Apache has a low-inertia main rotor-head system, a factor determined by the mass of the blade and how easily it gains or loses momentum. The key to autorotation is how effective the pilot is in controlling the rotor speed when dropping. I ascended and, on command, lowered the collective all the way to cut all power to the rotor head, making it easier for the blades to turn in the descent. The task was to hold the helicopter stable as we began to drop. My first attempts were awful and needed intervention from Rich, who had returned as my instructor for this part of the course. On attempt number four, it was looking good. We dropped like a brick, but in a stable manner, before recovering, with my sweat glands at full pelt, at the given height. From there, I now had to do the same while adding in landing checks, turning into the wind and picking somewhere to set her down.

The final sortie before the IHT was confined areas, which means landing in a tight spot. The dimensions of the Apache, with barely any room to spare, had been cut into woodland. With my eyes on stalks, I descended inch by inch between the walls of leaves and branches, blade tips almost cutting them. And on touchdown, it was right back up again. More sweat.

The night before the IHT, Rob didn't seem himself. We chatted for hours, and it was clear that he had way too much on his plate. I hoped he would get through, but I am sorry to say he didn't make it, which I know was more due to his frame of mind than anything else. I passed, but Rob's troubles took the shine off things.

Next up, 'the Bag'. Unique to the Apache, this phase is about blacking out the rear cockpit. It forces the student to rely only on the sights and sensors via symbology provided through the monocle. The Americans came up with the idea after finding the day-to-night training transition too much of a leap for trainee pilots.

The Bag phase involved eight hours and three sorties. It didn't sound a lot but after just ten minutes I couldn't wait for it to end. Plastic panels, Velcro strips and glue are used to cover the windows, and just getting into a freshly blacked-out little box is enough to fire up the dread. I felt sick right away, enclosed alone in an ink-black cube under orders to fly the gunship well, or fail the course.

With Scotty in the front seat, I finished the checks and now, with the monocle illuminated point blank in my right eye, I breathed in deep and looked it all over. I'd heard that a pilot's depth perception goes haywire in the early Bag stages, and now I knew for sure. As I began my ground taxi I was overwhelmed with the feeling that the helicopter was about to topple over or crash. My senses were simmering, in some kind of panic mode, giving me whatever information they could, yet it was clashing with what the symbology was saying. The job right now was to learn to trust what you don't know, to learn to ignore what you do know. It felt like a hell of an ask. I turned the first corner, sitting in my dark bubble, and the huge machine lurched to one side, leaning way out. By instinct, I rapidly overcompensated and the aircraft flung the other way like a metronome.

From the front, that familiar phrase.

'It's all noddy.'

Cheers Scotty. Words of wisdom there.

Anyway, I somehow got the Apache out of the dispersal without writing it off. From there, the PNVS was my eyes. It uses infrared imaging, which creates an initially very-bloody-confusing heat map of what's around you. And just to make the picture that little bit trickier, the flight data is overlaid.

As we had been taught, the PNVS turret on the aircraft's nose was perfectly tuned to my head movements. The weird thing was that, when looking down, it's as if you are looking straight through the floor. What you are seeing is the infra-red feedback from the night system 13 feet away at the front of the aircraft. This bizarre remote-viewing situation can lead to what's known as parallax error, the apparent difference in the position of an object viewed along two different lines of sight. So I had to bear in mind that if I saw an obstruction or other feature in a certain place, it might not be in that place at all.

Aircraft movement is displayed in the form of a vector line. In daytime, the vector line combines with outside references to make it clear on which axis the aircraft is moving and by how much. Now all I had was the vector line. And, just to add to the fun, it has a time delay which meant I was already on the move before it showed that I was moving.

I was feeling sick on that day, sick with the pressure of it all, mentally shredded and dreading having to do it all again. I came away from that messy Bag sortie wondering, for the first time, if I might make it my last.

And the second one didn't go much better, flying circuits over Salisbury Plain. Scotty gave me a location where I should come to a hover and commence an exercise but I could barely work out where it was. The third sortie was pretty much a revision of the last. And still I wasn't feeling good about any of it.

The following day and it was time to meet up with my old pal Baz for the Bag Check to see how I'd fared. And that didn't go well either. I failed and got placed on what was called air warning (AW). And even now, just writing those doom-laden words sends a shiver down my spine. Someone once told me that all the best pilots have been on AW. I didn't believe them. The idea is that AW ensures struggling but competent students get additional flight hours and, in my case, I was given five. I'd be examined again after that and if I failed again, I'd be signed up for a test with the overall commander, who would decide my fate. But I couldn't think about that. For now, I'd been given a lifeline. I reframed it all, told myself I could either dig deep or give up. I knew which one it would be.

Nick W, the OC leading my first AW sortie, was a hugely experienced instructor. He told me afterwards that my problem was that I couldn't 'see the wood for the trees'. I was sweating, literally, over the little details and that was making me lose sight of the bigger picture. I knew he was right. Our second sortie proved it. That was when my head finally clicked into gear. And when it came to the third sortie, all two hours of it, I was knackered but starting to get the hang of things. Anyway, Bag Phase? Been there, done that, passed.

Next up was Night Phase, including reversionary night flying, which I had always loved. If there's a perfect place for me, it's looking down over the lights of the towns and villages, watching car headlights snake along roads, seeing the flash of blue light in the distance because even an emergency looks peaceful in the night sky.

Night flying in the Apache involves the TADS and PNVS systems acting together, even though both systems are independent. TADS is packed with tech, including stabilised electro-optical sensors, a thermographic camera and a monochrome daylight television camera. It has a laser rangefinder and laser target designator. Like PNVS, the movements of TADS can be slaved to the head movements of the crew. This allows the FLIR (forward-looking infrared) to be projected on to the crew's helmet-mounted display, the monocle.

Compared to the Bag Phase, this was relatively straightforward. After several sorties, we deployed to the wilds of Wales to experience how the aircraft performed in windy, mountainous terrain. The scenery was beautiful, and yet more breathtaking when dived into and danced around at speed. For a helicopter pilot, winds and various currents caused by immovable mountains are our best friends and worst enemies. Updrafts provide at times astonishing additional lift, while downdrafts, which can hit around 2,000fpm, can force the unpleasant merging of helmet with cockpit ceiling.

The final key section of training was Weaponeering, in which we student pilots got our first sense of just how hostile an Apache can get. Initial sorties were in the sim until we were competent enough to complete the weapon-handling test (WHT).

That 30mm automatic M230E1 chain gun, or area weapon system (AWS), blasts out 600 (+/– 25) rounds per minute. Depending on operational requirement, the Apache itself carries either guided Hellfire anti-tank missiles on a four-rail launcher (sixteen in total) or a combination of both missile and nineteen unguided 70mm rockets in pods (seventy-six total), each packed with a mix of flechette (tungsten dart), and high-explosive incendiary semi-armour piercing (HEISAP) or point-detonating (PD) warheads. The firepower of a fully armed Apache is beyond anything the world had ever seen from a helicopter before.

It's worth knowing that the Apache is a very stable aircraft in the hover, which helps when firing weapons (simulated or otherwise). And I was about to find this out on the sim with a young officer called Rory C, who made up for his lack of aviation experience by being an all-round ambitious guy and quality team player. We kicked off with the chain gun. As pilot, I could place my monocle crosshair onto the target with a set range, slave the gun to my helmet-mounted display (HMD) and, with ten rounds selected, press the trigger. Once all the rounds were on their way, I could check one of the MPD screens displaying the TADS picture highlighting the target area. After seeing the fall of shot I could assess and adjust accordingly. It was a very quick way of getting rounds to the target area. Once a simulation was completed, Rory and I would then swap seats.

From there we moved on to simulated rockets and missiles, the latter being the more fearsome. Two types of missile: the laser-guided semi-automatic line of sight (SAL); and the radio frequency (RF) version fired from the data provided by the FCR. The AH-64D Longbow Apache is equipped with the Northrop Grumman millimetre-wave Longbow radar, which means it can spot radar-emitting threats whatever the weather conditions. Inside thirty seconds it can determine the location, speed and direction of travel of up to 256 targets, will prioritise the top 16 and present them to the crew who have access to 16 missiles.

We learned that SAL is more accurate, a missile ripping away and heading for its target at hundreds of metres per second, guided by the laser maintained by the front-seat operator. The laser must stay constantly on the target otherwise the missile ends up like a cat chasing a laser beam.

Live firing the 30mm, after Rory and I passed the WHT, involved waiting for my instructor Nick, in the back seat, to establish a stable hover. I'd run through pre-firing checks, ensure I had the correct target and range, select the number of rounds and check that the safety officer on the ground was happy.

Permission received, I'd arm the aircraft by flipping the safety catch reading from SAFE to LIVE, and declare, 'Firing now.'

The thump-thump-thump of the rounds, the side-to-side rocking, the thick scent of freshly-fired ammunition, the feeling of immense power in your hands – none of it could be replicated in the simulator.

Three further weapons sorties involved nap-of-the-earth night flights using all available sensors. I'd get tasked with stealthily creeping into a planned position to search using FCR then identify using TADS and store items of interest in the computer. Once cleared to fire, I'd pick the most effective weapon system and go through the motions of letting rip. And the final two sorties saw students operating as a pair in some formation flying.

For the FHT I was given targets and had to collect and send information to Rory to destroy these within specific parameters. If in the back seat, and working as a team, Rory could put the laser on the target and I'd fire the missile that hits where the beam stops. The lasers were coded for particular missiles to keep everything as clean as possible, and once I knew which laser code he was using I could programme the missile accordingly. It was complicated, a steep learning curve on the sim and in the real aircraft, but we both got into our stride and found that we worked well together.

For CTR training, we covered formation flying, flying on headings and tactical lead changes, as well as 90- and 180-degree course changes to simulate turning towards advancing air threats. Up to this point all weapons engagements had been from a static position, but now we would move on to running and diving profiles. Both involved the aircraft engaging a target at speed and height, and would certainly provide a key foundation of our work if, for example, we were sent to Afghanistan, as rumour had it we would.

The amount of media coverage the Apache was getting during all this was immense. Those rumours were building fast about deploying to Afghanistan. In 2005 the prestigious annual RAF Leuchars Airshow on Scotland's east coast requested Apaches for static display. For some reason, I was picked to oversee events that weekend. All went well, with more than 60,000 visiting and I'm pretty sure all of them called by the Apache stand. Lots of questions were asked of our team and, if someone seemed shy, I used an old phrase to remind them, 'There is no such thing as a stupid question.' Funny thing is, I now know that sentiment to be wrong. For at one point, a chap who was very obviously a plane spotter – thick glasses, lenses, camera around his neck, military webbing pouches round his waist that contained nothing but spare footwear – pointed at the FCR dome and asked, 'Is that where you keep the spare tyre?' I restrained myself to a laugh when in reality I wanted to fall over. I told him (truthfully) it was a radar.

As it happened, our team had won the prize for the best static stand. We were given our award in the VIP tent by Carol Vorderman, who had somehow sneaked in, literally, under the radar.

The course ended with electronic warfare (EW), involving offensive and defensive sorties at RAF Spadeadam in Cumbria, the only electronic-warfare tactics facility in Europe. The Apache is equipped with a multitude of mind-bendingly advanced EW sensors, including those that detect laser, missile and radar threats. To counteract such threats, UK Apaches are fitted with the BAE Systems helicopter integrated defensive aids suite (HIDAS), which includes flares that fire off to trick heat-seeking missiles coming your way.

To simulate the threats, RAF Spadeadam unleashed its working ex-Soviet vehicles that were once driven by the enemy. They were in operation throughout the ranges, hunting us using their systems as we evaded them using ours.

Before deploying to Oman to complete the final phase of environmental training, we got into the live-firing package at Otterburn Ranges in Northumberland. And so, 46 rockets and 360 rounds of 30mm later, the weapons package was complete. And after a few more sorties, CTR was over.

In Afghanistan, war was just beginning.

Chapter Fourteen

INTO BATTLE. AFGHANISTAN, 2006

I MADE A BADGE for myself as a way of saying 'up yours' to a major. Leaked emails from him, splashed across the British press, made clear his thoughts after the first six months of army engagement in Afghanistan. He said the RAF had been 'utterly, utterly useless' so far, focusing his rage on a female pilot who almost hit a British compound with phosphorus rockets before strafing the perimeter and 'missing the enemy by 200 metres'. To be fair, it didn't sound as though she was on top of her game (which is probably why she was in the RAF...)

Worse than that, he tore a strip off Apache pilots from 656 Squadron AAC. Their behaviour in theatre was 'maverick', he said, and they were all 'egotistical'. He saved his warm praise for troops from 3 Para which, coincidentally, was his own unit. While he might have had a point about one or two of 656 Squadron's pilots, his assessment lacked subtlety. And so, inspired by him, my badge, hand-crafted just before I was due to deploy, read 'Not Egotistical – Just Great.'

The press was routinely carrying reports about what was going on out in Afghanistan and the army grapevine was filling in the picture. None of us were kidding ourselves. We were heading for all-out war against a revitalised, fearless enemy who had nothing to lose and much to gain.

It was the spring of 2006 when the UK first dispatched troops to southern Afghanistan, some 3,000 of them. A small number had already been there for five years as part of an international security assistance force (ISAF) tasked with finding the leaders of al-Qaeda after 9/11. By the end of the year, the Taliban had been close to finished and ISAF stayed in place to assist with security as a new government took power.

Yet the Taliban retreat proved to be more like a Taliban rethink. With their eyes on the prize of taking over the nation, they recruited non-stop in towns and villages with messages about imperialist invaders, about the will of Allah, about old enmities finally coming to a head. ISAF had stayed around precisely because of that sort of messaging, knowing that extreme fundamentalists don't just drift off into the ether. But the groundwork being carried out by the Taliban turned out to more substantial than expected.

When the excrement began closing in on the fan, Mohammad Daoud, governor of Helmand, one of thirty-four Afghan provinces, insisted that ISAF troops be deployed everywhere that was at risk of Taliban attack. As he got his way, the insurgents went hell for leather to get their way. What had looked like token ISAF forces fought like lions when called on. They slowed the Taliban advance but could not hold out indefinitely. Meanwhile back in the West, and among our US allies in particular, no one was in the mood to let the Taliban and their medieval plans win control of a sovereign state. So an increase in ISAF's involvement was signed off.

Initially 'platoon houses' were set up, small outlying bases which would be frequently resupplied. The idea was that they offered a discreet, non-confrontational presence, but in practice it didn't work out well. NATO troops, mostly British, ended up getting tied down in remote and increasingly dangerous locations across Helmand. The fighting, often close-quarter, only got heavier, and the casualties and loss of life in areas like Sangin, Nawzad, Musa Qala and Kajaki became unacceptable.

In 2006, the British set up a base in Helmand, in the south of the country. It was already clear the area was a Taliban hotbed, that getting a foothold on hostile ground would be high-stakes stuff. Indeed, Helmand was the most dangerous territory in all Afghanistan, which was exactly why we were sent there. We needed to be in the enemy's backyard to be able to know him better, to keep him in check, to push his resolve, to see the whites of his eyes and know the weight of his punch. Inevitably, every now and then, he would lash out at the infidel on his doorstep. And when he did, we needed him to know he would not get the better of us.

Helmand was something of an explosive puzzle inside an unstable labyrinth. Its thirteen vast districts take in around 1.5 million people across 1,000 villages. Its capital is Lashkargah, a city of around 200,000 people. And the province's most notable and priceless feature, the Helmand River, flows through the area's vast desert region. With the aid of the enormous Kajaki Dam, the river provides water for irrigation, for drinking, for sustaining life itself. Also priceless, to at least some of the population, is the annual poppy harvest. For when it comes to the world's opium (and thus heroin) supply, around forty-two per cent hails from Helmand. That's a lot of jobs for a lot of ordinary farmers and labourers who, in many cases, were well disposed to neither the Taliban nor the allies at a time when both were seeking to win hearts and minds.

Before that main deployment to Helmand, the Royal Engineers built Camp Bastion, some 40 kilometres north-west of Lashkargah, to serve as a main base, and built Camp Shorabak, for Afghan forces, near by. When at full scale and fully operational, Bastion was like a minor wonder of the world. Unfortunately, at the time I arrived, it hadn't quite reached that stage. And it was to there that I was ultimately heading in late 2006, flying on the no-frills overnight special with RAF Airways. I mean, not even a meal in a bag, which would usually be provided for merely a day at the ranges...

Ahead of descent into Kandahar, you could have heard a gnat fart on that plane. We'd been asked to don our helmets and get ready for darkness because all aircraft lights would be switched off in case some enterprising Taliban tried to hit the jackpot with a single rocket-propelled grenade (RPG). I suppose that was the moment, after having left England, that I found myself personally at war. Just after touchdown, my first impression was the tangy smell of shite, or something like it, along the lines of what you might smell after a farmer has sprayed slurry (liquid manure) over crops in the spring. I could only assume it was from the fields beyond the base.

Kandahar, built on a site near the city's airport, would be home for a couple of days while we orientated ourselves and attended the dozen or so briefings before moving on to Camp Bastion. Members of 656 Squadron showed us the accommodation. And that, mixed with the smell, just added to the joy. There was very little in the way of actual furniture, the chairs and tables fashioned from bits of wood, discarded plastic and broken boxes. None the less, knackered, we climbed into our camp beds and drifted off.

On the first day, with that same stench of shite all around, we set off in search of the mess halls. It was in doing so that we came across the source of the foul smell. It was a very large sewage works, dubbed 'the Sea of Tranquillity', near the accommodation blocks. It struck me that this was the middle of winter and still the thing was smelling like that – I could only assume that you'd need a gas mask in mid-summer. Whose bright idea had it been to site it there?

Initial briefings covered some Afghan history, conventions on airspace and various house rules. When we were freed up for lunch,

Vince H, Pete L, Pete D and myself piled into one of the Land Rovers in search of The Boardwalk, where we'd heard we could get grub.

We found it because, despite being in the middle of the desert, it was basically an American mall. I couldn't quite believe it. We're talking half a square mile of glass-fronted stores, coffee shops, flashing neon signs, Mamma Mia's Pizzeria, The Green Bean Café ('Honor First, Coffee Second'). There was a barber shop, an AT&T call centre and a cyber café where you could video-chat with those back home. The location screened nightly sports games – basketball, hockey, baseball – attended, for the most part, by US and Canadian service personnel in shorts. The place even boasted multiple wi-fi networks and ATM machines. If this was how the Americans did war, I'd love to know how they did peace. The Boardwalk would have been exactly like an American mall apart from the fact that all the punters were in uniform, many of them were heavily armed, and there was an international war going on just over the perimeter fence. For skirmishes were routinely taking place close by, with lives lost literally only minutes from where soldiers sat.

We talked among ourselves that Saturday afternoon about our proximity to the continuing loss of life and the irony of Taliban strongholds just a couple of miles away, and all while eating double-dipped chocolate ice cream. Occasionally a jet fighter would shoot through the sky while letting loose a stream of white flares designed to confound heat-seeking enemy missiles. And while I enjoyed both the spectacle and the ice cream very much, I can't pretend that I didn't feel embarrassed. There were, we knew, Paras, Irish Rangers and other British fighting troops putting their lives on the line to hold off wave after wave of Taliban attacks just a short drive away.

It was in Kandahar that I picked up on the term 'looking ally', British Army slang for personnel in the field who had lost their way when it came to personal grooming. All of us had begun to notice unwashed, unshaven guys with caps that looked like they'd been used as slippers. These were the guys who had been in country a while, who had returned to base and hadn't quite got around to taking a shower. Initially I thought they were Special Forces between low-profile taskings. But, no, that batch of dishevelled guys turned out to be an RAF Regiment who thought they were Special Forces but had been entrusted only with patrolling the perimeter fence of Kandahar while real battles raged near by. I felt embarrassed for them.

That afternoon we sat down for a lecture on rules of engagement (ROE). At some point, we knew, we were going to press triggers, to send bullets and bombs thundering towards human beings. ROE are the internal rules or directives that define the circumstances, conditions, degree, and manner in which the use of force, or actions which might be construed as provocative, may be applied. We had to get this right. If we took life and it was not justified under ROE, there was every chance we would face severe consequences. That included being subject to prosecution under criminal, military, human-rights and even international law.

Possibilities were put to us. Debate ensued. One man's idea of what was justified was not necessarily the same as that of the next man. We talked then of grey-area situations, and it was in those that we reached the agreement that our seniors had hoped we would. If ever you are not sure, you don't. Where there is doubt, there is no doubt. I can tell you now that before I left for Afghanistan and before I boarded a single combat aircraft during three tours, I held fast to that rule.

There were two ways to get to Camp Bastion from Kandahar. You could fly your own aircraft or take the daily C-130 flight. Unfortunately, our helicopters were already there so, with all our kit packed up, the squadron piled aboard the C-130. Helmets on and earplugs in, we set off on a deliberately turbulent flightpath as the pilot made random moves to avoid potential Taliban engagements. By the time we had levelled off it was almost time to descend again.

And off we went once more, shaking and slaloming, trying to be as unpredictable as possible.

Disembarking alongside the runway for our home for the next three months, I noticed no smell of shite. This was, I was sure, a good sign. I noticed too the dust blowing everywhere, the rows and rows of tents of various sizes, the full beam of the sun on everything, and how everything in sight seemed to be the same shade of dull brown.

We formed a human chain and unloaded the C-130 as helicopters churned overhead, and two Apaches took to the air from a nearby small concrete runway. Within minutes, the C-130 was being loaded up once more with men and material and away it went, back to Kandahar.

Accommodation was a tent within a multitude of tents joined at a central spine. Each of the eight camp cots, or sleeping pods, was overhung by a mosquito net. To make mine more homely, I had brought a small quilt and fitted sheet. I had also picked up a prayer mat along the way to use as a little bedside rug so I could pretend the place was decorated. And I got myself some empty metal ammo boxes to use as a shelf for the most important item in my possession, the laptop.

We chatted that evening with 656 Squadron members and they didn't sugar-coat it. We would go on to spend the next few days looking over video of some of their engagements, their gun tape footage and talking over the lessons learned. It all rang a few bells. Our CTR training had been good.

There would be four Apache flights, and by flight I mean two aircraft. Our flight would consist of the OC, Mike M, who was paired with Jules P in one aircraft while I was paired with 'Binary Boy' Nick E in the other. There would be four duty cycles of three days each, and not all strictly involving flying Apaches: very high readiness (VHR); days off; air testing; deliberate operations. And repeat.

VHR, meaning ready to go day or night, would mirror how I operated in Northern Ireland. It amounts to being constantly ready for a phone call from Operations requesting support with resupply, casevac, troops in contact (TIC) or anything else that might arise. It was a sure-fire way of spending your time with no idea of what the next minute might bring.

Air testing typically involved flying to Kandahar (KAF) to help get serviced aircraft shifted back to Bastion. It was all about keeping the rotation of helicopters going in light of maintenance requirements.

The fourth duty cycle, deliberate operations, involved Bastion-based crews being primed to plan, implement and otherwise support deep-strike and Special Forces missions.

Each aircraft type had its own callsign, with the Chinooks allocated Doorman and the Apaches getting, at first, Wildman. And each duty got its own number. So when an Apache flight was on VHR, our flight's callsigns were Wildman 50 and Wildman 51. As tours came and went, so did the callsigns. Eventually we would get one that really captured the essence of the Apache, although naturally it was no reflection on the men inside – Ugly.

After completing a live-fire package on the ranges, including firing our first live missile, 656 Squadron began disengaging. It took a week. And, just like that, our squadron was in the hot seat.

Our first duty was VHR. Mike, Jules, Nick and I moved to the VHR tent for the three-day shift. It contained four single beds with green plastic mattresses and just the bedding we brought along. There was a PlayStation, a TV and DVD player, a small fridge for water and, outside the tent, the standard array of crap yet practical furniture fashioned from boxes and crates, all loosely arranged into something that resembled a sitting area. From that point on, if we were there, or anywhere else close by – shower, toilet, in the cookhouse getting grub – we had to have our radios with us.

The most important item of all was a small field telephone that sat on a desk by the tent entrance. It was linked to the ops room and to other sections involved in the same duty. As it turned out, we didn't have to wait long for it to ring. The four of us were settling in when the call came. We stopped. And counted.

One ring was a call to the ops room, and we should ignore it. Two rings for the technicians. Three for the immediate response team (IRT) – the Chinook crews living next door. And when they were needed, it was likely we would be asked to support them. And four rings specifically for VHR crews.

Ring ring ring.

The IRT team. We were getting ready to go.

Ring ring ring ring.

'VHR.'

'Operations here. Escort required for immediate resupply. One aircraft. Kajaki area.'

Those were the days. An escort of just a single Apache was considered enough to back up a Chinook in 2006. That was going to change.

We'd already agreed that if a single escort was needed, Nick and I would go.

The pair of us bolted out to the VHR Land Rover, parked just metres away. I fired up the engine, revved hard and sped off along the dirt road, hazards flashing in dazzling sunshine. Others were around, other personnel who seemed startled by my driving. I turned left and left again, skidding, spinning, launching waves of dust over buildings and tents. One furious officer ran out of a building, signalling for me to slow down. I generously forgave him for not knowing what VHR meant. Sucking diesel fumes and spitting dirt, we dashed on and turned right, braking to a stop with a broadside last conducted by Starsky and Hutch. I'd been told that the drive from the VHR tent took three minutes. It didn't any more.

Nick ran to the ops room, I ran to the flight line, towards the silent dark dragon waiting in one of six VHR bays, each segregated by high concrete blast walls. One of those grey walls featured a colourful regimental mural by 656 Squadron. Ours would be alongside it in time.

I ducked over to my locker, grabbed my helmet. Back out and ground crew, or groundies, were at work, one having already removed the internal heat protectors from the windscreen. I climbed up, opened the back cockpit, pulled out my body armour, secured it, closed the zips. Ten minutes since the call. I clambered in and, before strapping down, called to the groundie to tell him I was starting the APU. Once that was up and running I ran through flight checks while awaiting Nick. And, Christ, it was hot. That wasn't something I'd factored in, not something I'd been warned about. The heat shields had only just come off yet I could have roasted a horse in there. The black metal monocle burned when it touched the side of my face. The controls were hot to the touch.

Nick appeared, scaling up like Spiderman, pulling on his gear, securing himself in the front, racing through weapons checks. He issued a brief description of what he had just learned – just a bit of where, a little bit of what. But the priority was to get airborne.

We made contact with the Chinook. And, with both aircraft ready, away it went with us following in a fast running take-off. Once over the perimeter fence, Nick armed the HIDAS. This was always left late to ensure that even if a heat-seeking missile came for us, no decoy flares would be fired into the camp.

Operating height achieved, we checked all was in order once more. It had been twenty minutes since the phone rang – not bad for a first call-out. In the distance, a thick, lush green band of vegetation snaked through the dry sand. Through it ran the sparkling, life-giving Helmand River. The rich burst of life, of fields, farms and trees surrounding it, known as the Green Zone, looked almost out of place from up there. But its beauty, we knew, was deceptive.

Nothing in the largely barren badlands of Helmand gave as much cover to the enemy as that river, which ran the full length of the unbiddable province, and the vegetation that lined it. Yet that same river offered critical support to countless local people and to the numerous fortified military bases and outposts, British included.

We were heading north to Kajaki Dam, to the location of the further flung British base. We saw the crystal-blue waters of the dam from miles out, another geographic jewel from a bird's eye view. The dam itself, providing so much power, was a constant target for enemy forces (EF) and one of the most hostile regions of the extremely hostile region of Helmand.

Kajaki, like every other area of the war zone, was under the control of its own joint terminal attack controller (JTAC) on the ground who, in theory, had all the information about what was going on. It was essential to establish communication about active armed activity, or TICs, involving friendly forces (FF). If there was, we could be flying into red airspace in which fast jets were shooting through and dropping ordnance. And for red, read danger.

Once cleared, I ramped up the speed to get ahead of the Chinook. I needed Nick to get eyes on the landing site, to scan for enemy ahead of the big aircraft's arrival. All clear, and the Chinook began its descent down a route pre-cleared by the JTAC. We remained in the overhead for Nick to observe the terrain through the TADS, the search screen for potential targets. After a quick unload, the Chinook lifted and we got back in formation. Now for a straightforward return to base.

Then a call from the JTAC in Sangin. Forward operating base (FOB) Robinson was taking mortar fire. Would we assist in a search for the firing point? We checked fuel. We were good. We checked with the Chinook. They were okay to return to Bastion without support.

'Roger.'

FOB Robinson was just south of Sangin, east of the Green

Zone. Coming into the area, Nick scanned with the TADS – and there was a lot to take in. Lots of ordinary people doing lots of ordinary things. Lots of farms, animals, bicycles, cars. We had suddenly found ourselves right above the complicated picture that was both Afghanistan and the Afghanistan War. Everyday life was everywhere, yet conflict was everywhere too. It struck me how much we had to learn.

Nick scanned more, moving from grid reference to grid reference in search of the unlikely, in search of the odd man out. Minutes passed and nothing. Yet the JTAC was certain we were looking in the right area. I flew the Apache as steadily as I could, a configuration which ensured the TADS could stay within azimuth limits and therefore not lose sight of the target area. It kept us high enough and far enough away to avoid drawing attention. And still Nick kept looking.

'There's a fella taking a shit there,' he said.

Both of us looked at the guy.

'Dear me. No need for that,' I answered.

It seemed an unpleasant and unnecessary thing to do by the roadside, especially when so close to large compounds, to people's homes. Could he not have... –

Wait.

We were looking for anything out of the ordinary. He was crouching down, in the shitting position, yet a closer zoom suggested something different. His hands were at his face, as if holding something, maybe binoculars, to his eyes. And he was looking towards FOB Robinson.

I used my own Mark I eyeball to orientate towards his location. Beside him there was very large dark patch of ground. A deeper zoom and it looked like the patch might be a hole, perhaps some form of well. It was massive, maybe the size of a bus, and we could see now that it was deep too. As we weighed all this up, we took stock of a car parked around fifty metres away.

Nick said, 'Do you think mortars are being fired from inside the hole?'

Good question. It was certainly big enough.

We felt we had enough to justify sending off a few warning shots and put forward our argument. The JTAC cleared it. We ran through some checks before Nick selected a ten-round burst. He aimed 100 metres from our man and fired.

The hard drumming of rounds pumping from the 30mm cannon beneath our feet. The aircraft lifted as the big gun recoiled and the rich scent of cordite filled the cockpit. Heavy seconds ticked by as the bullets sped from 2 kilometres out. I was sure that the squatting man was about to shit himself for real.

A clustered explosion of mud, dust, sand, dirt as ten rounds precision-punched the earth. The thud of impact, the ripping-up of ground – all more than enough to change a man's mind. Except that this man did not move.

'Whoa!' I said, almost stunned. 'He didn't even flinch.'

Word on the radio. Another mortar bomb had landed just shy of the perimeter wall at FOB Robinson. It was coming from somewhere within our sights.

'Right then,' Nick said.

He cut the distance and fired again. Ten bullets thumped the ground fifty metres away from our man, in front and just to the right of him. Even if he was blind and deaf, he'd have felt them hammer the soil.

Yet he did not move.

'Okay,' said Nick, advising all concerned. 'Increasing to a twenty-round burst, same area.'

The strike was twice as fierce, and closing in on the crouching figure. He got the message. He was up and running fast, dashing towards the car. Heavy fire followed him, a line of 30mm tracking his path. Skirting the car, he sprinted into a large compound and vanished. The fastest man in flip-flops.

We maintained our position, waited for feedback. In a few minutes the JTAC confirmed the mortar fire had ceased, at least for now. That was all they needed. Troops would get to the suspicious hole. We were good to go. I turned the Apache towards Bastion and headed back for the debrief, to explain exactly what had happened, what we did and why. Word came soon after that the hole was indeed the site of a mortar firing pit. It would be shut down. It had been a good first VHR sortie.

In fact, those first three days were all good. Phone calls came and went, sleep was on and off, and we adjusted well to it all. We learned fast how to rest lightly, how to wake up fully after more than one ring, how to be out of bed and grabbing what we needed on three. The fourth ring, more often than not, came as we were at the door, ready to sprint to the Land Rover.

'VHR.'

'Operations here... '

Days off were about reading, chilling, taking part in Operation Massive – the British Army's on-tour exercise programme designed to keep troops fit, build muscle and send us home looking like Thor. Bastion at that time was still developing and had no more than – and this list is full and complete – a NAAFI and a Pizza Hut. And I don't ever remember the Pizza Hut being open in all the time I served there.

After time off, we would move back to KAF to help with air testing and/or the ground runs needed to ensure the aircraft were in good order. On one occasion, we were to swap two helicopters, flying them to KAF to collect Apaches to bring back to Bastion. For a change, I flew with Jules and Mike was crewed with Nick.

We were ten miles from KAF when the aircraft central warning panel displayed an engine fault, described as a computer malfunction. We'd seen this only in the sim before. One engine was good but, in all the complexity of what was going on, it looked like the other might shut down. To be safe we elected to shut down the affected engine ourselves and conduct a running landing. It had our hearts racing but we kept nice and calm, as did the Apache. Once the technicians got to work, they were able to provide more detail about the issue. Elements of sunglasses had been ingested into the engine. They were in bad shape after retrieval. They were shit quality anyway, so we knew they didn't belong to any aircrew.

I'd always try to make a couple of calls each evening, keen to talk to Tracey, the welcome new love in my life. It was good to hear news from home, even just to hear her voice. It's hard to overstate the importance of having that connection, of being able to reach out to dependable loved ones when the rest of your life is uncertain.

I'd met Tracey while serving at Dishforth, North Yorkshire, in 2006. She was a fitness instructor at a large gym facility, and after a day of tormenting unfit people she often helped out behind the bar of a local pub. It's important to say that she has often claimed I approached her for her number, when the truth is that she just gave me hers. So, now that's been written here, the matter is settled.

At Bastion one evening I was sauntering the short distance to the phone booths, probably to assure her of just that, when sirens began blaring. Then instructions over the tannoy:

'Op Minimise. Op Minimise. Op Minimise.'

I would be making no phone call. Op Minimise is an operational procedure, an order from the Ministry of Defence that suspends all communications facilities. It's usually in the event of a serious or fatal incident, to ensure that no sensitive information reaches the press or anyone else before an official notification by the MoD.

In the case above, I'm sorry to say that a family back home would be getting the gravest of news. It wasn't the last time I would hear those words over the tannoy.

Towards the end of that first tour, news came of Operation Bagi. Long in the planning, this was a full battle-group mission to get a logistics convoy and an air-portable bridge into Sangin. The bridge would span the Helmand River and open a safe route to the west.

It came at a time when the Taliban were showing enhanced war skills, and was to take place in a location where they were many in number. Well aware of this, the army would put everything it could into getting it right. Maximum resources would be allocated to the job, fixed-wing aircraft and helicopters included.

Our role was to support the convoy rolling into Sangin. On the ground it would be escorted by the Household Cavalry Regiment (HCR), whilst elements of the Paras already in Sangin were to push north and south, swamping the area with troops to stop Taliban attempts to infiltrate or attack. We were providing overhead cover throughout, ready to neutralise any enemy positions if the need arose.

We knew from intel that as soon as we lifted off from Bastion someone would be watching or 'dicking' us, and that they would call ahead to whatever area they thought we were heading. Which is why we set off east before, much further out, turning north. We held off the west of Sangin until we could see the convoy moving in from the east. From a pre-planned point, we were called forward. At the same time, the Paras left base and split into two large elements.

The element heading south had a lot of work to do. They were tasked with clearing three buildings that were well known Taliban firing points. Chief among those was the enormous Chinese Restaurant, so called because of its garish pagoda-like décor. The other two buildings lay just to the east. Sangin had been deadly ground for months, with heavy fighting taking place in pockets all over the city. So it didn't take long before the gunfire broke out. Our controlling JTAC advised it was mostly coming from the Chinese Restaurant area, notably from beyond a large wall to its rear.

The JTAC cleared both Apaches to engage and suppress. While Mike and Jules set up for a Hellfire missile strike on the building (which was not in fact a restaurant), Nick spotted two individuals behind the wall. They were holding a weapon and firing through holes towards the Paras.

'Where's Mike?' Nick was asking it.

I could see the other Apache to my left.

'He's off on our nine o'clock. We are well clear.'

Nick actioned the gun, selected twenty rounds and fired. The deep rumble again, the gun's recoil forcing us back like we'd hit waves. This time, however, he was aiming only to kill.

The rounds fell short. Both men were up and running, belting into one of the smaller compounds. At the same time, Mike unleashed a Hellfire, sending it pounding into the front of the Chinese Restaurant. Jules peeled their aircraft away yet the JTAC immediately requested another missile strike. This time it was to hit a small superstructure, a possible firing point on the building's roof.

Our position was better for that job, and I advised I could turn and commence the run-in. Mike moved on in search of the insurgents who had dashed away, and of the many others in the area. This missile attack run would be tight. We had no more than a couple of kilometres to make the engagement, which isn't far in an Apache. I slowed. Nick began pre-fire checks. With the right trigger, he fired the laser, locking the missile onto its path towards the rooftop superstructure.

'Okay,' I said, 'all good. Clear to fire.'

While continuing to fire the laser, Nick snatched at the missile trigger with his left hand. A sharp clunk from the rail to my right. followed by an explosive whoosh and it was away, a puff of exhaust appearing directly ahead. Seconds later, fifty kilos of fury struck and the small outhouse was blown apart. Hot mud and dust filled the screen, fading away to reveal debris.

Mike was engaging targets off to the east, close to where the two fighters had fled. We made contact and agreed to fly a wheel formation, a large orbit to allow both aircraft to keep eyes on the target area. To avoid collision, I would be 500 feet higher.

Troops were still being fired at from inside the huge Chinese Restaurant. We could have had no idea how many EF were in there, how much they had in the way of munitions, or how long this assault could go on for. All we knew was that we had a bridge to put in place.

Then the JTAC made the call, announcing that the restaurant should be JDAM-ed by the fixed-wing aircraft on hand. And a JDAM (joint direct-attack munition), in case you didn't know, is a precision kit that turns heavy-duty dumb bombs into smart bombs. Basically it makes for a bloody big 1,000lb bomb, about the size of a wheelie bin – but moves much faster. We cleared off to the west to watch the show.

Over the radio, 'Bomb away.'

And everything seemed to fall silent for what felt like minutes. Then, like a glitch in the matrix, the picture changed in a heartbeat. The Chinese Restaurant seemed to lift right into the air before it was smashed to smithereens.

'Wow,' I said, 'impressive.'

Insurgents were on the move. Whatever plan they had was not going well. But I'd learn they were never short of a Plan B. At all times, they sought to blindside FF, to attack from anywhere but the front. And that was a favourite tactic when pushed away from one location. When they were scattering, we had to watch everywhere.

Nick spotted a handful trying this very tactic. They had gathered at an irrigation ditch and were slowly, stealthily, climbing to the top. They were well covered by trees and knew it. Fully aware of the Apaches above, they were seeking to secure a strike point from which they could hit and then run for cover in the trees.

Before we could engage, the JTAC cleared a mortar strike on the woods. That meant red airspace for us – we had to get out of there. We hadn't got far before the mortar hit. Chunks of timber soared into the air like confetti, dust and mud and bark and splinters shot in every direction. Our eyes firmly on the scene, it was clear that some of the men would not be standing up again. Others managed it, ran as best they could, some nursing wounds.

We asked for urgent clearance to engage. It took minutes. In that time, insurgents hell-bent on killing British troops were vanishing one by one into the thick of trees further away. When the all-clear did come, two Apaches turned their 30mm cannon on the enemy. Dozens of rounds ravaged through the trees, ripping through whatever they hit. I don't know how many had made it that far, but it was the last place they would ever be.

The JTAC came back with urgent news. A British casualty. The immediate-response team had been alerted; it was going to take twenty minutes to arrive. In the meantime, the wounded man was to be moved back to Sangin to await the Chinook. We offered to meet the IRT, escort it in. Mike and Jules would remain in the overhead. I'm glad to say the IRT came quickly and left fast without incident.

And all the while, Operation Bagi was developing, moving forward, succeeding. By the end of the fight, the convoy had safely arrived and the prefabricated bridge was being installed. It had been a hectic operation, the first early wild one I was involved with. Each Apache had fired a standard K1-type Hellfire missile and each had unleashed more than 150 rounds of 30mm.

But whatever success war may sometimes bring, loss is never far away. On 2 September 2006, while our flight was conducting maintenance flights at KAF, tragic news came in from not far away. An RAF Nimrod had suffered an in-flight fire and exploded in mid-air. It crashed just outside Kandahar. All fourteen on board were killed. The crash, during a reconnaissance flight, was the biggest single loss of life suffered by the British military since the Falklands War. It was one thing to lose a member of the British forces to enemy fire, but this was something else, a heartbreaking event on the grandest of scales.

Chapter Fifteen

SEVEN HOURS AT MUSA QALA, 2006

SOME DAYS LAST for ever. Because sometimes things happen that will never be forgotten.

This day, 6 September 2006, was a Wednesday, although I don't know whether I knew that. I was in the thick of the tour, fully adjusted to a new way of doing things. Weeks had no beginnings or ends, days had no standard wake-up point, no typical sleep time. Life's rhythm and routine had reformed as a random pattern of carnage, emergency, disruption, gain and loss. If there was a constant, it was that we were doing more of the moving forward than our enemy was, that his losses were greater than ours. My deepest hope was that it would stay that way, that we run him down, run him to the end, wear him down further than he ever wanted to go. Inevitably, there would be moments of glory for the British military. And, equally inevitably, there would be pain.

On that long day an incident took place at Kajaki Dam. A small infantry patrol had left their OP to move into the town below. They were investigating sightings of Taliban, looking into claims that they had set up checkpoints and were demanding money from drivers. There were women and children around in numbers. The only way to know more was to send a foot patrol down the hill.

A mine detonated as they went. The OP sent out a second team with medical equipment. Neither team could have known they were walking into a minefield. And ahead of the IRT arrival, another blast. As the Chinook attempted to touch down, it was waved away amid fears it, and the actions due to take place around it, would set off yet more mines. As it lifted without the casualties on board, the immense downdraft triggered yet another. And although the troops were left stranded, vulnerable and nursing serious wounds, it would be two hours before two US Blackhawk helicopters, equipped with winches, arrived to lift all to safety. Corporal Mark Wright of 3 Para died of his injuries before reaching Bastion, and seven others from the battalion were injured. Wright was posthumously awarded the George Cross. During the horror on the hill that day, and although severely wounded himself, he did all he could to save the lives of injured soldiers.

Several miles to the south, in the village of Musa Qala (MSQ), two soldiers from Easy Company of the Royal Irish Regiment were injured on that same day. Mortars had hit their base, scattering shrapnel in all directions. At the time Musa Qala, like Sangin, had been in the grip of almost daily Taliban attack and the Royal Irish had been brought in to support 3 Para. Dave W's Apache was in the overhead as the IRT Chinook arrived low and fast to assist. But insurgents had been waiting for it. A volley of lead raced upwards, four bullets striking the Chinook as it tried to land, one almost shearing off a rotor blade at the root. The shots were rapidly followed by two RPGs soaring up from the same location. Luckily both missed, one going under the aircraft, one over. The IRT had no choice but to abort and get back to Bastion. Initial plans were put together for a second attempt, this time at night. But the medic at MSQ had serious concerns. The casualties, he said, were in a bad way. They needed out of the base and into hospital immediately.

SEVEN HOURS AT MUSA QALA, 2006

The CO of 3 Para took the floor of the briefing room at Bastion. I watched as he laid it on the line. The enemy would be expecting the Chinook to return. As such, there was a heightened chance the aircraft, and its crew, could be lost. He wanted his soldiers retrieved but gravely explained that he understood if the Chinook pilot, a Royal Marines officer named Mark Hammond, did not want to return. Yet Mark did want to return, as did his co-pilot Mark D, a flying colleague from Brunei and recent transfer to the RAF. In fact, all the Chinook's crew wanted to return. They knew the risk and they would take it.

The plan now turned to a way of wrongfooting the enemy, of somehow masking the Chinook's approach. Someone in the room piped up with a straightforward idea.

'We need pre-emptive fire,' he said.

The suggestion was met, at first, by silence. All engagements come under ROE. And ROE had no loopholes. To shoot at people ahead of their making themselves targets went against everything we'd been taught. Given that the risk of injuring or killing civilians was high, clearance from high up was needed. Our CO was asked whether this idea might work. He did some thinking, talked over some ideas. Questions went further up the chain of command and soon it was agreed. The circumstances called for pre-emptive fire. We would be shooting our way in.

Our job was to create a narrow avenue of airspace to ensure the Chinook reached the base, that it could load up and get out as safely as possible. We were told that other air assets, including an A-10 Thunderbolt close air support jet and an AC-130 Spectre gunship, would likely be on hand.

Normally, just a single Apache would arrive ahead of a Chinook. This time we were doubling up. We would go first, full aggression, immediately engaging known firing points. Two more Apaches would shepherd the Chinook, resolutely protect it, ensure it got safely to ground, destroy anything that threatened to get in its way.

The IRT pilot led the brief. He said a major from the Paras would act as liaison officer between aviation and ground forces. Our flight would arrive by an unusual route ten minutes before the rest. After we had laid down some fire, my CPG Nick would give one or other of the required code words. One would mean we were confident we had neutralised the targets, the other would say the area remained hostile.

'What are the code words?' I asked Mark. I expected something like 'chilli,' meaning hot and therefore 'stay back', and 'ice', suggesting cold, meaning 'come ahead'.

'Mowlam and McAndrew.'

'Come again?'

'Think about it,' he said.

We did. He had been referencing the late Labour politician Mo Mowlam and the English glamour model Nell McAndrew.

Mark said, 'So, with Mowlam, you wouldn't. With McAndrew, you would. Right?'

Part of me expected the political-correctness police to come bursting through the door and make an arrest. They'd have to arrest all of us though, because everyone was laughing.

Mike and Jules rolled off the HALS, Nick and I following them up into the black sky. As the dark lands below blushed green, we fell into formation, higher than the other Apache and to its right. We would be flying at max chat, as fast as the engines would allow. Mike opened comms with the JTAC.

'Widow 65, this is Wildman 54. Two Apaches entering your area from the east. Confirm clear to enter and operate north of Sangin.'

'Wildman 54, this is Widow 65. Cleared in but hold east. We have an A-10 Warthog on an attack run.'

Right then, the night sky ahead of us came alight. Seemed like the A-10 had deposited an almighty bomb some distance from the base at MSQ, blowing all sorts of things apart and sparking an enormous blaze. That wasn't part of any plan we knew about. We learned only later that it had been a strafing run on an arms dump, and that the explosion had been Taliban weapons and munitions.

'Useful fire,' Nick said as the raging flames rose. 'It'll help orientate the Chinook and escort.'

From here, our timing had to be spot on. If we made a mess this end, the Chinook and escort could get held back while in the air, gifting the enemy yet more time. All we needed was our cue.

'Wildman 54. Widow 65. Area is now cold. You are cleared in.'

And we were off. The targets, or at least the positions, were just to the north-west of MSQ. There was no room for error in what lay ahead. Each aircraft involved would now be no more than a silhouette of heat on the screen. Mike and Nick scanned for targets on the TADS, Jules and I held tight to the agreed formation – one aircraft higher than the other.

As we ran in to towards the location, Mike confirmed he had the first target building on sight. Nick was still scanning for the same location, taking in a scene that looked hugely different than it did in daylight. The single hardest thing was to orientate our position relative to the ground, not helped by the fact we were constantly moving. Sometimes you can't tell from which direction you are looking at a building. Confusion comes easy up high over the desert in the dark with your eyes full of green lines.

'Got it,' Nick said, relieved.

The IRT was due in ten minutes.

Our target was a previously active, relatively small, mud-walled complex at the edge of a tree line. Two Apaches ran in on the attack heading. Mike fired a Hellfire, the split-second flash from the missile rail giving away his position. We watched as the warhead walloped the building, walls buckling live and on demand. Jules broke right. Our missile followed up, thumping out and off with a blinding burst of light, roaring towards the laser point. Now the sight of a building collapsing completely. And, up in our world, only the sound of the aircraft, and of me congratulating Nick.

Jules was in a wide slow orbit. I broke right to join him. We were to engage wood lines and culverts used as cover by the enemy. Thunder rolled from both aircraft, pulses of lightning from the underslung guns as high-explosive dual-purpose rounds sliced into the targets. As the cockpit filled with the sharp aroma of cordite, the JTAC advised that Taliban comms were silent.

'This may just have worked,' I said.

And still no movement, or any other response, from below.

'Doorman 26. This is Wildman 54. McAndrew. Repeat, McAndrew.'

The formation appeared, the Chinook dropping low, an Apache above in support. Our eyes back on the target areas, still nothing doing. And to keep it that way, we went again.

Another barrage of 30mm into the ditches, into the trees. If plans were being made down there, we were insisting they get unmade fast.

Mark Hammond, flying the Chinook, was now on short finals. The escorting Apaches broke off, formed a protective shield to the south right above the district centre as the big tandem-rotor machine touched down.

We pushed to the north, watching everything below, watching every second, ready to do whatever was needed. If Taliban were down there, and we knew they would not be far away, they knew now for sure that we were in the air. Yet there was still every chance they'd try something on the Chinook's departure.

Doorman advised that the casualties were on board. It was about to lift. And as it rose above the base walls, the night came alive – flashes everywhere, tracer fire from all directions, RPGs belting up towards the Chinook. Mark transitioned to the right as two RPGs screamed through the sky at his one o'clock. Mike had nailed the firing position. A Hellfire raced down in answer. As it hit, I saw tracer from a building twenty metres away. Nick hadn't seen it.

'I'm visual,' I shouted it. 'My HMD.'

'Go for it.'

For a brief second, I remember thinking I'd be the first ever UK Apache to engage the Taliban using this method, firing from my helmet, and not through the TADS. It was the fastest way for me to respond. It wasn't the most accurate option, but I hoped it was enough to suppress the fire. Monocle tracking my eye, I armed the weapon, put the crosshairs from my monocle onto the target area. If looks could kill. Ten, then twenty heavy rounds slammed down. Then again, another twenty for luck.

'Check my rounds, Nick.'

He slaved the TADS to the impact point.

'Okay,' I said, sure now that the rounds had fallen short. 'The building right beside them. That's the one.'

He took control of the gun and fired deep into the building. No more tracer from there, but it was flying everywhere from other locations. All Apaches and the Chinook were engaging, pouring hell as the enemy sought to tear one of us from the sky. The hornets' nest had been truly shaken. The IRT was trying hard to break away, to get its human cargo to hospital fast. As Mark finally made it beyond the town, angry tracer rounds were still rocketing his way. His escorts joined, offering cover, firing down as they went.

The firing died down and then ceased as they moved beyond range. Our two Apaches remained, prowling around in search of the next cue. We were coming close to bingo fuel, the calculated minimum fuel level we could reach before returning to base (RTB). An A-10 was due, readying to ride in and strafe the freshly identified firing points. As we took stock of the scene, multiple figures dashed from the scene, running for their lives into a cornfield. We turned their way, two actioned guns pointing right at them, pressure on triggers.

But insurgents or civilians? We couldn't know for sure.

Fuel at bingo, we pulled away from the triggers and moved out, clearing the airspace for the A-10. We'd set off just before midnight, after a refuel and rearm we finally landed back at Bastion just after 7 a.m. Four missiles and over 700 rounds of 30mm had been fired. The busiest night yet. And mission accomplished.

As a result of his actions on that day, not least that selfless decision to risk his life to get those injured men out of there, Major Mark Hammond was awarded the Distinguished Flying Cross. The 3 Para CO described it as 'a day of days.' Once again the helicopters had taken an enormous risk, and once again they had got away with it.

But there was learning to be done. Now we knew that the odds were shortening. How long should small numbers of troops stay holed up in isolated platoon houses, constantly dependent on helicopter resupply while on the enemy's doorstep? How long before the enemy took down a helicopter and secured themselves the propaganda victory of which they dreamed?

The Royal Irish Regiment's Easy Company and 3 Para had been under siege since July. There was a growing sense they were cornered, that any notion of winning hearts and minds in the district had vanished. These guys were something close to sitting ducks. They had courageously repelled wave after wave of attacks, some 100 in all, but that situation couldn't go on. The departure of a Danish contingent just weeks earlier had only led to a weakening of the base's defences. A rapid pull-out from the MSQ base moved up the agenda.

Talks began on the ground, community leaders sitting down with intermediaries, and with the military. The Taliban didn't want the base there, the troops inside didn't need to be there. Commitments were made on both sides. It took time, yet a local ceasefire was called and, although shaky, began to bed down after a few weeks. In mid-October 2006, the extraction took place.

They called it Operation Omer. I was airborne for eight hours, the longest I've ever flown in a day. My role was to ensure no one decided to make a nuisance of themselves, to stop it right away if they did. And what unfolded below were some of the most bizarre scenes I have ever witnessed.

By arrangement with village elders, Easy Company were to be evacuated in local jingly lorries, so named because of the noise made by the hundreds of decorative chains hanging from the bodywork. An elder joined troops on each lorry to ensure safe passage. Then, as the convoy of trucks slowly moved out of town, men who were clearly Taliban fighters watched from the roadside and followed in cars. It must have been a tense and nerve-racking business for everyone involved. However, the operation went smoothly without a shot being fired.

On that tour, Apaches alone had fired 10,835 rounds of 30mm, 108 rockets and 27 Hellfire missiles. And little did we know at the time, but we would be back in MSQ a year later.

Our 2006 tour was coming to an end. In the weeks ahead we were to hand back over to 656 Squadron. In the meantime, other squadrons in the UK were finishing Apache CTR in anticipation for their tour after 656 moved on. For now, we were looking forward to a couple of days in Cyprus, where all troops were to get a break to decompress before continuing the journey home.

Back in England, my heart filled up like an airship at being able to see Robyn and to be with Tracey and our dog Minty once again. It felt as if it had been so long, too long. I wondered if I had changed, if I would be able to disengage from the new way of life I had just left behind? I remember being slightly thrilled to see so much colour again, given I'd been stuck staring at various shades of light brown and luminous green for a while.

And I remember thinking how it was as though nothing had happened, as though nothing at all was going on some 4,000 miles away. Over there in Afghanistan people were running for their lives and shooting and bombing and killing and dying. Over there, gallant fellow countrymen were doing all they could for their comrades.

Over there, courage and self-sacrifice were on display like nowhere else on earth.

And back in dear old Blighty it was as though no one had noticed.

Chapter Sixteen

THE WOMAN IN THE BOAT. AFGHANISTAN, 2007

INTO JANUARY 2007 and the war in Afghanistan rumbled on while I got back to the daily grind of exercises and air testing. Every day I was keen to know what was going on out there, what was being asked of the AAC, what was being achieved. I can't say I wasn't missing the action out there, the sense of doing important things for a noble aim. Moving helicopters back and forth in England didn't quite cut it.

I learned that 656 Squadron, from 9 Regiment AAC, had replaced us for their second tour of Afghanistan. Meanwhile, 662 Squadron, from 3 Regiment AAC, over in Wattisham, were wrapping up on CTR. The plan was for 662 to relieve 656, and when the opportunity arose to join 662 Squadron in Helmand to share experiences, I signed up right away.

By now I was a warrant officer class one (WO1) and a weapons airborne instructor. This put me in charge of all weapons training as well as placing me front and centre during post-engagement debriefs. Throughout the tour, I'd be monitoring the squadron and keeping the pressure on to ensure standards stayed high.

I was to be part of 5 Flight along with my wingman pilot Baz, now a major, a qualified helicopter instructor and a first-class soldier. We'd flown together many times. My front-seater would be Alex W, a fresh-faced officer straight out of Sandhurst. He was twenty-five and the spitting image of Will Young, a once famous singer who won a once famous reality TV show called *Pop Idol*. I felt sorry for Alex and told him so. He was a good man but with little aviation and zero combat experience. That suited me well. He had no bad habits to break. Baz's front-seater was Tim P, a similarly untested dashing blond-haired, blue-eyed man of twenty-nine with a jawline like the north face of the Eiger. He probably wasn't used to being addressed as Ugly, but he'd need to get used to it. For that new callsign was now active, replacing Wildman, and it suited the Apache down to the ground.

Sangin was still under siege and had been since June of 2006. The town centre was so heavily populated with Taliban fighters and so clouded with the dust of battle that troops dubbed it Sangingrad, in reference to the Siege of Stalingrad. At the time, the situation had reached a kind of perilous stalemate. And that was the background to Operation Silver, set to launch in April 2007, in which more than 1,000 international forces would move in and relieve the town. NATO gave advance warning by dropping leaflets and local elders were urged to spread the word.

American troops kicked off Operation Silver with a heliborne assault at locations 5 kilometres to the south. At the same time, 250 Royal Marines from 42 Commando rolled in from the north in a column of armoured vehicles. As well as British and US forces, Danish, Estonian, Dutch and Canadian troops took part. Resistance was light. On 5 April, Coalition troops were in control of the town centre and it became clear that most locals and enemy had legged it. And although Taliban fighters were still in surrounding areas, the Afghan authorities were able to claim victory and declare the Siege of Sangin over.

I was on VHR duty on that day. By now I had developed a knack of being about to do something when the phone rang. The moment my arse touched the toilet seat, or just after I'd soaped up in the shower, I'd routinely get interrupted by an emergency. On this occasion, I was in the cookhouse and just about to get some seafood. My words to Baz at that moment were, 'Where do they get the fresh shrimp from in the desert?'

'Ops calling Delboy.'

Abandon shrimp. We shot out of our chairs, sprinted outside. I literally dived into the driver's seat, vehicle in motion as only half of Tim was on board. Down the dirt road, hazards blinking and dust flying. Braking hard, Alex and Tim jumped out, raced to the ops room. Baz and I ran the fifty metres to the Apaches. He was leading so headed for VHR Bay 1. I was on wing so peeled off for Bay 2.

Flight checks under way, we could have no idea what lay ahead. A TIC, casevac, resupply, a deep strike? Alex climbing the aircraft now, out of breath, getting inside, helmet on.

Radio crackle.

'Steve. Can you hear me?'

'Go ahead, Alex. What's the brief?'

'A Viking's been hit just south of Sangin. T1 casualty. Urgent casevac.'

T for triage. T3 needed care but can be delayed; T2 needs significant intervention within two to four hours; T1 needs medical attention now or the casualty will die.

The tracked all-terrain armoured vehicle had been ambushed moving from FOB Robinson towards Sangin centre. It had been hit hard by a large group of heavily armed insurgents. Local FF on the ground had moved in to protect the fractured Viking. In terms of firing from the air, this could get complicated.

'Ready,' I said, and in doing so I'd beat Baz to it, winning this match in our running bet. But that was far from important right now. I rolled forward, Baz followed, taxiing up alongside. We both accelerated, building speed until the nose of the aircraft dropped and the tail lifted into the horizontal. More speed now towards the end of the HALS. I pulled in the required power and both Apaches took to the air fast, the IRT Chinook lifting behind to follow us. Once clear of the boundary fence, Alex armed the defensive aid suite. Baz turned slightly left, taking a more northerly direction. I manoeuvred into the rear to get eyes on the Chinook behind. It could fly quicker, caught up with us and tucked in behind.

Sangin in the middle distance now, clearance required from the JTAC, callsign Widow 63.

'Hello Widow 63, this is Ugly 50 accompanied by Ugly 51. Requesting situation report and clearance to enter area for casevac from Sangin district centre.'

'Ugly 50 and 51. Widow 63. We have had an F-16 in the area. He has dropped one times JDAM on the vehicle. If you can establish in the overhead, I'll provide another update once I speak to the ground commander.'

Alex radioed to the Chinook, not on the Apache channel, advising it to hold off in open desert. The Uglies went into a right-hand wheel formation over the obvious smoke billowing out of the vehicle. Once evacuated, it had been wiped out to ensure nothing at all fell into enemy hands.

The blazing Viking was 2 kilometres from us, down to the right. Widow 63 advised that soldiers from the Royal Anglian Regiment were in the area. A twenty-strong enemy force had been seen moving to the south of the area, towards the Helmand River, in the direction of a heavily wooded area. Unlike British soldiers, these fighters were not easily identifiable by their uniforms. Their MO was always, when possible, to mingle with locals as they moved. But that didn't mean we wouldn't have targets.

Alex summed it up best, saying, 'You can't hide a PKM or an RPG in your tracksuit bottoms, mate.'

'True,' I said, 'but they're not Scousers so maybe they aren't wearing tracksuits.'

The JTAC was listening. Fortunately, he wasn't from Liverpool.

'Uglies. Widow 63. We think weapons have been dropped at some point and collected by a waiting vehicle.'

Scanning from several kilometres out, it was clear the streets down there were busy with people, men, women, children. It was hard to avoid the unhappy idea that the men who had attacked our troops would get to do it again.

'Anything out of place?' I asked, with both Tim and Alex combing through TADS images.

'Not yet,' said Tim, noting that no one seemed to be in a hurry. And then, 'Opposite side of the river, just to the south.'

Alex panned over the area, the potential destination of our vanished Taliban. Thick clumps of trees, a few tracks, buildings and bushes alongside the bank. Yet there was no one visible, which was strange in itself. Widow 63 advised the location had been used by EF in the past. But if they were going there, they'd first have to cross that fast-flowing river, which must have been 500 metres wide.

'A few boats around,' said Alex, scanning.

All eyes on stalks, Baz spotted a deep irrigation ditch leading off from the river and towards the point where the Viking had been ambushed. The enemy could be using that large ditch as a rat run to bring them back to the water's edge and allow escape by boat to the far bank. We needed a closer look.

Ugly 50 split to scan and we stayed put. Then a call from Tim – an empty boat had been seen leaving the far bank, was heading over. Then a second boat appearing briefly from under deep vegetation on that far bank, falling in behind, heading in the same direction. Both boats had by now disappeared under dense, overhanging foliage, both appearing to be travelling upriver, closing in on the other bank. Then nothing. Alex had kept eyes on the second boat and was trying to track its path, assuming it had continued to move in the same direction as the first boat. What we didn't know was that, once hidden from view, it had turned around.

Tim on the radio now. He'd spotted a third boat on the move, one he had noted earlier, but it had been empty then.

'Widow 63, Ugly 50. Third boat now has fighting-age males aboard.'

A white vehicle pulling up by the far riverbank. That had to be the rendezvous point. Close by, two unmanned boats tied up. We were dealing with a lot of moving, and not moving, parts at once.

'Ugly 50, Widow 63. Describe the occupants of the boat you can see.'

'Widow 63, Ugly 50. Four males with turban-style headdress, two with white tops, two with dark tops, two with backpacks. No visible weapons.'

I was sure they were the men we wanted. Or some of them, at least. But the area was huge, the situation complicated, the behaviours below both suspicious yet innocent at the same time. We needed more.

'Ugly 50. Ugly 51. We'll scan further downriver to see if there are any more boats or similar groups.'

Tim agreed. Alex and I turned south as Widow 63 said it could now confirm ground forces had spotted attackers dropping weapons and heading to the riverside in groups. And the descriptions of the men in the boat matched. Now another small knot of men in similar clothing spotted by the riverbank, as if waiting for a boat. This was unfolding fast.

Tim's response sounded like frustration.

'Widow 63, Ugly 50. Are you confirming you wish us to engage? Because if you are, I need clearance from the very top. These are unarmed men.'

'Okay,' Widow responded, 'stand by.'

The silence went on too long. The boat with the four men on

board moved under trees like the other two boats. All we had now was that group waiting by the ditch. The Apaches were waiting too, the Chinook still holding, a man in urgent need of medical care. But there was no way that IRT could be cleared in yet.

'Come on,' I said, 'what's the story here?'

'Ugly 50, Widow 63. From the very top, you are cleared to engage. We are confident these men are the Taliban that participated in the ambush.'

That was it.

I turned the aircraft towards Tim and Baz's position to see this attack. They ran slowly in, then smoke and fire flashes as the cannon let loose. Ten rounds at first. The targets by the riverbank, just the faintest of black figures on my screen, did not move. They had survived. A second burst from the angry aircraft, rounds thundering into the ground again. And still the men stayed put, still alive. Then a third burst. Where they were turned to blood and dust.

Ugly 50 swung to face the two boats tied up at the shoreline, doubtlessly part of the escape plan, and fired again. Instant kindling, like hot knives through butter.

As we set off in search of our absent fighters, the JTAC cleared in the Chinook. Not before time either. Its fuel was getting low.

A boat visible through a gap in the trees now, slowly motoring along, hugging the riverbank. A next target?

Tim called in, 'How many do you count Alex?'

'Three. I think?'

'I count four.'

And it disappeared again beneath the green.

'Wait,' said Tim. 'Another gap coming up.'

Alex zoomed in further with the TADS. As the boat appeared once more, another count.

'One, two, three, four,' he said. 'Tim. Definitely four.'

'I've got four as well.'

Alex asked my thoughts.

'Okay,' I said, 'similar boat, same number on board, same circumstances. It's good but we need clearance.'

'Widow 63, Ugly 51. I have sight now of one of the boats that now has four males on board. It's attempting to stick close to the riverbank using trees as cover. Confirm I am clear to engage?'

'Ugly 51. Widow 63. Stand by.'

Again the boat vanished beneath trees, to emerge again 50 metres further along.

'Ugly 51, Widow 63. You are cleared to engage.'

Alex ran through weapon checks, armed the gun, selected twenty rounds.

'Okay,' I said, just able to make out the boat's location passing under the leaves. 'They're closing in on the gap, Alex. Thirty metres. Twenty metres. Ten metres.'

Gunfire imminent.

'Ready to fire,' said Alex.

'Standby,' I said. 'Three, two, one – STOP STOP STOP!'

'What!'

A headscarf. I was sure of it. A woman's headscarf flapping in the wind. My heart was hammering. There was a woman on the boat, and the Taliban have no females on the front line.

'Fuck me!' Alex screamed, half a second from killing them all. 'I literally had pressure on the trigger.'

We watched, breathing deep, as the boat pulled up at the riverbank. An elderly man stood, reached out, tied up. He lifted a small motorbike from the floor of the vessel. The others helped as he climbed out with it, got on, started it up, turned to the others. As an innocent puff of exhaust smoke rose from behind him, the others were getting out of the boat. All three got on the bike behind him, including the woman, and in what was a deft balancing act, he began moving along and puttered away.

'Jesus Christ,' I said, before willing my mind to break away from the 'what ifs,' to move on to the next task.

Eyes back on the suspicious area over the river, the mini village that we were sure was the enemy's launch and landing ground. I could make out now what looked like yet another boat appearing from under trees, as if just arriving from the other side. Alex slaved the TADS. Fighting-age males on board. The second the riverbank came within reach, three alighted, the fourth following. We watched as they strolled along a dirt track towards a copse 100 metres away. We had now moved directly above them, our noise unavoidable. Yet none of them looked up.

The men entered the woods and, in a misjudgement, began changing clothes. With just a patchy canopy above them, we watched as one or two turned sweaters inside out, changing the colour. One individual pulled a spare top from a backpack before leaving the trees and walking off towards the little village. The other three remained, smoking, chatting, perhaps fooling themselves that they were out of danger.

A white vehicle, very likely the one we had seen earlier, came trundling towards the woods. It passed the point where the men stood, U-turned and stopped. The driver got out, began walking towards the trio in the trees.

Alex advised Ugly 50 and Widow 63.

'Requesting clearance to engage,' he added, urgency in his voice. It took seconds.

'Cleared to engage.'

We would wait for the driver to get closer to the others, then open up. For the second time that day, Alex armed the aircraft. He placed the TADS crosshairs on the driver, applying slight pressure on the thumb controller. The man was tracked by the sights as he paced into the woods. He waved, called out to the others. They signalled back, gathered themselves. All four began heading to the car when first Alex, then the cannon, spoke.

'Firing.'

The recoil was phenomenal, almost seeming to push the Apache backwards, each pump like a parachute deploying behind. It might have been the combination of wind speed, maybe the angle of the weapon, but the nose of the Apache was getting uppercuts from a roaring giant. Twenty rounds rained into the trees, flashes on the TADS screen as hot metal severed branches, sent mud and splinters flying. As the picture cleared, nothing was moving. Seconds later, I spotted him.

'We have a runner.'

Alex had him in the sights, tracked him as he emerged from the woods, sprinted for his life.

'He's going for the car,' I said.

'Not if I can help it.'

Alex switched weapons. As the man got close, I turned the aircraft, facing the vehicle. It meant we were better aligned for a missile strike.

'All clear around,' I said.

An invisible laser beam landed on the vehicle. The missile, like a dog seeking scent, scanned for it, found it and barked back that it was ready to go. Alex fired and 70kg of bad news broke free from the rail. While the car's bonnet and roof were launched into the sky, the rest of it seemed to disintegrate. Several smaller explosions followed. We watched them, one by one, realising that the vehicle had been packed with munitions. A scan of the area around the car, now a crumpled mass of metal, revealed no sign that a man had been there at all. A look back to the trees now, and beneath the shorn canopy only the grim spectacle of bodies ripped apart. Better them than us.

We knew there had been others around, fundamentalists gambling their lives to kill infidels in British Army uniform. In the mood to bet, two Apache pilots made a plan. We moved out, making it look like we were homeward bound. After five miles we dropped low, arced around and returned. We reappeared fast, arriving over the same scene in search of more trouble. But there was no sign of targets, just people attempting to retrieve the dead, gathering them up for burial. It was time to go.

During the debrief it became clear that Baz had harboured severe doubts ahead of Ugly 50's engagement of that boat. He had been shocked by our close call with the woman in the headscarf and wondered whether he had been diligent enough. He spoke freely, saying that a cold dread inside him was suggesting that he may have wiped out a family. It was a natural thing to worry about, only normal to feel that niggling doubt. His mind was eased by what we saw on the taped Hi8 recording of the incident. Yet as we watched, as Baz began to feel less uncomfortable, the tape flickered, the images fading. It had softened in the extreme heat and got chewed up as it unspooled. A rare occurrence, yet known to happen. Unfortunately for Baz, it took some time for him to be able to rest.

Our aircraft each fired over 160 rounds of 30mm in that engagement. The fighters we killed had ambushed a British convoy, badly wounding a British soldier – one of our own. There was no question whether it was right to hit back hard, yet even coming to terms with that rightness of duty can take time. After the heat of battle it can at times take a mindshift to think of the enemy's lifeless remains, of the scorched ground where he had stood, of the mangled vehicle in which he had sat, and categorise these only as success. Images of death have a habit of staying fresh while other memories fade. Resolution becomes personal, with each of us involved finding our own way to knowing that the right thing has been done, that some lives are taken for a greater good.

No experienced, honourable soldier enjoys those reflections, but must learn to take comfort in knowing that he did his duty. Baz did his duty on that day, but the reassurance he needed to find could only come from within himself. I, Tim and Alex are certain he did the right thing.

Chapter Seventeen

101 MINUTES AT RAHIM KALAY, 2007

HELMAND, 6 JUNE, 8.14 a.m.. Summer in the desert. It's like the sun's on steroids. There's a permanent, viscous film of sweat on the skin. Sometimes I can almost feel the sand and grit being baked into my limbs. I'd go crazy without taking a shower once, twice, maybe three times a day. Wash away the dirt and grime, then reset.

That day, 6 June 2007, marked exactly sixty-three years since D-Day, when soldiers from the Glider Pilot Regiment, the Oxfordshire and Buckinghamshire Light Infantry and the Royal Engineers flew their way into history with the midnight capture of two strategic Normandy bridges. They landed in darkness within thirty-seven yards of what became known as Pegasus Bridge. They took control and held on hard, hamstringing the enemy by preventing German armour from crossing to attack the main invasion force. Pegasus Bridge was one of the most astonishing British coups of the Second World War.

Those legends were on my mind that morning as I flip-flopped towards the shower, a towel around my waist – but the shower would have to wait. An urgent tasking alert. About turn.

I raced to the VHR tent, pulled on trousers and a tee-shirt,

grabbed socks and boots and ran barefoot to the revving Land
Rover. Baz throttled it, wheels spitting dust as I leapt in. Socks on.
Boots half on. Trousers undone. Tee-shirt inside out. No pants.
Commando Jones could have no idea that the gruelling day ahead
would be one both he and the Taliban would never forget.

Front-seaters Tim and Alex got the mission brief. Baz and I
dashed to the aircraft, launched into pre-flight checks. We were
to escort the IRT's Chinook to the outskirts of a Helmand village
called Rahim Kalay, north of Gereshk. No problem. Both Apaches
accelerated hard down the HALS and up, both airborne eighteen
minutes after the launch call.

Tim opened communication with JTAC, Widow 79, at the
scene. It sounded messy. Rahim Kalay was a tough little Taliban
stronghold. Troops approaching from the west had been pinned
down by heavy mortar fire. American F-15 fighters had launched
a couple of bombing raids yet nothing but the tension was shifting
– and that was only going up. There had been British casualties.
The Chinook needed to get in, get them and get out safely. The
plan was that Ugly 50 – Tim and Baz – would keep eyes on the big
helicopter as it descended while Alex and I – Ugly 51 – would keep
watch over the hostile terrain from the air.

Troops were under fire as we closed in, but not for long. As soon
as we were spotted from a mile or more out, the gunfire stopped.
It usually did when the Taliban knew Apaches – or Mosquitoes,
as they were now calling them – were moving in. They knew
how dangerous we were, that we operated way slower than jets,
that we could loiter for longer high above them, that we could
pinpoint them, finish them.

The background: 1st Battalion, Worcestershire and Sherwood
Foresters (1WSF) and a number of Czech special forces had been
conducting Operation Gashey, a search-and-destroy for Taliban
firing and defensive positions. In support was Widow 79, the
controlling JTAC for the Upper Garesh Valley (UGV).

Things had kicked off hard while Widow 79 was awaiting F-15s, callsign Dude 15 and 16, the immediate on-call fast jet assets. Intense mortar fire had targeted forward elements of 1WSF. Two possible fire points had been identified – one to the north of the village, one to the south.

On arrival, Dude 16 went south. It identified three males repositioning a mortar barrel and engaged with a 500lb bomb. Two were killed. The third man broke for a dense tree line across a narrow river. Meanwhile, Dude 15 in the north identified four males covering up what looked like a mortar firing pit. At least one was armed. They had raced into a building for cover when the jet showed up. Dude 15 wiped it out.

Yet there had been no let-up. Intensive small-arms and RPG fire kept rattling out towards 1WSF. The best intel said there were fighters both inside the village and within that tree line to the south. Dude 16 had made an early bid to dominate the theatre and shut this down. The F-15 ran a low-level pass firing flares. The theory was that the pyrotechnics might encourage insurgents to clear out so we could take the village. It failed. They weren't budging.

The IRT and escorting Apaches took twenty minutes to arrive from Bastion. As the shooting stopped, 1WSF and Czech colleagues wasted no time in taking advantage of the lull. Step by step, they pushed further east towards Rahim Kalay.

Knowing there was every chance of bullets or mortars tearing towards our troops, we kept our eyes peeled. Up front, Alex scanned the area on the TADS. I held the aircraft steady as I watched with the best bit of kit I had – the Mark I eyeball. Up here, from the enemy's point of view, we were much easier to see than they were to us down there. It was a given that we were being observed.

Rahim Kalay looked like plenty of other small Afghan villages I'd seen. A collection of compounds of various sizes, a jigsaw of beige-coloured dwellings, courtyards and alleyways that at first made little sense to Western eyes. The only splashes of colour were from trees, patches of crops or grassland, or the occasional vehicle. I ran my eyes over it all, trying to get a handle on the terrain.

Roughly speaking, this square mile of a village was split north to south by a slaloming road. To the immediate east of the road, a cluster of three huge, adjacent compounds of the typical style – stout, thick-walled mud constructions with large outside spaces, two of them with a handful of smaller buildings within the walls. They seemed so close at first, all at odd angles to one another, that they might be interconnected, but further inspection revealed that each had its own perimeter. There was a kind of free-flowing design style going on which didn't help when it came to scanning for exits, portals, firing holes in those high perimeter walls.

All of these compounds stood on raised ground, each with some overlook of the properties across the winding dirt road to the west, where our troops were static for now. There was every chance, I knew, that the enemy was firing from behind those walls. I figured that if some of the compounds were built on top of a network of caves, then Rahim Kalay could prove to be a tough nut to crack. All I knew for sure was that very often things were not what they might seem. Yet necessity and experience were proving to be a shrewd teacher in these matters. My instincts had been getting sharper, my eyes drawn faster to points of potential threat. Or so I hoped, at least.

I tracked the dusty, winding road that bisected the village as it dropped to the south and gave way to a wooden footbridge. The bridge served as the only crossing point over a sparkling, meandering river that ran from west to east, seeming to underline the little village. Just south of the water I could see the tree-lined riverbank that was causing concern. Some of it was thick woodland which revealed nothing to me from this bird's-eye view. If this little puzzle of a place was going to keep being as stubborn as it had been so far, the enemy was playing with a strong hand.

After a few minutes, the Chinook climbed back up without

incident. It confirmed it was happy to head back to Bastion unescorted. We confirmed that it might be wise for us to hang on for a while, just to see whether two Apaches could screw up a Taliban plan or two.

There was no immediate agreement to do anything but observe. As the Chinook shrank into the distant sky, my eyes once more traced building outlines, probed shadows, doorways, riverbanks, tree lines.

'Where are you?' I was saying it, quietly, slowly, as calmly as I could, saying it in the knowledge that the enemy were down there somewhere with British blood on their hands.

But the Taliban had proved to be quick learners. They had been watching how Apaches behaved for a while, and knew how long we could hang around before we'd need to refuel. Down there somewhere, someone would have the stopwatch ticking. To take out these Mosquitoes, at least temporarily, all they had to do was be patient. We had a little over forty-five minutes to play with. Would they sit it out as the Foresters slowly but surely continued their advance?

Forty minutes went by. Not a shadow moved. We kept on sniffing, inching our way through the air, orbiting above, swooping around from half a mile out, moving back in, watching, waiting, hoping.

A call from Bastion. We were eating up fuel. The guns had been silent for too long. For us, this TIC was over. The assets should get back to base in case of another call-out.

'Shit. Where. Are. You?'

Widow 79 was not happy. Neither were we. All of us knew that as soon as we were out of sight, this would kick off again.

But orders are orders. We had to depart ASAP. Widow 79 and 1WSF would have to rely on fast jets again – and the much less detailed ground assessments they offered.

Just before we turned for home, Alex called out.

'Hey.'

He'd seen something.

'White estate car,' he said.

A great spot. It was at the bottom of the road down to the river, tucked in by a wall and some trees, just before the footbridge. The only car around. It looked as if it had been abandoned.

Alex zoomed out on TADS to get a fuller view of the area. Our guys were advancing from the west, planning to cross over that road towards the compounds on the eastern side. The track they were taking would lead them close to the footbridge, right where this car had been left. Neither of us spoke. We didn't need to. Our guts were telling us the same thing. Alex called it in to Widow 79. They marked the car's location on the map. Yet we had an order to obey. We turned noses to Bastion, tails to the Taliban.

And it took just minutes before everything kicked off again.

The Mosquitoes moved out and the mortars pounded down once more. The enemy had not been twiddling their thumbs. They'd figured out positions as best they could, reloaded everything they had and began hammering as hard as their weapons would allow. Over the next hour they launched something like twenty-seven mortar rounds alone.

Dude had been called home too. Fast air cover was now down to RAF Harriers, callsigns Recoil 41 and 4242. They cracked on, identified firing locations and precision bombed as best they could. Not unexpectedly, the Taliban kept packing up, moving, repositioning. And, not unexpectedly, one barrage of rockets came soaring out of a village location busy with women and children, forcing Recoil 41 to abort a bombing run. It was all a bit of a mess.

As time passed, as we tried to learn everything we could while sitting on our arses in Bastion, it became clear that more and more Taliban fronts were opening up. The insurgents were getting stronger, ever more ferocious. It seemed as if an increasing number of men with a mounting number of weapons were coming into play. RPGs were pounding down like never before. Small-arms fire was zipping constantly towards the troops. There was no doubt that resolve on the Taliban side was firm and getting firmer, but resolve on our side was as solid as steel. One of the 1WSF casualties had been pronounced dead on arrival at Bastion. He was Lance Corporal Paul Sandford, aged twenty-three.

By mid-morning Rahim Kalay had become an active battleground yet it was clear to everyone that the air support was mismatched. When one of the two Harriers flew back to the circling tanker to refuel, as they kept having to do, the other one was alone and enemy fire only increased. These jets were swift and effective, in and out, hard and fast. But they offered no window in terms of loiter time over target, and could relay very little detail in an increasingly complex theatre. The Taliban knew it. Jets weren't going to force their hand. But Mosquitoes could. We needed to be there. I've never been more ready, never more willing. I was sure it was coming. And this time I had my pants on.

The call came.

Airborne in minutes alongside Ugly 50 and charging back to Rahim Kalay. Widow 79 updated en route to say a Harrier had spotted three fighting-age males in one of the large compounds east of the road. Holes had been bored into the walls. The men had been looking through in the direction of the troops. There was just something like 300 metres between the friendlies and the Taliban. Our guys had gone static until more information came through. Mortar fire was still coming their way. The gravity of it all, the urgent bloody reality, weighed heavy as we were cleared in. This fight would have to end, one way or another. It was them or it was us.

My very first decision had been to get Alex to scan ahead with TADS. Typically, we'd not do that until we were pretty much established in the overhead, but I wanted every shred of information I could get as early as I could get it. As the live monochrome feed told us what it could, I spotted something.

'Alex,' I said. 'Go to the right.'

We were looking at the western side of the road, the same side where our troops had dug in. I'd spotted plumes of white smoke rising up fast from inside a compound. Yet there had been nothing to say any that mortar fire was coming from there. Ground forces were close to this location and they had been certain the mortars were coming from the east. Yet now, with TADS recentred, Alex and I could both see the same thing – a burst of smoke. Then another, another, and another.

'Widow 79, Ugly 51. Please advise each time a mortar lands.'

A minute later and Widow 79 told of an impact close by. Alex and I had watched a puff of smoke rise just a second before. And then again – smoke, impact; smoke, impact. Yet Widow 79 remained sure the mortars were coming from the compounds to the east on the other side of the road.

Then it hit me – smoke signals.

There must be spotters in the compound where the smoke is coming from. Could it be that they were letting the mortar team know when to fire? We briefed and I set off slowly to get in for a closer look, for a first peer over the compound's high, fortress-style mud wall. As ground inside the compound came into view from a distance out, neither Alex nor I could see anything.

Before we moved further in, we needed to be ready. Clearance to engage with 30mm was requested and swiftly granted. With the weapon actioned and Alex in search of a target, I crept forward some more. Whoever was down there, they were not spooked by the approaching Apache. Smoke plumes were still rising, mortars still landing as though in response. Ugly 50, also now with eyes on, backed up my theory. The smoke was the signal to fire.

As the black belly of the Apache came into view above the compound, the full spread of the sections of the inner courtyard showed themselves. We were sure someone would run, that a manned firing tube would become visible, maybe that we'd rumble a camouflaged firing point. Whatever was about to catch our eye, we wanted to hammer it into Hell.

Hearts pounding yet still with nothing clear, nothing obvious, nothing even suspicious. The only movement in the whole place was that of an old man seated alone at the side of a clay pot. Another full look over, another search for Taliban signallers, but nothing. Then eyes back on the old man cooking his lunch by the fire. I watched as he reached over and lifted the lid on that pot. And a belch of smoke headed skywards.

'Jesus Christ,' I said.

What were the odds? He did it again. Lifted the lid. Stirred his pot. Another puff of smoke. Yet that man had no part to play in the war beyond the walls; quite apart from anything else, he had no view of what was going on outside. The only connection was coincidentally that the mortar rounds were coming just as often as he was tending to his grub. Since we had no reason to add lead to his meal we backed away.

Widow 79 requested that Ugly 50 move to the north of the trio of adjacent compounds on the eastern side of the road, and that we move to the south. I climbed the aircraft up another 500 feet to ensure adequate deconfliction. We were going to be working closely together above this village. If I was going down in Helmand today, I was bloody sure it wouldn't be because I'd crashed into an Apache.

As we moved towards where the enemy was based, the rate of mortar fire dropped. We were still some distance out but what was now coming into full view looked like some sort of medieval citadel, the kind of structure whose design likely hadn't changed in a millennium. Moving in to get a handle on the detail of it all, I could see one of the compounds was to the north, one to the south, one to the east. The eastern one, the furthest from the friendly troops, was vast, by far the largest, aircraft-hangar size, something like 650 by 650-foot of roofed building with just a patch of forecourt.

Alex scanned it all on TADS. Other than random clusters of chickens, neither of us could see any signs of life in any area – but that changed in seconds. We spotted a lone man in the northern compound, his back against the inside perimeter wall. Right beside him, also leaning against the wall, was some kind of object covered with a white sheet. We watched from some distance back as two more men appeared from a long, dome-roofed building across the yard and walked towards him. All three were of fighting age, and all in local dress. From a half mile out, the TADS revealed an animated discussion getting under way. Lots of gestures towards the troops' positions, no indication that they had taken stock of the Apaches. The leaning man turned around, faced the wall. In doing so he gave away the position of a hole he was using to observe troop positions. He turned back to the two other males, giving what looked like the thumbs-up. The two males turned and walked back towards the big dome-shaped structure.

'AK,' said Alex.

He was right. A Kalashnikov assault rifle was strapped to the back of one of the walking men. He and his friend disappeared. The spotter, with the white sheet beside him, remained.

We briefed Widow 79 and Ugly 50, advised that the lone man was again peering through the portal. Ugly 50, closer to the guy in question, requested warning shots to gauge his reaction. Widow 79 cleared it. Tim fired a ten-round burst, hitting dirt about 300 metres north, smashing ground outside the perimeter wall. The guy didn't flinch.

Tim adjusted his TADS. More heavy rounds slammed into the earth, this time just 150 metres away. And still no reaction to the ground-shaking danger just beyond the wall. All the subject's attention remained on scoping out troop positions.

'Widow 79, Ugly 50. Individual still in place. Not moving. Request clearance to engage.'

'Ugly 50, Widow 79. You are clear to engage with 30mm.'

This would get his attention. Twenty high-explosive rounds slammed down around him. Part of the wall exploded – dust, dirt and dried mud everywhere. Freaked-out chickens scarpered in all directions. He reached down, pulled the white sheet away revealing a PKM machine gun. He grabbed it, raced to the dome-shaped building. And that was when the shit hit the fan. The place burst into life, with small-arms fire blasting out towards the east.

'Widow 79, Ugly 50. We have stirred the hornets' nest.'

We kept watch on that one dome-shaped building where our trio had based themselves. It ran parallel to an identical structure and both were joined at one end by a broad, flat-roofed corridor. That big goalpost-shaped building could have been hiding any amount of Taliban, any number of weapons. All we knew for sure was that there were at least two firearms and three guys in there.

'Ugly 50, Ugly 51. Widow 79. You are cleared to engage.'

Both aircraft now with 30mm actioned. Alex guided our underslung cannon into position. Its high-explosive rounds are enough to tear open light-skinned combat vehicles. Now we'd get to see them rip holes through roofs in Rahim Kalay. I held the helicopter steady as Alex pressed the trigger, the big gun pulsing under our feet, unplanned skylights on the way for the two dome-shaped sections of the building.

But incredibly, those rounds did no damage, just bouncing right off. There was dirt and dust and noise but nothing to say that we were breaking through. It was a reminder that some of these walls and ceilings are several feet thick, and have been baked in the desert sun for years. They're as tough or tougher than double brick walls.

'We need something bigger,' I said.

Tim cleared a Hellfire missile engagement. Both aircraft would reset to the north, launch, run in together. Ugly 50 would engage the building on the left, we'd take the one on the right.

Baz peeled off, heading for a point about two miles beyond. I followed, tucked into their right-hand side, turned, slowed up, giving Alex time to prepare. Launch was imminent. Alex advised all checks were completed. Tim advised the same for Ugly 50. He fired first. I watched the missile scream off the rail, saw it climb to establish its flight profile. It would take around eight seconds to hit. We were next.

'Alex,' I said. 'Fire.'

A thump as our missile came to life, the whoosh as it rocketed away. We needed two hard strikes for this to work, to blow holes into that hideout. Black fireworks as the first missile struck. A building was burst open, a chunk of roof collapsing inwards in a heartbeat. Another second ticked by. Another impact imminent.

Any second now.

Any second now...

Where was our missile?

Unstoppable, high-speed questions charged into my head. Has Alex screwed up? Has he not held the crosshairs on the target? Has he missed? Has that bloody thing gone rogue?

Where the hell was our missile?

It's like time halts. We'd sent a missile flying into the middle distance, but where was it now? It was taking too long. There's no telling how bad this could get. There's no training away the cold terror that grips when you fear you're in the biggest fuck-up of your life. In those slow, heavy seconds before some impact somewhere, I could only hope it was all in my head, that my brain was just gaming out the worst possible outcome.

The answer was definitive – BOOM! Another instantaneous thick, dark, cloud, another hole punched into another part of the building. Our Hellfire was bang on target. It had been a matter of three, maybe just two seconds, but those seconds did not pass easy.

'Thank Christ for that,' I whispered, taking a breath.

An armed man was sprinting now, racing from the eastern

compound to open ground in the western compound. He was heading towards a small building. Alex tracked him all the way. A fast request to engage.

'Come on,' I said, knowing we can take this guy, hoping Alex can keep him dead centre of the crosshairs.

A fast response.

'Clear to engage.'

Rounds slammed the ground all around the man. He hit the earth face first, vanished into the foggy confusion of desert conflict. It would take time before we'd know if we'd served the kind of justice war offers, if we'd ended this deadly stranger's life. The Apache engine rumbled on as we orbited, hoping to see imminent harsh, hard proof that he was no longer a threat.

But he was up, running through the dust cloud and into the shelter of the nearest building, ready to fight again. Alex fixed on his location, somewhere in that little fort. At the same time Ugly 50 to the north had opened up on enemies at the top end of the hangar-sized building. I looked their way, back to the instruments, back to the TADS.

And there he was again, running from his hideout. He was going back the way he came. He darted through a doorway in the perimeter wall and back into the eastern compound.

'Engage!' I said, but it was all too fast, too dusty, too unexpected.

By now I was thinking that the eastern compound is the heart of it all. That's where they're coming from, where they're going to. That big hangar, I was sure, is Rahim Kalay's Taliban HQ. And, looking it over again, it seemed to have only one doorway.

I pulled hard at the controls, banking the big aircraft around. I wanted to see everything I could of that entrance. With the TADS zoomed in, I saw a second doorway. And right there, crouched low, in the hope of not being spotted, another enemy fighter.

I alerted Alex. He put him in the crosshairs. I ensured a stable platform, balanced my feet on the pedals, ran my eyes over the instruments. All was well. I looked towards our target. There was movement just across from him.

'Stop!' I said, Alex releasing the trigger. 'A donkey!'

A flippin' donkey was just across from the man in the shadows, standing still, looking towards him. I can only think that the guy really wished the donkey wasn't around, fearing it would give his position away. He had no idea it had probably just saved his life. I had no qualms about shooting a guy who wanted to kill British soldiers, no problem blowing him to kingdom come if it came to it. But we're not animal killers. We held fire.

Suddenly a fat man came running from the HQ building, a PKM in his hands, dashing as fast as his belly would allow. He raced right past our crouching Taliban and onto an open track leading towards the riverbank. And because we hadn't unleashed hell on the donkey, the cannon was good to go. Alex fired off twenty rounds. The earth exploded around the man. Dust everywhere. It was like we'd dropped a bomb. Whatever was left down there now, it was no longer a threat.

'He's not getting up,' I said, unnecessarily.

The breeze carried away the last of the cloud and, incredibly, our man was getting up.

'Holy crap,' I said, or maybe thought. 'Hardcore or what?!'

We watched in amazement as that seemingly bulletproof man with a bulging BMI grabbed his weapon, stepped away and dived athletically into a small cave entrance right beside him, almost underneath the compound. As he went, Alex rattled out another twenty. Cannon shells smashed into rock, spitting shards and sparks into the air. But he was gone. Some of the rounds had hit a small building further back. Two armed men came bounding out. One had an RPG on his shoulder, both were running like hell. They were at the riverbank in a couple of seconds, clearly breaking for the tree line on the other side. We already had information that more Taliban were in there.

'Engage them!'

I'd said it loud.

These two guys would be in the water in no time. And that river wasn't at all wide. If they made it to the tree line, they'd every chance of getting into a hide, of getting away. The adrenalin was making me want to fire off every weapon we had. I wanted these bastards dead.

'Come on – engage them, Alex!'

He was trying to get it right. They'd come fast, out of the blue. The gun sights were still on the cave. Alex had to reset, track the new target, get the crosshairs on, keep them on. Zoom too close and you'll lose sight and have to go looking once more. Don't zoom close enough and it's harder to accurately adjust the 30mm rounds. That's when mistakes get made. Yet we had just seconds to play with. We couldn't let them escape, RPG intact. Who knows how many British or American troops they'd go on to kill? My hands were squeezing controls, muscles tensed, long seconds of toothless fury as the enemy fled.

They leapt into the waist-deep water, weapons high, and began wading to the other side. Relief now as Alex fired, metal hailstones crashing into water. Streams of spray shot up like fountains. Waves around both men crashed together. One fell forward. The other didn't look back, scrambled to the bank, made for the trees. Twenty more rounds came his way. Bright flashes as timber was torn apart, our target literally running for his life as his dead comrade floated away.

Near by, Tim and Baz, fresh from engagements to the north, swooped in and opened up, scores of rounds hammering into the tree line, sparks and splinters everywhere. But how deep had our man gone? How many more Taliban were in there? The cannons were no longer the best tools for the job. We didn't know where to shoot.

A short discussion between Widow 79 and two Uglies. We agreed on flechettes. We'd set up for a rocket shot, each rocket packing tens of 6-inch tungsten darts. When discharged from the housing canister after firing, they'd rain down like a lethal canopy, each impacting at something like 2,000mph.

But we had to think about the spread of those things. If we fired, say, six or eight rockets, we'd be committing to hundreds of individual strikes. A lot of room for error in there. How wide a spread would it be? Just how much damage were we about to do? No Uglies had fired flechettes in anger before. And among everything we learned from training, we knew that every engagement is unique. We were about to take on a colossal responsibility. Yet we all knew that handing victory to our armed insurgent, and who knows how many of his colleagues down there with him, was a heavier burden. We had to get on with it. One way or another, this attack would further weaken the enemy. There was every chance it would ultimately spare British or American lives.

'Ensure all are under cover,' I said, advising all friendlies of an imminent strike.

Alex armed the aircraft. As pilot, I'd be responsible for firing this ferocious blanket of darts. I tuned in to the sensations in my feet, my hands, everything in my eyeline as I worked to align the aircraft. I needed this to go well, needed it to help bring this battle to a close. Finger on the trigger. TADS sight steady. Feedback from the pedals told me of the helicopter's natural tendency to yaw away, and if I didn't keep it in check the rockets could easily slide or swing off target. Christ knows how bad that could end up.

Ten things on my mind gelled into one. I took a breath, focused on dead straight flight. The rocket-steering cursor met the TADS crosshairs, then crosshairs on the target. A split second of alignment, a fraction of time in which to get this right. I pressed the trigger. Thump thump thump – the rockets left their pods, roared away. Just down range, visible black-powder charges, the canisters on each rocket blowing open. Tungsten darts in play, racing ahead of the housing, each gathering immense kinetic energy. Dozens of flying spikes, a terrible, lethal torrent ripping into foliage, piercing timber, stabbing ground. Darts on the extremities rained down in a cylindrical pattern, impacting throughout the tree line area, striking dry wadi wall, arid soil. Nothing moved afterwards but for branches swaying from the steel storm, falling leaves, and a light cloud of dust that vanished to nothing. It had been a well-controlled hit. I couldn't know at the time how many insurgents I'd just killed.

We shifted our focus back to the hangar-sized building, the suspected eastern compound HQ. Small fires, sparked by the earlier missile strikes, were burning near by. Some back-and-forth comms with Widow 79. All agreed that the building was a base for the fighters, that some were in there now. Questions sprang up. Might there be a cave entrance accessible from within that building? Could the enemy be hiding beneath it? It was just too big not to hold secrets, and could be too sturdy to give them up to the Uglies.

Widow 79 advised that an F-15 had just checked in. A solution could be on the cards.

'Dude, Widow 79. What ordnance do you have aboard? I have a large complex that needs to be destroyed.'

'Widow 79, Dude. I have two by one thousand JDAMs if that helps.'

'That'll do nicely. Ready to copy coordinates.'

We'd need to get out of there. Baz and I pushed to the south. We didn't know exactly how large this explosion was going to be, but we knew it would be getting on for biblical.

Eyes on the building from a good distance away. Dude completed preparations and then, charging through blue sky, he called it.

'Bomb away.'

That 1,000lb JDAM was so damn big I caught sight of it before impact. And wallop – the building seemed to lift into the air. The roof ripped apart and the walls buckled as the whole structure turned to hot, dusty, dancing rubble. Things just were not going the Taliban's way today.

With not a sinner in sight, the key remaining issue ahead of further troop advances was the abandoned car that Alex had spotted near the bridge. Every instinct told us it posed a threat. For friendlies to move towards the now flattened HQ building, we'd need to get rid of it.

Tim volunteered to hit the car in a Hellfire strike. He used image auto-track to put a cursor on the target and help stabilise the TADS. Yet laser tracking is easily lost if the picture becomes obscured. And, sure enough, the IAT broke lock. For a moment we had a rogue Hellfire on our hands, laser guiding from Ugly 50 lost due to a plume of exhaust from the missile motor. Tim met the challenge fast. He put crosshairs back on the target, guided it in, hit the suspect vehicle.

Call me a perfectionist, but it wasn't the best of strikes. Nevertheless, after watching the car sizzle for a while, it was clear that the missile had done the job. The strike triggered a handful of smaller explosions, so we now knew for sure there had been some nasty surprises awaiting FF. A follow-up patrol would go on to find elements of C3 plastic explosive in the wrecked vehicle and confirmed that there had been RPGs in the boot.

Layered with sweat, we checked our weapons state. No surprise at all that we were almost Winchester – all out of ammo. Not a single 30mm round remained, not a single rocket and just one Hellfire on the rack. In terms of fuel, if we didn't head back to Bastion inside ten minutes, we wouldn't make it.

The engagement had been our heaviest so far, one that had loaded our memories with unforgettable scenes, and had forced on us decisions that we'd pull apart in the debrief and hoped we would never live to regret. The Battle of Rahim Kalay had been a nerve-shredding 101 minutes that somehow felt like 15. Between both aircraft, we had fired over 600 rounds of 30mm, three

Hellfire missiles and eighteen rockets. That day, 6 June 2007, had been one when a Taliban advantage turned into its biggest defeat to date in the Green Zone.

On the drive to the debrief after arrival at Bastion we were still trying to collect our thoughts, still trying to let our muscles relax, when we were waved down by a member of the Royal Military Police on patrol.

'Yes mate?' I inquired, wondering if he needed a lift.

'Sir,' he said, 'I noticed you're not wearing a seat belt.'

It took me a moment to process it. I don't think I had the energy to laugh or yell or even to begin explaining how utterly insignificant his words seemed on this day.

'Mate,' I said, 'twenty kilometres up the road there are people losing their lives, and this is what you're worried about? Get real.'

'We're only doing our jobs, sir,' he said stiffly.

Us too.

We would learn later, via an update from Widow 79, just how heavy a price our work had forced the enemy to pay.

When 1WSF finally pushed into the centre of Rahim Kalay it was completely quiet with no signs of small arms or RPG. The destroyed car had been right in the way of their line of advance, lying in the middle of the road which would have caused many casualties if this had been used as a roadside bomb. After pushing into the main compound and caves we found many dead Taliban.

The one Taliban that had been engaged at the entrance of the cave was found dead just inside, it must have been the adrenalin that had him get back up and then climb inside. Upon examining the caves many arms and ammunition were found, along with many other entrances and exits all over the compound highlighting how it was possible to move around without being seen.

A supporting friendly unit then pushed out to a tree line just south of the compound over the river where both callsigns had engaged men running into it from the small building. They found approximately nine Taliban dead with no apparent injuries apart from a very small but clean entry and exit wound, as a result of the flechette darts fired from the Apache rockets. Also, in the wood line there were thousands of rounds of ammunition, many different weapons, food, sleeping bags and other equipment indicating the insurgents had been lying in wait for some time. There were also signs that bushes had been cut down to provide clear individual firing arcs towards any advancing Coalition troops.

We held the village of Rahim Kalay for a further 24 hours and held a meeting with the village elders, one of which was a representative of the local Taliban who confirmed there had been 41 Taliban dead with a further 34 unaccounted for. It had been the biggest defeat the Taliban had ever encountered in the green zone with the destruction of at least two mortar-based plate teams and at least two complete cells of Taliban. Which if correlated as correct, a force of that size in both the compound and fortified surrounding areas could have resulted in the biggest loss of life to British soldiers.

Not long after one of the Chinook aircrews passed us an X-ray from a makeshift enemy field hospital built into one of the trench systems in Rahim Kalay. It showed the clear image of a man's body, the unmistakeable silhouette of a flechette dart embedded deep within.

On the back, one of the aircrew had written:

'Never in the field of human conflict has so much been fired at so many by so few.'

It was as good a summary as any of that mission in Afghanistan.

Yet the heavy day didn't end there. After the two-hour debrief it was right back to the VHR tent to finish the duty. As night fell, we talked over the intensity of it all, of the hammer blow we knew we'd delivered from the sky.

A phone call. Baz and I were up and running again to the aircraft while Alex and Tim collected the basic brief – who, what, where. A TIC was under way in the Helmand town of Sangin – immediate support required.

As we closed in on the target area, the night seemed somehow to be blacker, heavier than we were used to. Our right eyes surveyed the sharp, green images from the PNVS in the back while Tim and Alex manned the TADS, scanning the terrain.

I slowed up as a plan was put in place. To ensure deconfliction with Baz's aircraft just ahead, I was to climb 500 feet before establishing the orbit. That distance of open night air was the only protective barrier the two Apaches would have between each other. We would both be constantly moving, as we always must over hostile ground, and two orbiting helicopters at night are one step from disaster.

As expected, Taliban fighters fell silent when the Mosquitoes showed up. But, unlike in daytime, hiding places and movements often proved easier to identify because people appear as hotspots in night-vision imagery.

We were up there for about thirty minutes with nothing to see when something unexpected happened. A large aircraft, out of nowhere, on my PNVS. My monocle rapidly filled with the shape and size of this thing. It was close – way too close – maybe just a hundred feet away, crossing left to right.

'What the fuck was that!?'

I'd roared it out before jumping on the radio. Had anyone else seen this thing? What the hell's going on? There had been no notification at all.

To my horror I learned it was my wingman. Our Apaches had almost collided.

'Check height,' I called to Baz over the radio.

He checked and confessed he had somehow climbed 200 feet. I checked too – and had to confess I'd somehow descended by 200 feet.

Over the thirty minutes, we had both departed from our orbit heights. If we hadn't realised, we would have been on a collision course.

Given that nothing was doing and that the four of us had almost just killed each other, the all-clear was given to return to Bastion. There was no doubt we were all drained, no doubt that we had all come close to turning a day of victory into one of disaster. Rahim Kalay had exhausted us and no one had said it out loud. It was one of those 'I learnt about flying from that' moments. I would never make the same mistake again.

Following the events in Rahim Kalay on that day, FOB Sandford was established on the outskirts of the village. It was named after Lance Corporal Paul Sandford of the 1st Battalion, Worcestershire and Sherwood Foresters Regiment, who fell there on that morning of 6 June 2007.

Although the area had always been considered a Taliban stronghold, British and other troops stationed at Rahim Kalay would go on to make considerable inroads in terms of gaining the trust of local people.

With the help of residents, security was improved and improvised explosive devices (IEDs) were cleared allowing farmers to return to work in what had once been one of the most unstable locations in Afghanistan's most hostile province.

FOB Sandford would go on to be renamed FOB Rahim and, later, Patrol Base Rahim before it was closed. In time, Rahim Kalay fell back into Taliban hands, as did the rest of Afghanistan in 2021.

Chapter Eighteen

DANGER CLOSE – OPERATION CHAKUSH, 2007

A N INTEL BRIEFING. Nothing out of the ordinary.

EF shocked and feel threatened still. Massive absence of enemy in Gereshk and Upper Gereshk Valley due to losses they have suffered.

EF retreating into the mountainous areas east of Helmand River, via Zumbelay, Khogyadi Miramandaw and Pasaw.

Reports of 150 enemy fighters trapped in the hills, and running low on ammunition and food.

Reports of EF pushing suicide bombers into Haidarabad.

Haidarabad had become something of a refuge for Taliban on-the-run after the wipe out at Rahim Kalay. Further pressure had hit them via the Afghan National Army-led Operation Tufaan. British attention was now focusing on the area. The thinking was that if we could crush them at Haidarabad, the enemy would have lost his last foothold in the Upper Gereshk Valley. After that, just 10 per cent of the Helmand River Valley, Musa Qala to the north and southern pockets around Garmsir, could reasonably be said to be under complete Taliban control.

A decisive hammer blow was needed, a major ground and air offensive. It came in the form of Operation Chakush, the Pashtun word for hammer. Infantry from the Royal Anglian Regiment and the Worcestershire and Sherwood Foresters were given the task and all four flights of 662 Squadron would play a part.

Ground forces were to stake out a perimeter to the east of the settlement overnight. At dawn, Chinooks would land troops on to bridges leading over canals and into the town. More would be landed in the open spaces to the east, the prediction being that surprised Taliban would flee eastwards and into their sights. It was an important and ambitious plan, but for me and Alex in Ugly 51, and Baz and Tim in Ugly 50, it looked like we would not be at the sharp end. We were lined up to escort a Chinook for the dawn bridge drop and, as far as we could tell, that would be it.

On approach, flashes from a firefight were already piercing the black night, with artillery walloping target points in the town ahead of an advance. Baz and Tim orbited overhead as we stuck close to the Chinook, eyes peeled. Dust scattered and formed a cloud, encasing the giant aircraft as it descended towards the landing zone (LZ). Then a flash. Our eyes flicked to the wooded bank above the town side of the canal. An RPG was tearing towards the Chinook. Then another flash – a second RPG. Then a third.

We called out over the radio.

'Break left! Break left! Incoming RPGs! Incoming RPGs!'

The enemy had timed their attack well. They must have been tipped off. Their advantage created our nightmare – but their firing created our target. RPGs exploded in air as the Chinook adjusted, shrapnel thumping the underside. Ugly 50, with infrared vision on the firing point, let loose with 30mm. We joined in. As the Chinook committed to touchdown, both Apaches were pouring hot fire into the woods.

We watched as Royal Anglians raced from the rear of the Chinook and took up defensive positions as it lifted away. As they moved forward to secure the bridge, we turned for Bastion, duty done. There was every chance that, as planned, Operation Chakush would see the town cleared within hours. There was also every chance we had just seen our last action of the tour. We were just days from going home.

But Taliban are at their fiercest when cornered. They were heavily tooled up, holding tight to positions all along the canal banks. The plan to seize the bridges rapidly began to falter. It seemed that every crossing point was in some way overlooked by a well-supplied enemy firing point. Reports were coming in that buildings had been booby-trapped and approach roads mined, that ground troops were finding it hard to hold position, let alone advance. EF were on the move too, small groups darting from place to place, and armed insurgents were spotted at locations to the rear of British forces, shutting down forward momentum. Yet despite the mayhem, despite our keenness to battle back, we had to sit tight in Bastion.

We were sleeping when the next call came. Operation Chakush was ongoing, we were told. Colleagues in 2 Flight had come under heavy attack during a resupply and were low on fuel. By the time we got back out there, twenty-four hours from the launch of the mission, troops had still not crossed the bridges – and it had been predicted that they'd do that in an hour.

Tim opened comms with Widow tactical operations centre to get the full picture, and to ask where we were most needed. The reply was, basically, everywhere.

We split up. Ugly 50 peeled off towards Widow 74. His unit was pinned down, under heavy gunfire from within a compound and unable to get onto the bridge. Ugly 50 spotted a white Toyota, with men unloading bagged-up RPGs and carrying them into the building. In the compound itself, the figure of a Taliban commander looking towards the bridge and issuing orders into a radio. That was more than enough. Cannon fire crashed down, immediately followed by a Hellfire strike from 4 kilometres out, then a flechette rocket strike to finish the job. And on to the next bridge. It was there, while launching another attack, that an Ugly 50 Hellfire went rogue before striking close to a Royal Anglian position. It hit just 50 metres away, which is nowhere close to a safe distance. Luckily the infantry were in an armoured Viking at the time. A second attempt went better.

Further along, we were hammering 30mm into enemy positions, creating chances where possible for friendlies to inch forwards. Where the resistance was strongest, we were hitting external firing points with flechettes and buildings with Hellfires. As the enemy was pressed back, before moving to the next defensive position and regrouping, friendlies began taking compounds. IEDs were detonating. Close-quarter skirmishes were kicking off. And on we pushed again, driving aggressively forward, taking the hard-headed town inch by inch. The ground was flashing like a pinball machine, the sky alive with American fast jets zipping by, with British Harriers raining down destruction as the bloody theatre rolled on.

We'd been badly wrong about having seen our last action of the tour.

By the time we hit bingo fuel, the effort, death and destruction were beyond what anyone had imagined. Ugly 50 had fired 5 Hellfires, 32 rockets and 240 rounds of 30mm. Our tally was 6 Hellfires, 28 rockets and 270 rounds.

But it wasn't a return to base – it was return to refuel, re-arm and return. The fight for Haidarabad still had some distance to run. It was all hands on deck now, even for those who had just arrived. Our squadron's replacements, due to take over in a couple of days, were new on base and already being asked to assist in ferrying fully loaded Apaches from KAF to Bastion. Back at the front lines, enemy manoeuvres were ongoing. Small, fast-moving groups were posing threats to supply lines, to casevac operations, to the lives of troops.

We went up in wheel formation over the canals, electronic and human eyes scanning for moving targets, for any enemy position. Within seconds our fresh stocks of missiles, rockets and cannon shells were in use. We struck over and over again, tearing open buildings, pummelling insurgents into the earth, striking hard and fast. By the time supplies ran low once more, we had clocked up five hours over that battleground.

After another resupply, we were under orders to take up VHR duties. Operation Chakush, despite the intensity of the fight, was not the only show in town. In Garmsir, to the south, a heavy engagement had kicked off. Now after midnight, the flight was needed to escort a Chinook on a casevac, a pickup in open desert. After that, some all-important rest – if only for a couple of hours. For at 5 a.m. we were up and running again, this time escorting a Chinook on a resupply to Haidarabad, where troops had cut off enemy routes on the far side of the town. It turned out to be a quiet tasking and dared us to think that Chakush was finally coming together.

Yet on the way back, with plans for a hearty breakfast, Haidarabad kicked off once more. We refuelled and, maxed up with weapons and amunition, took off on that now familiar route.

Three Widows were requesting air support. When we worked out the locations, it was clear that although the ferocity of the fighting may have lessened for a time, not much had changed. British troops were still not over all the bridges. We were tasked with heading to places where we had already been to continue the assaults. This time around the enemy was more cautious, now fully aware that Mosquitoes had been coming in heavy-handed and hungry.

Oddly enough, on scanning one battle-scarred bridge area below, we spotted a line of feet underneath bushes. We were looking at a row of sandals, boots, Nikes – a full range of random footwear attached to the feet of men who believed they had hidden themselves from view by lying under bushes. Unfortunately for them, they had given the game away. A burst of 30mm cannon fire made the point. They wouldn't need those shoes again.

The Apaches were proving vital. Friendly mortar teams were striking hard, targeting as best they could. Yet they had limited vision compared to the view we had of the battlefield. There were moments when ground forces didn't get it, and at one point we were even asked to get out of the area so they could fire off mortars. I had to impress upon one mortar team commander that I could see the enemy, and that my services might prove a more accurate option.

None the less, ground forces were working with a profound and steely determination. As insurgents were being pushed back, bit by bit, street by street, they were leaving mines behind, booby-trapping every building they could and British troops were handling it, pressing ever deeper. In the air, we were receiving intel that a large number of surface-to-air missiles (SAMs) had been delivered to enemy positions. Without a doubt, they were meant for us.

As this now second day of the operation rumbled on, we were tasked with relieving a flight at a village called Shorakyan, 5 kilometres north-east of Haidarabad, as part of the wider Operation Chakush. Widow 75 there, sounding remarkably calm about it all, advised that his unit had crossed a bridge while advancing towards two compounds. They had been under the cover of trees when, 50 metres from the compounds, a large enemy unit had opened fire, pinning them down. FF had been left with nowhere to run, just open fields on either side. And EF were doing what they could to get closer.

I could see the enemy had a maze of trenches and bunkers from which to operate. Worse was that the tree line sheltering friendlies ran all the way to the compounds, meaning that the

Taliban had a route to them that could spell disaster. On the far side of a river to the east, 2 Royal Tank Regiment (2RTR) was arriving in a column of Mastiff protected patrol vehicles (PPVs) – heavily fortified personnel vehicles, each fitted with a .50in heavy machine gun. Yet they were more than a kilometre from the scene and for them to reach the friendlies while everyone stayed safe would be one hell of an ask.

We kicked off with some cannon fire to test the enemy's resistance, raking through the tree line to the south of the larger of the two enemy compounds. But then a call came in from Bastion operations: more imminent danger elsewhere.

'Ugly. This is Zero Bravo. We've lost all contact with a Widow. They're cut off, down to a handful of men, and we haven't heard from them for several minutes. We think they've been captured or are in imminent danger of capture. This is now your priority mission.'

'Roger that, Zero Bravo. What's his callsign?'

'We're unsure, Ugly. Try them all. Find them. Out.'

Widow tactical operations centre, on request, found no one reporting imminent danger or capture. But Bastion insisted someone was in serious bother.

And not far below us, just a few minutes before, hadn't the cool tones of Widow 75 advised, in the most easygoing way, he was in deep shit?

'Widow 75. Ugly. Tell us again, just how bad is your situation?'

'Hey Ugly. Well, you could say we're in a spot of bother. There's four guys down here, including me. The Afghan National Army (ANA) have all run away, the enemy have us surrounded on three sides, they're fifty metres close in all buildings and the tree line, we're running short on ammo, and up to our nuts in water. Other than that, the sun's shining and it's a great day.'

'Zero Bravo, this is Ugly. We've found the missing Widow. We're with him and on station and we'll see how we can help.'

'Ugly. This is Zero Bravo. Thank God for that. Good work. Whatever it takes stay with them, okay. Out.'

Earlier one of the twenty ANA troops advancing with British soldiers had suffered a flesh wound as they began crossing the bridge. His nineteen comrades had kindly volunteered to escort him back to safety, leaving four friendlies behind. By now those four were in an irrigation ditch, low on ammo and almost out of options. They remained hidden, yet the enemy was so close they could hear them cat-calling, making monkey noises, threading their way through trees towards them.

'Ugly. Widow 75. The bastards are coming for us. I can hear them coming down through the tree line. I need fire on the tree line now, Ugly. Now.'

'Roger that. Engaging now. Keep your bloody heads down.'

None of us were in a good place at that moment. As Ugly 50 kept eyes on, my Apache was about to send heavy fire deep into woods where our exhausted colleagues were holed up. Yet we had no choice. And, as the black Mosquito's gun blazed, twenty cannon rounds ravaged trees, timber exploding in all directions.

'Ugly. I need more fire, they're still coming. I need you to cover us. And closer, Ugly, get your fire in closer!'

'Roger, firing now.'

This time both Apaches pumped bullets into the thick, green canopy near where it met the compound wall.

A call from Widow 75.

'Yeah! Just there! That's the right place. Hit them Ugly, put more rounds into that position.'

We went into a wheel, each firing at the woods then, with a little further, each firing into the compounds. And repeat. It was a lead rainstorm, although it would do little more than pause the men in stout compounds, in bunkers and trenches. And soon enough we would run out. We called on the Mastiffs, advised we could help direct their fire to enemy locations.

The heavy shots that followed freaked the hell out of Widow 75, much of the fire passing way too near. And they had other issues. Unseen Taliban were still leaving the compound, weaving their way through the woods – whooping, jeering, making monkey noises – still hell-bent on reaching the stranded British troops. We could not let that happen. We fired again, ammunition stocks depleting fast. I was at 160 rounds, Baz at 140.

An urgent talk. Hellfires or rockets, typically fired from 3–4 kilometres out, presented a 500-metre danger-close radius. There was no way we could risk it. But if we got near the targets, fired from directly above, we'd blow any trench or hideout to smithereens without making the same mess. At least that's how the physics worked. For the first time, we had to consider despatching heavy-duty munitions at pretty much point-blank range.

Every second we talked was another second lost. The enemy was getting ever closer to our men. We had to turn this whole thing around right away.

'Widow 75, Ugly. We're low on ammo. We're still here for you, but we've got to decide what's best to use. We're going to go in danger-close with Hellfires, plus rockets. You happy with that?'

'Roger, danger-close, happy with that. It's like the Haidarabad Zoo down here – they're making funny animal noises again. Plus, we're taking sustained incoming from the tree line, directly to the south of the main compound. See if you can't hit that.'

'Visual, tree line south of the main compound. We're attacking on a heading of 190, two Hellfires. Take cover.'

'Roger. Ground commander's initials are DG.'

Giving his initials meant he was giving consent for a danger-close strike. It signals that he knows the risk, that he's taking his share of responsibility.

In return, 'Roger, commander's initials are TP. Tipping in now. Engaging in thirty seconds. Out.'

'Roger, cleared to engage.'

I drove forward. At half a kilometre out, I sent the Apache into a steep dive. In seconds, Alex and I were heading right into the enemy compound, staring into the faces of men now looking up. They raised machine gun barrels our way, began firing as the Mosquito roared towards them. Alex had the crosshairs right on a bunker. He fired the laser, held it on the target, pulled the left-hand TADS grip trigger. Normally we'd wait some seconds to see the strike. This time we didn't have to. It was instant. I was flying into the shockwave of the explosion, flying right towards the blast. Smoke and dirty air filled the view below, one enemy location turned to dust. And I was still closing in.

Alex was roaring. 'Pull up! Pull up! Pull up!'

I was trying to.

My hand was wrenching back on the cyclic. The G-force was crushing my guts. A tight right turn, climbing again, whooshing beyond the tiny settlement and out over the desert. The exhilaration was unreal. But I hadn't time to think about it. I needed a situation report – and one that wouldn't rip apart the rest of my life.

'Widow 75, Ugly. Sitrep?'

'Ugly, Widow 75. Nice shooting. Nice flying. I'm deaf as a bloody post though. Any chance you can do that again for us?'

Damn, it was good to hear that laid-back voice.

'Roger. Coming in on a heading of 190, four flechette rockets. Make sure you're well in cover.'

As if he didn't know.

'Happy with that. Clear to engage.'

It was Ugly 50's turn to push all the limits. I readied my aircraft for a second run. This time they would know I was coming. They might even have something to hit back with. We were by now aware that Bastion was seeking an update. It was a case of us not having time to explain and not quite knowing what to say anyway. We had found ourselves a whole new way to fight in two days of constant fighting.

After Ugly 50's strike, we divebombed together for rocket attacks into the trees, Widow 75 yelling encouragement as the men who came to kill his unit were taken out.

Yet the Taliban kept going, more pressing into the woods, moving men and equipment around as the machines above them forced rethinks. We gave them multiple Hellfires, a barrage of rockets, hundreds of rounds of 30mm. The Mastiffs, now driving towards the compounds, were meeting heavy resistance from that eastern side. It was clear now that Taliban were dug in all along the riverbank at that end. It was clear they were never giving in.

Yet we were running low on weapons, running out of fuel. And, as we needed to talk about next moves, Widow 75 hit us with terrible news. The enemy were now charging down the tree line, a wall of well-armed raging men racing blindly towards our troops, never more ready to cut them to ribbons. The British, on their last magazines, had opened fire, fighting back from the ditches, the last stand they could make. But they all knew this could be it.

I turned hard, plunged downwards, aiming for the Taliban side of the narrowing space between friend and enemy. It was the last twenty-round burst of 30mm I had. Pulling out of the dive, we were Winchester. Ugly 50 had made the same manoeuvre and was now going for another attack run, this time with manual override on the HIDAS. His flares would not be used to trick heat-seekers. Instead, as they fanned out in searing bursts of white and rammed down into the same location, they were used to attack.

The call was made to Bastion. A quick update. Widow 75 was alive, we said, but the situation remained lethal. And we were all out of ammo. To hear in return that a relief flight was inbound was music to our ears. A rapid handover to the Apaches included us wishing Widow 75 the greatest of luck in what lay ahead. They had ridden it this far. Maybe they might just see this day through yet.

En route back, we listened as Widow 75 advised once again that yet more enemy were coming through the trees. Learning that a Harrier, callsign Recoil, was also on the way, he urged for it to hit the enemy with a colossal 540-pound airburst bomb. He said that, on detonation, all four would make a break for it, heading west then south to meet the Mastiffs. The new Apaches could cover the escape. The plan was fraught with danger, but then there wasn't exactly a lot of choice. By the time we touched down, initials were being exchanged once more. Groundies began refuelling and rearming us fast in the knowledge we might need to get right back out there.

'Widow 75, Recoil. Two minutes out.'

Last minute details were given. Potential last words were said.

'Confirmed.'

'Widow 75. Recoil. Running in now. Engaging in ten seconds. Keep your heads down.'

'Roger, clear to engage.'

'Bombs gone.'

The sky on fire, metal shards sent all directions in the airburst. Widow 75 was up and running, four exhausted, drenched, deafened men belting westwards as a bomb cloud burned behind them. As they reached an open field the enemy was up again, shooting from the compound with AKs and machine guns. They fired back with their last rounds, racing towards an unknown building for cover. An RPG shot out from the compound to give chase, disaster racing towards them as the Apaches opened up on the enemy. Even as the anti-tank bomb missed, cannon fire was ripping through the last of the Taliban positions. Widow 75, having found cover, said the enemy were running, leaping into the water. And it was with that news that Tim, Baz, Alex and I felt a tidal wave of relief wash over us. The four would make it to the Mastiffs.

We were hitting 5 p.m. Those past six hours had been among the hardest, wildest of our lives. For those four men on the ground, the whole day had been a test of courage and endurance beyond comprehension. As for us four aircrew, we emerged from the aircraft like zombies, barely able to speak, even to walk. Everyone involved – aircrew, groundies, technicians, ground troops – had played a key part in the process of getting those men out of there.

The tally for Operation Chakush showed that Ugly 50 had fired off 11 Hellfires, 74 rockets, and 1,050 rounds of 30mm. Our aircraft, Ugly 51, had fired 9 Hellfires, 49 rockets and 730 rounds of 30mm. Ugly 50 had also fired off 34 decoy flares.

It took three days, but Haidarabad was taken and the operation came to a close. A new base, FOB Arnhem, was established. Some days, later Widow 75 came to visit the Apache base at Bastion. His name was Sergeant Dave Greenland of the Royal Anglians. We played him the gun-tapes, let him see what it had looked like from our end. He told us that the scariest thing in that whole day of scares had been when our Apaches dived down firing rockets. He said his men had caught sight of small tungsten darts ripping through woods and striking the water in the same ditch in which they had been stranded.

Chapter Nineteen

GETTING UGLY. AFGHANISTAN, 2008

I THOUGHT IT MIGHT get easier to say goodbye, but now I knew that was wishful thinking. As the departure date to return for my third tour closed in, I'd worked to clear my mind, get on with some exercise, prepare myself for whatever might come in the three months ahead. Yet the emptiness in my gut would only grow. And while I was trying to focus on what I needed to do, loved ones were trying to adjust. When soldiers get out into the field, they have colleagues and routines and access to a culture of support built into the British Army across hundreds of years. Truth is, it's those left at home who have it worse.

I knew that Tracey, despite the brave face she put on it, was hurting as I left. We had moved in together after my return from that second tour and now I was away again, off for another hundred days, leaving her home alone in Hadleigh, Suffolk. I found her farewell cards, two of them, hidden in my luggage when unpacking at Bastion. There were seven other guys in the tent at the same time. I had to break away and take a moment to myself. It never gets any easier.

May 2008. I was back with my original squadron, 664, and with a new flight. Tim P had moved on to become a flying instructor with the corps and I knew how much he had to offer. Alex and Baz were in theatre and my squadron was taking over from theirs. Along with my friend Pete L, I now had the great responsibility of commanding my own flight of two Apaches. We were the first NCOs ever to get that honour and it was something I had longed for. Yet I felt a great weight on my shoulders. I was directly responsible for the wellbeing of others under my command. Nothing was more important to me than getting everyone through what lay ahead and home in one piece. I had no plans to let anyone down – not my team, their loved ones, nor my OC, Paul T, who had selected me for the role – and not myself either.

In the rear of my No. 2 aircraft team would be Colin, a red-headed maestro and a safe pair of hands with a stock of nifty one-liners. In the front seat was Steve L, or 'Lunny', a reliable young captain with two tours to his name and, also, ginger hair. In my aircraft was Pete A, or 'Ackers', a man with a plan to fly commercial airliners and who was best described as being everything I'm not – tall, square-jawed, witty and completely incontinent (only one of those is not true). I couldn't have asked for a better flight.

Ahead of deployment, we had some further training in Arizona, but the flight out from RAF South Cerney, near Brize Norton, had annoyingly been delayed by four hours. Everything had been on hold ahead of the return of Prince Harry from his top-secret first tour of Afghanistan. The whole thing was a pain in the arse but we didn't blame the guy for it.

That journey, incidentally, had another delay when, after landing in Minneapolis for refuelling, all 100 of us were told the aircraft had developed a problem and we'd have to stay overnight. The hotel we stayed at was hosting a sci-fi convention and I remember not knowing quite what to say as I rode the elevator with Chewbacca. One whole floor was packed with aliens and space pilots of all shapes and sizes, some showing off their intergalactic lasers, phasers and what not. Our arrival, in mere desert combats, seemed to them to be run-of-the-mill.

But those three weeks out there in the US of A were good, not least for the sense of pride that came when random strangers approached to say 'Thank you for your service.' Little acts like that mean a good deal to soldiers from anywhere. Spread the word.

The intelligence picture in theatre was in flux. Although the Taliban were intent on retaking Musa Qala, they had been relatively inactive in recent months. In part, they were reeling from losses of equipment and manpower. But their apparent docility was also being put down to the poppy harvest. They didn't want to do anything that might interrupt it, and indeed many were involved in working the farms.

Now that the harvest was coming to an end, however, expectations were high that things would kick off. The Taliban may have suffered serious losses, but their resolve was undiminished. All Coalition troops were advised to expect at least small-arms fire incidents, chiefly those based at smaller out-stations often manned by either ANA or Afghan National Police (ANP). Air threat to aviation, the briefings made clear, continued with EF constantly seeking to source new man-portable air defence systems (MANPADS), including RPGs.

Now leading pre-flight joint mission briefs (JMBs), I talked through all aspects of a task ahead. We were to escort two Sea King helicopters, Daydreamer 16 and 17, from Bastion to deliver generators, water and other supplies to locations across Helmand. The job had been added in as part of my flight's area familiarisation sortie, or famil, which helped the crew learn or refresh their knowledge of the area.

'Auto,' I called as we cleared the base in Ugly 54, confirming that potentially lifesaving HIDAS had been armed. With Ugly 55, we climbed to our respective operating heights and into the route towards the drop-off point ten minutes away just south of Sangin.

Looking down, I could see how Bastion had expanded and been upgraded in the nine months that I'd been away.

The JTAC were advising ahead, confirming secure landing points before Daydreamer 16 and 17 began descent. On the ground below us, everyone raced to unload passengers and freight. With aircraft stationary on the ground, the risk to man and machine is at a high point. An RPG or mortar from the wood line could be disastrous. I remember being anxious on this first flight of that third tour, hoping hard that it would be a non-event, wanting at least to get the seat warm before having to engage the enemy. It took thirty seconds and the Sea Kings were ready to lift back into the comfort zone. Daydreamer 16 and 17 returned to Bastion while the Uglies continued on the famil, opening comms with JTACs along the way.

Heading over Sangin, an urgent call from Nordesman 22. Grid references were given. Taliban were moving into position, gearing up for an attack on a friendly patrol in the area. As our focus shifted, the JTAC advised that a key combat indicator was in place – women, children and uninvolved men were leaving the area in numbers.

Looking on grid references from 5 kilometres out, we noted a complex of compounds but no sign of life within. We scouted the wood line near by, yet nothing doing. And still not a weapon had been fired. Time ticked past. No emerging threats. And I had a famil to finish, the essential opening sortie. I advised Nordesman 22 we needed to move on. They advised that enemy radio intercepts were indicating an attack as soon as the Mosquitoes left. Nothing had changed.

But I was in a bind. I had to get this duty done, to give my flight at least an idea of the lie of the land. And another order had come in, to escort two Chinooks resupplying stations. I advised Nordesman 22 that we weren't the only Apaches around, to request support through the chain of command. On hearing that, Ackers in the back radioed home base, telling them they might want to stand up a crew.

We broke away to act as guardian angels for the resupply aircraft. The route was to Sangin then to the further out FOB Inkerman, followed by a final stop over at FOB Robinson. Something was already telling me this day might just get lively.

The first Chinook, callsign Black Cat 20, landed at FOB Robinson and lifted without incident, heading east. Orbiting for a while, hypnotically circling over the beige world below, my mind slid away from that earlier gut feeling, thoughts of Tracey and homecoming and leaving, thoughts of –

'Engine two fire.'

Holy shit!

'Engine two fire. Engine two fire.'

The aircraft's audio warning.

'What the fuck?'

Had we been hit?

My heart had burst into a sprint, my mind ablaze with confusion in a second. I looked around, down at the panel. The red fire warning light for Engine Two, now brighter than I ever saw on the sim, that warning louder than I ever heard before. It was hot as hell outside, the midday sun scorching everything for miles, and an engine burning. We were twenty-five minutes from Bastion, 3 kilometres from FOB Robinson and over an area that was as hostile as it comes.

But had we been hit?

Pressing the fire button arms the relevant engine fire bottle, smothering the machinery in retardant. Yet doing so immediately disables fuel to that engine. So right away I'd drop to one engine. The Apache can fly well on one engine. I'd practised doing so in sterile sim conditions, but the real thing is a whole different boiling kettle of fish.

Ten seconds had passed. There was no choice. Whatever fire was going on, however it had come about, would only be getting worse. I hit the button, committed to shutting down half the power. Then nothing. It seemed like ages. Had I done the right thing?

'Engine Two out.'

I knew that much. Yet the light was still on, the warning still alive, sensors still detecting flames. The helicopter was still burning. The remaining option was to arm the fire bottle for Engine One, override its default and compel it to target Engine Two. If this didn't work, I'd have to drop fast. I set the command, hit the button.

'Come on,' I said, to myself.

Ackers was cool as can be in the back, saying nothing. He knew I was busy.

A heavily pregnant pause as several long seconds ground past. The warning light dimmed and went out. And I could breathe again. Now all I needed was no more fires because I was all out of extinguisher.

As captain, I had to make the call whether to put down in the desert, move further out from the hostile Green Zone and land or else make the full journey for home. I sat in silence for a moment, looking in all directions.

'Okay,' I said. I knew I would have to land. Bastion was too far. We had at least one undiagnosed mechanical fault. One more and we'd have to go down, no matter what. And, trust me, we would not get a friendly welcome on the turf between us and Bastion. We were 3km from FOB Robinson. We might just be able to get closer.

'How you doing, Ackers?'

We hadn't communicated since the warning light came on.

'More importantly,' he asked back, 'how are you doing?'

He was already in the picture, fully updated on the drama. I didn't know how.

'You told me,' he said.

I'd given a running commentary all the way through but

couldn't remember saying a word to him. Yet he'd already adjusted functions for single engine flight. He'd already planned to aim for Robinson.

'Oh,' I said. 'Right.'

He'd lowered the speed, meaning we were moving not too fast, not too slow. But he was unable to keep the aircraft flying straight and level. We were within normal limits for single engine operations, yet whether we liked it or not we were descending. To demand any more power from that one engine would push it beyond limits. The Apache was fully loaded with weapons, the outside temperature was blistering, the air density thick as soup and we were slowly descending into enemy territory.

We had to lighten the load. Dumping fuel was not an option. It would have to be ammunition. The aircraft could, on command, jettison all weapons stores on the outside of the pylon wings. Doing so would be enough to get us to Robinson. At the rate we were dropping, we'd be hitting the ground in ten minutes.

'Where can we dump munitions?'

We were over some trees, alongside a residential area. There were dust trails, a couple of cars, a motorbike, some market stalls here and there. People were shopping, walking, chatting. It was no good. I called it off.

We could only hope that Lady Luck was with us as we began that long descent towards FOB Robinson. As we drew closer, we could see one of the resupply Chinooks on our intended LS, unloading men and materials.

'Black Cat 20. Ugly 54. I'm going to need your full attention.'

As we lost height, hoping against hope that the Apache would make it, we could see the panic kick in. Equipment, bergens and boxes were getting flung out of the Chinook. Black Cat 20 was airborne and clear in thirty seconds. It was brilliantly handled.

Yet for some insane reason the freshly deplaned personnel were now meandering in among the swirling dust, leisurely collecting kit, seemingly with no idea of what was happening. There is no horn on an Apache because no one in the world ever thought it might be needed, given that it makes quite a lot of noise. If the troops had bothered looking towards the increasing racket above them, they would have seen a ten-tonne lump of steel coming their way. As the dust cleared, the full view of the base, of the daunting 105mm light field guns fixed around its internal perimeter wall. As we committed, we spotted two more of the mighty weapons, their barrels to the sky, which seemed to have appeared from nowhere. Neither of us had seen them. We could not be sure we could clear them.

'Come right,' I said, seriously fearing the Apache was sinking so fast it would strike one weapon with God knows what consequences.

'Come right,' I said again, 'get between them.'

There would be enough space for us to fit, to avoid having to take the chance on clearing them. But now we had gathered speed on the descent. We were too fast for a running landing, not enough room for it. The only feasible strategy was to slow and let the helicopter drop once past that internal wall.

As the aircraft commander I could have elected to take control and fly, but Ackers had all my faith in those final moments. I was sure he had the skill to complete this flight. We cleared the external 30-foot Hesco protection wall, heading between the guns. He decelerated, forcing our only engine to handle holding us up as our momentum vanished. With just metres to go, that engine was screaming.

Amazingly, just ahead of us, with seconds left, we realised four men were cleaning a 105 mm gun. How could they not know? Was everyone deaf around here?

'People left come right!'

Ackers was too focused to be able to see the madness that I could see. He cleared the wall safely, but the aircraft so close to the ground now that we were in full brown-out from the dust cloud.

Using instruments alone, he dropped us to the earth. As that back wheel hit hard, Ackers pulled the last ounce of power the aircraft had to slow it down. The relief was tangible as it stopped. For a moment, it rolled backwards, into a rut, but that only made me smile as we shut down. As the air cleared, we could see those four still cleaning that gun.

Black Cat 21 was alongside in minutes. We were to board and get straight back to Bastion, twenty-five minutes away. I made safe all the weapons systems, scrambled around collecting maps, weapons, helmets, all the classified equipment and said goodbye to our stricken Ugly.

We were sure the Taliban would know of the situation soon enough. A Mosquito parked on their doorstep, just 400 metres off the Green Zone. They rarely had an opportunity like that. How long before they tried to blow the shit out of it with mortars and RPGs? Our aircraft had just increased the danger for FOB Robinson.

My OC, Paul, was waiting along with the squadron CO, Lieutenant Colonel Neil, who had by chance flown into Bastion that morning. There was no small talk. We needed to get Ugly back as fast as possible. Two options: Have her stripped down and lifted below a Chinook or Halo aircraft; or have her inspected and worked on by technicians with a view to flying her home.

Understandably, FOB Robinson's base commander wanted it gone. He had enough to deal with. He said certain Taliban hotspots had a direct line of sight on to the Apache, or at least on to its high radar dome. A plan was agreed to hide it behind three large ISO containers, but that could only be as temporary as possible. With the opium harvest coming to an end, a lot more of the enemy were coming into circulation.

After much deliberation, inspections, and after all the relevant data had been downloaded and analysed by the makers Boeing, the decision was to fly her out of FOB Robinson on May 14. There were concerns regarding the state of the good engine and the main gearbox but having her lifted had yet more unknowns and was potentially more dangerous.

Volunteers were needed to get the job done. My hand was up first. Major Alex G, a vastly experienced ex-test pilot, would be the other crew member. We reviewed an aerial photo of the FOB. There had as yet been no fire directed towards the Apache, but that left us in the dark as to whether the enemy was on to it or not. We set out to learn everything we could about nearby Taliban locations and previous firing points to help figure out the best departure route. From there, we reviewed the weather, especially wind speed and direction. Then on to what actions to take if the affected, but now rested, engine had a similar fault. What if the overworked good engine failed too? What if that stressed-out gearbox failed? What if enemy fire came during departure? With it all talked over and planned out, I fell into bed the night before like a dead man.

An early start. I hadn't slept long, too many what ifs running through my mind. We boarded the Sea King at 8 a.m. Alex smirked as I looked over at him. I laughed, smirked back. It seems like moments before the hiss of the sand came again, whipped up in the downwash. The pair of us leapt out.

The Apache was 50 metres to my right, the ISO containers just removed. It was a sad sight. Her black paint was covered in a layer of brown dust. I'd never seen an Apache look so forlorn, so abandoned and neglected. I approached, reached out, patted her on the side.

'Gonna get you out of here, girl,' I said, then hoped Alex hadn't heard.

We began a thorough but hurried pre-flight walk around, loaded in our kit and buckled up. A briefing had advised that Taliban had been viewing the aircraft from a few kilometres away. If they had been preparing to give the Apache a rough send-off, we were about to find out. Christ only knew what might be coming our way. The 105mm light guns near the aircraft had been removed to give us a bit more room should we need to come back down fast. In the sky above us, another Apache was due. The plan was it would show at the allotted time, that its noise would mask the start-up of the grounded aircraft, that it would discourage potential attackers. But other urgent commitments came up. That support aircraft would be late. Alex and I shrugged it off. We were going now.

Alex started the engines and the instruments came alive. It started sweetly but we could not lift before a final inspection. With both engines running and rotor blades turning, those minutes seemed like a lifetime. I felt so exposed, instinct telling me to get the hell away. All our training told us aircraft were the prime targets, that they had to get in and out fast or people could get killed. We were sitting ducks.

Before the all-clear, we were advised that an Apache was on the way from Bastion. The timing was good. In the arriving support aircraft above were Nick B and Ackers. Yet, even then, we still had no clearance. Time was pressing on, the technician was still working and, we were sure, the enemy could have made an elaborate painting of the scene by now. Then, at last, thumbs up from the ground.

'Let's go,' I said.

Alex slowly pulled power. I monitored the gauges. The aircraft became light on its wheels as sand was whipped up.

'All temperatures and pressures good, continue,' I called.

'Roger,' he said, 'climbing.'

She was refreshingly light, having been stripped of all but the most essential equipment to lower the weight. She floated upwards with ease as the sand bubble closed around us.

'I still have references left,' I called.

'Roger. Transitioning.'

Alex pushed forward on the cyclic, we gained forward speed and cleared the dust cloud. The path from here would avoid possible enemy locations and put us into the wind as much as possible. The journey home went without a hitch.

I went on from there to write Ackers up for consideration for some form of flying award. I'm glad to say he was granted a Green Endorsement for his top-class professionalism during that emergency.

Intelligence briefing:

The poppy harvest is almost at a close, EF activity is expected to increase, recent enemy actions small scale asymmetric harassing attacks with little sustained contact.

EF are unsure of FF intentions and therefore are under instruction to remain within the Green Zone and protect any stronghold or opium factories. EF intention is still to retake Musa Qala and preparations are continuing to be reported.

Reports indicate EF lack basic necessities and that money made from opium sales that were reserved for ammunition was being used to buy more medical supplies.

Air Threat to Aviation: Still extant, EF intention is to still purchase more Man Portable Air Defence Systems (MANPADS); recent finds in Garmasir have highlighted that EF seem to have a vast quantity of RPGs, heads and stocks.

VHR duty repeatedly involved call-outs for soldiers who were badly dehydrated, who had been struck down with diarrhoea and vomiting. The warning to use alcohol gels and drink only bottled water was constant, but some cases of the squirts (from both ends) still occurred.

That very issue arose on 17 May, after an intelligence briefing had referenced the deteriorating situation in Musa Qala. MSQ was perhaps then the Taliban's most sought after prize in Helmand. 3 Para were in theatre there and facing RPG and small arms attacks day and night. Casualties were not infrequent.

The callsign for the day was Ugly 50, myself and Ackers heading north to that diarrhoea and vomiting call in Kajaki. In a hot desert environment, that patient needs out of there fast for rehydration. The operation was swift, arriving at the same time as the SH to avoid giving the enemy any notice. The casualty was up and out in minutes.

En route back, Base Ops requested we escort SH Black Cat 22 on routine tasking from Bastion to Lashkar Gar, the capital of Helmand, where the HQ for UK forces was based. The Chinook was to pick up VIPs and take them to the drop-off point at MSQ district centre via FOB Edinburgh. Due to the threat briefing, the plan was to go low, climb while over the Green Zone, and descend again on the other side heading into MSQ. Black Cat 22 was directed to hold to the west until Ugly 50 could guarantee the LS was clear.

Widow 44, the JTAC in MSQ, updated with intel. It had interceptions advising that Taliban were preparing what was described as 'their big gun' to engage what they referred to as a heavy – aka a Chinook. Big gun meant either an RPG or some form of anti-aircraft weapon. A few minutes later and Widow 44 advised that latest radio chatter was making it clear that insurgents were moving into position. We had to balance the information. The Taliban were very often on the move, very often shifting various weapons to new positions, and equally often these reports came to nothing. But they did seem to be ahead of us on this occasion.

We advised Black Cat 22. It wasn't able to pick up on Widow 44's briefings, so we passed them on and talked it over. The decision was made that, with the threat coming from the south of the area, Black Cat 22 should approach from the north-west.

The Chinook swung around, flying low over open desert, advising 'Three minutes to run-in.'

We could just about see it approaching from our position over MSQ district centre. Our attention was also on areas of concern to the west and south. If the enemy became visible or made any moves, we needed to clear him out of there fast to protect the approaching Chinook. But three minutes isn't a lot of time.

I was piloting, eyes peeled, that elevated rear cockpit offering the better view. Ackers was programming grids into the computer, slaving his sights, looking them over. At times there can only be one pair of eyes looking outside.

'Two minutes to run in.'

'Roger.'

Ackers asked me to position for the final grid. I turned the aircraft to offer the best angle and he scanned the area. Nothing doing.

Even though the Chinook is a big beast, it's surprisingly hard to keep track of one when you're also airborne. I turned back from assisting with the grid, looked out again for that approaching dot on the horizon. I couldn't see it. My heart slammed.

'I've lost... '

I caught it again. Sighed with relief. I was more tensed up than I thought.

'It's fine. Nothing. Visual again, coming from the west.'

'One minute to run in.'

'Ugly 50, Widow 44. EF in place, big gun ready.'

'Roger.'

As far as we knew, they were in the south, some distance away. And besides, Taliban could be anywhere down there. There were a million places for them to hide – compounds, ditches, tree lines, vehicles, in among groups of ordinary people.

'Thirty seconds to run in.'

The last stages of the Chinook's flight saw it coming off the desert and over the Green Zone surrounding the district centre.

Radio crackle.

'Declaring an emergency.'

It was Black Cat 22.

'Ackers,' I called, turning the aircraft towards the Chinook. 'Something's wrong.'

Black Cat 22 was turning, swooping round 180 degrees over the Green Zone and heading back to the desert.

'We've taken fire. Possible RPG, multiple small arms.'

'Roger. Report what you can. Are all okay?'

'All okay. But suspect severe damage to one or more rotor blades. We'll try to land back at FOB Edinburgh.'

Ackers slaved the sights to potential Taliban firing points. I pushed us towards the area, eyes on the Chinook. Luckily it didn't have far to go. I radioed operations back at Bastion.

'Zero Bravo, Ugly 50. Black Cat 22 has been engaged, hit by several weapon types in the area north of Musa Qala. Black Cat 22 en route to FOB Edinburgh. Have eyes on a possible firing point.'

'Roger. Wait out.'

'Roger.'

Minutes passed by. We needed to know if the Chinook was okay, and hoped to get clear directions on where to engage the enemy. My fingers were drumming.

'Ugly 50, Widow 44. Black Cat 22 now safely on the ground. A huge hole in the rear pylon about the size of a football. Several small bullet holes in the rear of the aircraft too.'

With the Chinook safe, it was time to hunt. Widow 44 gave us reports of possible enemy sightings from a friendly tower position. We had a grid reference. It narrowed the picture nicely. We moved out, Ackers slaving the 127-times magnification sight. The location was a single compound, about four buildings. As he watched through the sight, a 4x4 utility was pulling in, parking in shadows under trees. A man got out, began covering up whatever was in the rear with a tarpaulin sheet. He looked up at our orbiting aircraft, put his hand out, waved across the road. Two children appeared from the compound entrance and dashed to his side. He looked back up before walking into the building with the kids.

We didn't have enough to allow us to open fire before the

children appeared, and doing so was out of the question after they had. But everything about the man's behaviour suggested he was at least one of the men we wanted. We advised Widow 44. Hopefully a ground patrol could search the vehicle and the compound. Widow 44 advised that a Dude callsign was coming on station so we were free to move out.

Heading back, we flew slowly past FOB Edinburgh and the damaged Chinook, filming the aircraft. The hole was some two feet in diameter, just behind the rear main rotor blades. Most likely it had been an RPG strike. Fortunately, it hit where the aircraft skin is soft and went straight through without detonating.

Back at the briefing we were told that the VIP on board Black Cat 22 had been the provisional governor of Helmand, Governor Managal. He was a figure of defiance, hated by the Taliban, a man with no tribal loyalties and, a rarity for the region, one who wasn't corrupt. He had been changing things for the better in Helmand, especially in Musa Qala, and had been on his way to open a new mosque built by both locals and British.

Unfortunately, as a show of defiance towards the Taliban, he had advertised that he was going to be there on the day. Dick!

The Sun, 19 May 2008:

A HERO pilot safely crash-landed an RAF Chinook helicopter after a Taliban RPG smashed its tail.

Sources said it was a 'miracle' no one was hurt – and praised the crew.

The chopper was carrying British diplomats and Helmand governor Gulab Managal to a meeting with province elders.

Terrorists attacked as it tried to land in Musa Qala, a stronghold taken by Our Boys last year. The helicopter's body and the rear rotor were badly damaged, a military spokesman said. It must be repaired where it landed in Forward Operating Base Edinburgh near the town.

The Beast awaiting the call . . . AgustaWestland AH1 Apache Longbow of the Army Air Corps at Camp Bastion, Helmand Province, Afghanistan.

'Binary Boy' Nick E and the author (rear seat) strapped in and ready to go on a VHR sortie, Afghanistan, September 2006. The helmet-mounted monocle can be seen at each pilot's right eye.

5 Flight, 662 Squadron AAC at Camp Bastion, 2007; author at far right. One Hellfire missile and a box of 30mm cannon ammunition in the foreground.

Groundcrew loading a Hellfire missile onto its rail, also showing a partly loaded pod of 70mm rockets.

The author holding a flechette dart, which are contained within a 70mm rocket; note the sun blind in the cockpit window.

A rare aerial shot of the underside of an Apache, showing the 30mm M230E1 chain gun at the front.

The Boardwalk shopping mall at KAF; among other things, it contained branches of Subway, Pizza Hut and Burger King.

Camp Bastion in Helmand Province, 2008 – at that date the huge military base was still growing.

Above: Camp Bastion – the UK's contribution to troops' morale. It too included a Pizza Hut.

Right: The outside rest area for VHR crews at Bastion, with home-made table and seating.

VHR crews' sleeping area – no expense spared.

Above: Sunset over Camp Bastion, August 2006.

Right: A typical Afghan village in Helmand, showing the walled compounds.

The Green Zone from the air. The Helmand River flows the length of the province from north-east to south-west.

Rahim Kalay, June 2007: the remains of the white car destroyed by a Hellfire missile.

Concealed Taliban trench at Rahim Kalay, photographed after the battle.

The village after the battle, with the destroyed car at right.

Top: The author firing a salvo of rockets from his aircraft, Helmand, 2008. *(© Sky News)*

Middle: RAF Chinooks taking off on a mission from Camp Bastion.

Left: Lieutenant H. Wales with his Apache instructors, including the author, at Middle Wallop.

WO1 Steve Jones and his
aircraft at Camp Bastion,
Afghanistan in 2008.

Managal blasted the 'cowardly attack'.

One soldier said: 'It could have been a disaster. The pilot did an amazing job to get away and land safely.'

Flight Lieutenant Alex 'Frenchie' Duncan, the RAF pilot, was awarded the DFC.

Chapter Twenty

HELICOPTER DOWN IN DEVON, 2008

THE INITIAL TV reports said an army helicopter, a Lynx, had crashed in the UK. Word spread fast through Bastion. The details changed. Not a Lynx, a Squirrel. All in the AAC knew Squirrels operated only from Shawbury, in Shropshire, and Middle Wallop. The crash happened in the south-west of England, suggesting it was a training sortie. One crewman had been killed; one was critical in hospital. We knew nothing else. I went to bed feeling sick.

The next day, arriving for air testing at Kandahar, Pete L approached, looking pale and shaky.

'You okay, Pete?'

'No. It was Vince Hussell in that crash. He's dead.'

I felt weak, dropped the kit from my hands, almost collapsed. The news was like being hit by the England rugby scrum. A close friend had been killed.

'And, Steve,' he said, 'the other crew, a guy called Lieutenant Mark Reynolds. He's died too.'

One of the victims I knew very well, the other I had never met.

But the personal loss, the loss to the corps, to the British Army, was huge. I'd known Vince for over eight years. After his second Afghan tour, he'd taken the flying instructor course at Shawbury. Being killed on operations under enemy fire would be hard enough to deal with. Yet somehow his death by accident on home ground made it incomprehensible. And what of the families, of Vince's wife, Liz, and their sons? Back in the UK, AAC personnel rallied around them all, did everything they could. I know the support shown in those days from soldiers like Pete D, Redders, Garie and JJ, was extraordinary, offering comfort, as well as gratitude for the efforts of the lost men. Despite my sadness, I was proud of everyone involved, not least of the life and work of my much-missed mate Vince.

Yet, as Vince himself would have said, there was a job to be done. A Special Forces (SF) operation was being scheduled for somewhere in southern Afghanistan and my name was on the list of participants. This would be the first time an Apache flight had been asked to assist in such an operation. Due to the distances involved, the aircraft would have to land at night on a dry lakebed to refuel and, if required, re-arm. By its nature, it would be an unfamiliar place. And up to twelve other aircraft would be involved. Right away we knew we were looking at a logistical riddle.

Ackers and I met Colin and Lunny ahead of a minimal brief. After that, some forced sleep. We needed to get as much rest as possible, if we could. It was very likely that things would kick off soon and it was anyone's guess as to how long for.

We were up at 2.30 a.m. I'd maybe had an hour or so of kip. I kept thinking of Vince, of the unknown immediately ahead, and of Vince again. It was as though my mind was stuck in a spiral.

That night was oppressively dark. We had fitted NVGs ahead of time, knowing they would complement the Apache's default night-vision system (NVS) – two systems are better than one.

The initial flight down would take about an hour, heading further south from base than I'd ever been before. When we were around 5 kilometres from the lakebed, Ackers said he could see aircraft below.

'What?' I was puzzled. 'You sure?'

'Yep,' he said, rechecking his screen, 'Three aircraft on the ground in my right two o'clock.'

It didn't make sense.

I contacted the on-call tactical landing zone (TLZ) controller.

'Ah,' I was informed, 'You've flown over the landing zone.'

Bloody hell.

The grid reference we'd been given was out. Thank Christ Ackers spotted the three aircraft or we'd have been flying miles off course. We reoriented, needing to get on to the right patch of ground swiftly.

A call from the TLZ protection party.

'Vehicle approaching from the north.'

The Apaches were asked to check it out. We located it, along a dirt track around 3 kilometres beyond the lakebed. By then it was stationary. With sights slaved on it from 2 kilometres out, we couldn't see what kind of vehicle it was, but it had line of sight to the dry lake. We updated the TLZ commander. We could guess, but we had no evidence of who might be on board the vehicle. And anyway, if I or Lunny were to open fire, this hush-hush game we were playing would be over.

Five minutes later, the vehicle moved off, first heading deeper south towards the lakebed, before making a slow U-turn and driving away. We'd have to live with whatever just happened, if anything had happened at all.

Back to the plan. Get on to the TLZ landing spot. All perfectly clear in a diagram but very different from up there on that impenetrable night. Things look further away or closer than they might be, sometimes seem small or bigger than you imagined. There is no end to the tricks your perception might play. It didn't help that we'd had so little rest.

As I led both aircraft from the south, we were advised that a C-130 was coming. We had ten minutes to get safely onto the ground, one shot to get onto the right spot. If we missed it, we'd be on a strip about to be occupied by a C-130.

Infrared strobes, visible only on NVG, marked the refuel point. Yet using NVG, and not NVS, while flying effectively blacked out the symbology – height, speed, distance and all the rest of it. Ackers said he would fly NVS, I'd talk him down using NVG. We landed well, with a slight bump and almost zero forward speed. A ground marshal arrived, beckoned us forward. The pumps came into view, each around 100 metres in length. The whole refuel system had been dropped off there some two hours before as part of the complex logistics for the longer-range operation.

All sorted, we departed for the holding point, a thirty-minute flight south. We paused 15 kilometres north of the target area, holding back to avoid alerting the enemy. From this point, for reasons of efficiency, all comms would go through Reaper – the UK's new and gigantic unmanned aerial vehicle (UAV, also known as a drone) high above the target area and armed with Hellfire missiles. It had a live video downlink with instantaneous video feed from its sensor pod and was being flown, with the aid of satellites, by the RAF from a base in the Nevada desert thousands of miles away. The comms systems on board were cutting edge. When I opened talks with a ground callsign from 15 kilometres away, the message was being relayed 8,000 miles via satellites to the US and back again in the blink of an eye.

Possible enemy sightings meant Rolex plus 30 minutes – with Rolex meaning an adjustment to the predetermined start time. So now, instead of the 3 a.m. start, we were looking at 3.30 a.m. But what was the job?

SF had been dropped some distance away, all tabbing in to their relevant start points. At the agreed time, all the units would simultaneously assault a set of Taliban compounds with orders to arrest where possible, kill if necessary. Once complete, troops would fall back to a prearranged pickup point for extraction.

Air support included F-15 fighter/bomber jets circling above as well as AC-130 Spectre gunships, UAVs and Apaches, all separated by height, a stacked-high army ready to handle whatever the moonless night might bring.

Updates came via Reaper. SF on the ground had come across four armed men in an enemy observation position. All four had been killed. Guns had been used. That potentially turned everything Kinetic early on — meaning that if any enemy were still sleeping, they wouldn't be for long. Yet the four insurgents had died some distance from the main base. Was our presence still unknown?

Another thirty-minute delay. Not good news. Gas-guzzling Apaches cannot hang around for long. Lunny and Colin agreed to fly back to the TLZ to refuel. In the meantime, word came that the compounds were coming alive. Things had indeed gone Kinetic. More reports coming through, more decisions moving up the chain of command. Another delay. By the time Lunny and Colin arrived back, Ackers and I were no further forward, still orbiting, literally turning aviation fuel into noise.

And then bedlam.

That ink-black sky ahead came alive with red flashes, tracer fire, explosions on the ground. An AC-130 gunship holding above had been called on. The rate of fire from its Gatling gun was dazzling. But the Apaches had no warning. The comms from the JTAC, passing through Reaper, had failed. Only the gunship was getting the messages. The JTAC, callsign Mayhem 04, made fast moves to higher ground to bring us all on board.

Radio reports came in thick and fast. Enemy had been sighted running from buildings in all directions. SF were still down there somewhere, stealthy, hidden. Their quiet mission was now a full-on engagement.

Enemy in a wood line to the north. I identified it on the map, a short distance from our location. I advised Mayhem 04. Ugly 52 and 53 were cleared in to fire flechettes, a sure-fire way of making a wide, deep, deadly strike in the dark.

Ackers was more than ready. 'Finally, some action,' he said.

'Let's hope so.'

And then, with heavy gunfire below, 'Hold.'

Christ!

Lunny on the radio, 'What the fuck?'

'Don't know.'

Armed enemy hiding by a compound wall.

I shouted it, 'Then let's go for them instead. 30mm gun, take them out, cut risk of collateral.'

'Hold.' It was JTAC again.

'For fuck's sake.'

An airburst of weapons. Another one. We were like spectators at a shooting match. And now word that Reaper, with no one on board, had been cleared to Hellfire a building.

The flipping thing was on its first engagement with British forces. Understandably they wanted to test it during real-world action – but two Apaches with more effective Hellfire types, designed for buildings and bunkers, were pissing around turning circles in the sky.

I got back on the radio. 'Mayhem 04, Ugly 52. Our Hellfires are a better match for this.'

But no. All was in hand. We had been upstaged by a remote-control robot. Low on fuel, I advised Mayhem I'd need to get back to the TLZ, that both Apaches were in challenging positions in terms of fuel. Ackers and I had a feeling this might turn their attention to us, make them realise that you use it or lose it.

Mayhem reverted to clear both Apaches back for refuel, then cleared us on to Bastion.

'Ah bollocks,' Ackers yelled. 'That backfired.'

On the plus side – and I always try to find one – we had limits on our flying hours. There was no point wasting them during a contact in which we were playing no part. We spent seven hours on that mission, seven hours farting about, seven hours being treated like the dodgy uncle at a wedding.

Eight days later, and another example of the enemy's vicious resolve, another reason for us to want to pound them into the dirt. There was a large explosion in Musa Qala. Up to nine KIA by a suspected suicide bomber. Initial reports suggested that the casualties were combined ISAF and Afghan forces. It was later confirmed that all were ANA, victims of an act of madness by one individual and cowardice by those who commanded him to do it.

Medical air assets, tasked elsewhere at the time, were unable to collect the dead right away. As harsh as it sounds, the dead don't need to be evacuated as urgently as wounded casualties.

The area was live and dangerous. To avoid risking aircraft and crews, the decision was taken to move the dead via vehicle to the nearest FOB, which was Edinburgh, around forty-five minutes away. That happened within a few hours.

The ANA, understandably, wanted their fallen comrades collected from FOB Edinburgh as soon as possible. It's imperative in Muslim tradition for bodies to be buried within twenty-four hours. But those hours were ticking by and nothing was happening. The ANA were getting more frustrated. Eventually a Chinook managed to divert towards FOB Edinburgh, brought the bodies to Kandahar ahead of an onwards flight to Kabul. The bodies, heated in the sun of Musa Qala and stored in shade at FOB Edinburgh for over six hours, had been deteriorating. The smell of death through the body bags was enough to turn the stomachs of the medical team. My heart went out to those soldiers, to their loved ones, to all involved. I had come to know that while sometimes my mind was ablaze with thoughts of waging war, at other times I felt wearied by the horrors of it all.

And yet my friend Vince had not even been in theatre when his good life was lost. It was bittersweet to learn that Pete L and I were allowed to return to the UK for his funeral after a request from his widow, Liz, for us both to attend. She asked me if I would say a few words.

As we departed Bastion for KAF, I asked myself what should I say at a mate's funeral? Should I speak from the heart, from the head? I sat by the open door of that flight, low level, fast gliding over desert and villages, weaving in and out. I remember looking at Afghan people in their homes, looking down into compounds, into gardens, into outdoor bedrooms, onto washing lines, wells, pavements and gathering places, looking from new, shorter distances, taking stock of the easy practicality of so many lives in the midst of this seemingly intractable conflict. Children without toys, women without liberty, families with almost nothing but a goat or two, a small plot of land and each other. Some people waved, some ran in fear, some called on others to look up.

There was standing room only at the rear of the cathedral for the first military funeral I had attended. It was truly moving to see so many fellow soldiers from all corners of the UK to lay that fine man to rest. And it was hard to see his coffin for the first time, for both Pete and I to see the cold, silent evidence of what we never wanted to be true.

Vince's eldest son bravely stood in front of more than four hundred people to read a powerful piece about his dad. And then it was me, trying hard to keep control just as Vince's fine young lad had done.

Telling a few tales of joy turned out to be as tough as reflecting on the sadness, the loss, the wrongness of it all. I finished with a poem written by a son to mark the death of his airman father.

Flight is freedom in its purest form,
To dance with the clouds which follow a storm

HELICOPTER DOWN IN DEVON, 2008

To roll and glide, to wheel and spin;
To feel the joy that swells within;

To leave the earth with its troubles and fly,
And know the warmth of a clear spring sky,
Then back to earth at the end of the day
Released from the tensions which melted away.

Should my end come while I am in flight,
Whether brightest day or darkest night,
Spare me your pity and shrug off the pain,
Secure in the knowledge that I'd do it again,

For each of us is created to die,
And within me I know,
I was born to fly.

Gary Claude Stoker

Four rings on the bat phone.

'Troops in contact, Lashkar Gah. Requesting one aircraft.'

Ackers and I belted outside, heading for the Ops Room.

I jumped into the back of the aircraft, started the APU and pre-flight checks. Ackers was there in minutes.

'What's the score?' I said, rotor turning faster, temperatures and pressures declaring themselves.

'PRT under contact from just to their south. Fighting-age males moving in and around a compound.'

The provincial reconstruction team (PRT) needed air support. We were happy to help. Whatever other information there was, we'd pick up along the way. To get going all we needed was a radio frequency, a callsign and a location.

The PRT, set up to help local government in Helmand, had

been through hell. Four British members had been killed on 16 June, six days earlier. They included the first British servicewoman to die in that war, Corporal Sarah Bryant of the Intelligence Corps. We were in no mood to play nice.

We shot into the sky pulling maximum power on both engines, arriving overhead inside fifteen minutes. All we needed now was some good luck to ensure the undulating terrain didn't hamstring the comms. All too often the insight and instruction from the ground would be interrupted by simple geography. On past occasions we had ended up pissing around for ages, waiting for messages.

We were in luck. The comms worked fine. Sadly, the same couldn't be said for the JTAC. Amber 54A wasn't fully qualified, and wasn't on top of the terminology and procedures when working with air. This was going to slow us up.

He gave us a grid, the suspected enemy firing position from thirty minutes ago. Ackers slaved the TADS to the coordinates. We were looking at a small compound close to a wood line. One armed man on the roof was looking up at us. I spotted another two in the compound's garden, both armed. I smiled down. I was certainly happy to see them and more than happy to ruin their day. Yet their clothing wasn't typical, their actions unrushed, their confident demeanour telling me to take extra care.

By this point, confusion was standard. ANA patrols could be anywhere, might have already moved in to investigate the shooting. Undercover Afghan cops could be anywhere too. And so could the Taliban. The JTAC was usually, but not always, fully in the picture. And I had a feeling this JTAC might be less informed than most. My smile became a frown. Who were these guys?

I asked for more information. What weapons had been sighted? Had they been seen before? What routes were the shooters thought to have taken? In a situation demanding that every action be immediate, every answer was taking ages.

And then, from JTAC – 'Friendlies.'

Not Taliban. We'd wasted time watching them.

Fresh instructions. A wider orbit taking in an area further south. Then a new grid reference, a possible enemy firing point, small arms and mortars may be on site.

My left eye caught movement. Some form of ruckus at the side of a white estate car. But that was 1 kilometre away. I couldn't be sure what I was looking at. Ackers's head was buried in the keypad. I looked again, asked him to do the same. He was taking a radio call.

Around eight people in all, but hard to be sure. One guy was being pushed away from the car by two others. The gang began piling into the vehicle. The last guy to clamber aboard, I was sure, had a long-barrelled weapon. But had I really seen that? I blinked, cleared my vision as best I could. The car door had closed.

'Ackers,' I called. 'Ackers!'

He was still on the call. We had four radios in the aircraft, and there were times when all of them were screaming for attention in the same moment. Sometimes you have to decide what order to handle the demand.

'Ackers!'

He heard me over the din.

'Steve?'

I told him about the car load. He slaved the TADS to my helmet. The vehicle was now speeding off with its heavy human cargo, heading away from the friendlies, dirt clouds in its wake. I asked myself again what had I seen? There was at least one weapon in that car, right? I told Ackers I was pretty sure I had seen a gun. But I couldn't start taking life on the strength of that. Yet Taliban had just been shooting at British forces. We had to flush out the situation. Warning shots might reveal their intentions. And their intentions would reveal their ID.

With the aircraft in a good firing position, The JTAC cleared it. Ackers actioned the gun and selected a twenty-round burst. The aircraft shuddered as the first rounds went 300 metres ahead of the car. Allowing for the car's speed, they should hit 100 metres ahead of it. And, in a couple of seconds, they did just that. The car kept going, tearing through the dust. The Apache pulsed again as Ackers fired twenty more, this time much closer to the car. They landed in a perfect parallel line, as if tracking the vehicle. It braked hard. We counted eight men who jumped out, every one of them now visible with weapons. This was like hitting the jackpot – but only if they were enemy fighters. Several looked up. They raised hands, as if to wave us away. The actions of friendlies? Yet they could also be the actions of Taliban who knew we would not shoot to kill unless we were sure. Some of the men pulled backpacks from the car, put them on, began marching to high ground 100 metres to the north, in the direction of FF. Amber 54A had no information on friendly patrols, none on the movements of SF.

We opted for two more ten round bursts by the side of the car. The situation meant we just didn't trust these armed men enough to allow them to approach friendly positions. But, of course, warning shots weren't going to stop them, whether EF or FF. So, we sat in limbo, with the thoughts of slain comrades on our minds, as eight armed men walked. We needed this resolved. Amber requested us to engage the abandoned vehicle, its doors and boot left wide open. We said no. This didn't feel right.

Ops came on the call seeking every detail we could provide. We reported back on the progress of the men for half an hour. The JTAC sent out a patrol vehicle to meet them. After a slow approach, a conversation took place, ending with handshakes. Those men were on our side.

Back at the debrief, it was confirmed no one had been made aware of this rogue patrol. They were undercover police who had in fact gone so rogue that they had hijacked a man's car earlier on. At least we hadn't blown it up. Still, it was small wonder that the local population had precious little confidence in their coppers.

Just a day later, I and colleagues had the sad duty of saying a final farewell to five of our own. Ramp repatriation parades had become something of an all-too-frequent fixture in Afghanistan. In this case, it was held for five Paras KIA, three by suicide bomber and two who had died in an ambush. The turnout was enormous, with soldiers from all regiments and ISAF nations in ranks of seventeen, whereas they would typically be in ranks of three.

It's never easy to watch the efficient military way of saying goodbye, the ceremony underpinning the pain and holding it all together, the precision timing evenly releasing the emotional flow. We say goodbye to friends and strangers this way, to those who stepped forward and stepped up all the way, right to the end. The respect for these men shines through the straight faces of experienced troops. And it's that lack of emotional indulgence that gives such events the pride and power they deserve.

A lone piper led the cortège of five Union Flag-draped coffins, each with the lost warrior's maroon beret and belt on top. The CO of 2 Para spoke about each in turn, making every word count as he summed up five outstanding, brief lives before the Last Post and the rock-solid silence that followed.

I was by now mid-tour. It had been a gruelling journey, frustrating and heartbreaking, loaded with loss and despair and self-reflection. This would, I was sure, be the last time I was in this country in uniform. I wanted to make the most of what lay ahead of me in this war, whatever that might mean, whatever might be asked of me. I wanted to fight in the name of lost troops, in the name of the nation that sent me here. And yet I was longing for home, to give and get kindness and care, to share good things.

The arrival of some journalists had me thinking about what it was people back in the UK were thinking about us. Sky News were embedded in Bastion and at the Colchester Garrison in England as part of a documentary called *For Queen and Country*. It was to be dedicated to the memory of the 100 British servicemen and women who had died serving their country in Afghanistan. Reporters were tagging along with troops in various situations while deployed on Operation Herrick.

My squadron was asked whether we could lay on a live-fire display of the various weapon types. Rob and I went for it. We sent off rockets while flying at different speeds and angles to help the camera guys get the best shots. We Hellfired some old ISO containers and bits of tanks and blasted off a few bursts of 10 then 100 rounds from the underslung cannon. When possible, we spent the next week glued to the telly and cheered whenever we saw the Ugly in 'action'.

Part of the documentary focused on how much we valued the support of our own families and friends, and the support of our fellow countrymen, too. There was a sense that people back home were growing weary of the war, that it played almost no part in their lives, almost no part in who they were.

For military personnel, it can be uncomfortable to know their duties play second fiddle to some so-called celeb who has had a breakdown because their camera phone didn't work, while colleagues go home in body bags. Yet the flag placed over the remains of those newly fallen is the same one we carry on our arms every day. We take comfort in knowing that whatever forces connect us to that flag, to our home and to her people, they will endure.

Chapter Twenty-One

'FORGET ABOUT THE CODE WORDS.' AFGHANISTAN, 2008

A S BRITISH EFFORTS increased, patrols grew larger and often penetrated deeper into what had been enemy territory. And, in turn, Taliban IEDs increased in number. The more men and women they saw, the more the enemy retreated to bases and foxholes to prime booby-trap devices or prepare suicide belts. It was easier for them to send some poor sucker to his death than confront us, much easier to hide explosive charges and slink away than the alternative. Almost every time they engaged in person with weapons, they came off worse.

By this stage in the war, most Helmand villagers were craving normal life. They were fed up with the Taliban demanding money or forcing them from their homes, fed up with them drawing fire right to their doorsteps. It also seemed that the enemy was running low on fresh blood and was working hard to draw in young fanatics from the slums of Pakistan with a promise of a gun and, in the event of death, everlasting bliss in Paradise. Yet many of the chiefs were still out there, the bigwigs giving the orders and making the cash who thought nothing of sending their fellow Muslims to their deaths. It made good sense that whenever such a proverbial snake was located, we would be called on to remove its head.

The mood in the squadron had dipped, the losses of war felt much deeper than the gains. I'd been there this time around for 50 days, 250 days in all across three tours, and it had started to grind. Tracey told me she had made a chart, that she was crossing off the days until my return and just learning that damn near killed me. There is something truly unsatisfying about expressing love down a phone line or in a letter. We laughed about me missing the simple joys of the British summer while noting that it usually pisses rain for most of it. And I laughed to myself at the thought of English rain, at how I would love for it to come teeming down and quench the hot dirt of this desert life. I'd walk in that for miles. I could imagine few things more lovely than walking with Robyn, with Tracey and Minty as the rain bucketed down on us from above.

Queues for toilets, queues for showering, queues for shaving, queues for food, for phones, for the Internet. Sandstorms. Plastic plates. Sweaty pits. Camp cots. Farting roommates. Dull grub.

Seven weeks to go.

The tannoy bursting into life. They'd only installed that thing three weeks ago. Few of us could work out what half the messages were. Something about the NAAFI and cookhouse.

'Avoid them both,' someone clarified.

'Good idea,' I replied.

It turned out that a car had been parked up alongside the NAAFI and cookhouse, and that no one was coming to claim it. It had been brought in by a local trader during the weekly jingly 'tat' market held in the camp, the source of all the crap cigarettes, encased scorpion ashtrays and scratched bootleg DVDs and CDs. All vehicles, people and stock were searched on entry, but you can't be too careful. The area was cordoned off and the bomb-disposal team moved in fast, inspected the vehicle and then blew it up in a controlled explosion. In the event, there was nothing suspicious. That said, we did feel it had been right to take out the thousands of pairs of knock-off Oakley sunglasses bound to have been on board. In fact, some of the crew had hoped to be asked to hit the thing with a Hellfire, accidentally miss and take out the NAAFI, but it wasn't to be. Anyway, the poor man who owned the car was located, had the Riot Act read to him and was ordered to collect what was left of it

By the time I began my duty on 2 July, Pete L, Redders and Alex G had left for the UK, making room in the coming days for less experienced crew. Ackers took the opportunity to move into Pete's flight with Dave L, setting him up nicely for a command appointment as a flight commander for his next tour. I wished him well.

For now, I was back on VHR with Nick E. I'd taken the Apache course with him and we crewed together during CTR and our first Afghanistan tour. Nick was a great guy to have in the aircraft, apart from the fact that he seemed unable to close his mouth during gun engagements. A weird quirk of his and a weird thing for me to remember about him. Luckily, on this day, he'd be in the back so if there was shooting, it would be me. It gave me an opportunity to show him how to shoot with gob shut.

Four rings on the bat phone. The watchkeeper on the other end was Andy, who was almost as popular as Geordie, one of the other watchkeepers.

To announce the emergency, he said, 'Steve. Only if you are interested and only if you think I'm better at this than Geordie, then I have a job.'

The Land Rover. Nick bounding out for the Apache, me running into the ops room. Andy's big grin only lasted a second. No more messing around.

'Troops in contact around FOB Gibraltar. Civilians seen moving out of the area. Small-arms fire and RPGs followed after that.'

I noted the grids, frequencies and callsigns of friendly controllers, then belted out to the flight line. Nick was already strapped in, the gas turbine-powered APU running to allow pre-flight checks and start the aircon unit to cool the cockpits and avionics. He made the air traffic calls and we climbed for FOB Gibraltar.

All was quiet when we arrived which, as we knew, was typical when Mosquitoes appeared. Nick orbited as we watched for movement at suspected firing points.

Another call, asking us, if we had the JTAC's blessing, to break away for Kajaki and another TIC. We received the blessing.

On approach, Widow 64 asked Nick to hold over the lake until mortar fire had ceased. The ground was familiar. I'd been in combat close to here with Ackers, our aircraft firing two Hellfires into a nearby compound. As the mortars stopped and we moved in on the grids, it hit me that that one of them was just south-west of that compound. It was, I could only assume, a new base after the last one was blown to bits. Not long before our arrival there had been a 500lb-bomb strike by FF just to the north, taking down much of the compound's north wall. The southern wall, we could see, had visible portals. I knew by now they served first and foremost as information-gathering and firing points.

Four males had been seen there and in the small woods near by. Significantly, one of them was believed to be medium-level Taliban commander. Widow 64 advised there were no civilians in the area. I asked for clearance to fire warning shots at the compound's southernmost building and received the okay.

The Apache shook as the cannon shells were hammered out, a ten-round burst striking alongside the structure. No sign of anyone doing anything. I adjusted and fired thirty into the roof. It ripped open and collapsed like a dusty landslide in seconds. The other hiding place had been the trees. I trained the weapon on the edge of the woods, pumped ten rounds deep into the foliage, dragging the weapon along, Ugly shuddering as the rounds drew a dotted line.

I couldn't know if I'd killed anyone, if those bullets had made a difference, if they had stopped something or started something. But one hour later I did know, via an intel briefing, that the Taliban commander had been in the building when the roof came in. He had survived. If I'd known he was in there, I'd have kept on firing.

Two days later and my backseater was Kelvin B, on his first tour, when we were called to a TIC south-west of Lashkar Gah. I'd never supported ground troops in the area before. The layout was US-style, communities living in blocks, the town and its canal and dam system built with American dollars back in the 1960s. The place seemed very green compared to many other towns, and while that made it prettier it also made it trickier. Taliban loved a hiding place, and this area had more than most.

Amber 64A, today's JTAC, advised us that due to a radio fault we were 'talking in red', meaning that the comms might be insecure, that others could be listening in. It also meant that we should talk in pre-established code. He then advised that a six-vehicle friendly convoy was static at a junction and taking fire from up to four positions. I punched in the grid for Amber 64A's position and slaved the sights. The TADS displayed live footage of several vehicles by a compound next to a canal junction. Kelvin positioned the aircraft in an orbit just to the east. Closing in, I asked Amber 64A to confirm his grid. He did. I inputted the coordinates into the keypad. It was 40 kilometres from where we were. He must have got that wrong.

'Amber 64A. Ugly 50. Please repeat grid.'

'Yeh.'

'Okay?'

It was getting frustrating.

'Repeat grid. Over.'

A minute passed. He got back. Stress in the voice. He repeated the same grid. Still 40 kilometres away.

'Seriously? What the. . .?'

Was this TIC somewhere else and we were flying around here talking in mangled code? I had to get this cleared up.

'Amber 64A this is Ugly 50. The grid you have given is approx forty kilometres from where I'm holding, confirm.'

Now Amber 40 joined in, a JTAC further out.

'Amber 64A. Grid is incorrect. Repeat, incorrect.'

'Ugly 50 this is Amber 64A. Listen, I'm under contact from multiple firing points and running around trying to gather all the ANA troops, which in all honesty is like trying to herd cats. I'm trying to get you a precise grid. Be patient with me.'

'Roger,' I said. 'If you are under contact forget about the code words, just talk in clear.'

He came back with the grid. It was 2 kilometres away. His earlier reference had been a single digit out, shunting the position far away. But it didn't matter. We had it right now.

Coming overhead, we were advised that the firing was dying down. The convoy began to move again. A minute later, the lead vehicle braked hard. Its occupants leapt out, lying down at the edge of the road to return fire. The troops in the following vehicles did the same. They must be coming under more fire.

'Ugly 50, Amber 64A. Contact from the north, ready for grid.'

'Don't worry about a grid, just tell me where.'

Taking a grid takes time. It has to be established, passed over, put into the weapons system, sights slaved, target located – we didn't have that kind of time.

'Tell me,' I said, 'Using the clock method from the lead vehicle, where is the firing point?'

'It's right two o'clock around three hundred metres, RPG and small arms.'

Kelvin could make out a wood line 500 metres beyond, past a

cornfield and by a compound. The road it was on ran parallel to the road on which the convoy was travelling. I was cleared to fire, aiming just shy of the trees. The cornfield took the brunt of ten rounds, my hand pulling them along in a single line. I opened up again, parking twenty rounds between the woods and the compound. Then twenty more into the base of the trees, the rounds shredding timber, bits of bark, dirt, branches and leaves flung into the air.

'Ugly 50, this is Amber 64A. Good rounds but we are now taking fire from a compound to our left ten o'clock position, at the end of the road.'

Kelvin put eyes on the location. I slaved the TADS to his monocle, to where he was looking. Juddering from under our feet as ten rounds bit the compound's eastern wall. Then twenty more. Chunks were smashed out of it, some rounds passing right through.

'Ugly 50, Amber 64A. All shooting has stopped.'

'Roger.'

Two more kilometres and the patrol would be on safe ground. As it prepared to move, another call.

'Ugly 50, Amber 64A. Incoming fire from both sides of the road now. We will not be stopping and will try and fight through. Follow us with fire into the wood lines that parallel the road. Fire when ready.'

I could hear the fear in his voice, knew it was escalating. The Taliban were giving this patrol all it could, pulling out the stops on this planned ambush, craving a small victory. The tree line was 100 metres from the patrol. It ran all the way to the next crossroads, around a kilometre. It would be a hell of a job to rip through it all.

'Ugly 50, Amber 64A. I have just witnessed some form of airburst behind your aircraft, believed to be RPG.'

A quick check. All aircraft indications were still good. We just didn't know how close the explosion had come to us but clearly EF, in their frustration, were engaging us too. It was well known that Taliban had modified their RPGs to use as a crude form of surface-to-air rocket designed to explode at a certain height. We had been lucky. But there was no time to dwell on it.

Kelvin calling, almost shouting into the radio, 'Steve, another RPG launch southern side wood line, my line of sight.'

'Roger, slaving.'

Thick woods. A small ditch running by the base of the trees. Two men in there, a third close by, all clear as day, all with AKs, all right in the crosshairs, our orbit bringing us up behind them. One of the men would stand up, fire, duck down, then they'd move and repeat. I actioned the missile. But our approach angle forced us to lose sight of the ditch. Kelvin battled to get the aircraft in a better position, flinging it back around fast. It took just seconds. But, as the ditch came back into view, they were gone.

'Shit!'

I de-actioned the Hellfire. It's a big missile, but a precision one too. A waste to fire it with no visible target.

'Kelvin. Still time for flechettes.'

He actioned them from the backseat. If the men had hidden in that ditch or were just within the trees, the darts would find them.

Clearance secured, Kelvin ran the Apache in, aligning the aircraft for a straight shot. He pushed the aircraft into a dive, held it steady, pulled the trigger. Hard, short bursts, then whooshes as four pairs of rockets detached from the aircraft and, amid blooms of black smoke, bulleted earthwards, the cockpit instantly filling with the scent of rocket fuel.

In that same second, three wise men ran from the wood line as dozens of darts left their housing canister. It was like watching heavy rain fall, little impact points all across the ground, all through the trees. The position from where the men had run was blanketed with tungsten darts. And so was the area where we last saw them. Hundreds of metal points, travelling at hundreds of miles an hour. We could see nothing, and knew nothing for sure. But I didn't rate their chances.

The situation had erupted now, firing points opening further along on both sides of road. I blasted twenty cannon rounds into one side, tearing a hard line through the woods, repeated the action on the other side. The convoy kept moving, gunfire from the vehicles into the trees, gunfire from the trees at the vehicles. I'd fired close to 300 rounds, the aircraft rocking with the rhythmic discharges. Then, out of nowhere, that big gun stopped.

'What the... ?'

Pressing the trigger. Hot mechanisms clicking, yet no response. A message flashing on screen: 'Gun Fail'.

'Gun's jammed,' I called. I'd never known it to happen. Yet we'd cleared the path as best we could, leaving trails of dust and still-dancing leaves for hundreds of yards. And the convoy was moving well, now beyond that particular danger zone, hastening on its way to Amber 40. We stayed above to ensure it got home safe.

The gun jam was examined back at Bastion. The cannon had somehow got locked into position out of safe limits and become unable to fire. I had fired thousands of rounds with that thing and found it to be a most dependable weapon, my weapon of choice. Still, it had not jammed earlier on, which allowed us to help our soldiers. And unlike the enemy, we had suffered no casualties.

Yet Taliban tails were up. We were hearing reports of financial incentives on offer for anyone killing ISAF forces. And although these guys were often motivated by some warped version of religious duty, the cash offers did seem to be putting fire in their bellies.

The daily briefings for all three services, led by the OC Paul T, followed the new standard format – threat updates; flight safety points; meteorological reports; latest incidents; latest intel; deliberate operations ahead; updates via the legends in Royal Electrical and Mechanical Engineers (REME) on the condition of aircraft; and closing with other camp matters of concern – expanding the wi-fi, the lack of computer terminals, the less than generous phone-call allowances, concerns about rubbish blowing onto the dispersal, use of lights at night – nothing was passed over as trivial. I remember one ending with Major Paul raising the deteriorating state of the toilets, saying that he was aware of too much 'bangers and mash' on display, urging people to flush properly. To be clear, the mash bit of 'bangers and mash' was the toilet paper...

The briefings were invaluable. All aviators listened carefully, for the intel was crucial. The names of well-known players would come up. We'd learn what they had been up to, where they might be, what they might be planning. The sources were high-end, some of them with often excellent access to the plans of Taliban warlords. And some of the information came via technical sources – drones, eavesdropping, interceptions. There was a sense very often that we had them ever more boxed in, that if we kept on this unrelenting pressure, if we continued to win hearts and minds, it was only a matter of time before the madmen of the Taliban were left with almost nothing.

On 6 July, word came in of one such madman we had heard of before, a high-value target (HVT) by the name of Bishmullah. He had a reputation as something of an IED expert, a proficient bomb-maker, skilled logistician and warlord with many fighters in his charge. Intel had been received on his location and SF had refreshed scenario plans for a well-informed search and arrest. Apaches were put on standby and advised that things could swing into action at any moment. We'd heard that before, however. These kinds of operations, involving the highest degree of precision in the detail, easily fall apart at the last minute. There was no point in getting overexcited.

Two hours later and things moved up a gear. Ackers and a newly arrived, yet experienced, Apache pilot, Dave L. were to set out for a location to the west, hold off, stay stealthy and await instructions. Ground troops were to be dropped at a location beyond and if push came to shove, the attack helicopter would be called in. Meanwhile, myself and Will D were to sit tight back at base, ready to go in support or to replace our colleagues.

Back in the ops room, a large video screen with a high-quality live feed from a UAV, callsign Cody 47, was put in place. Aircrew and ops staff pulled up chairs and watched as ground troops, visible as detailed thermal images, moved towards the target compounds, the drone orbiting above. It was like being at the cinema, except this was for real, happening now, and there was no popcorn. The troops formed up into lines while moving to their respective positions ahead of the assault.

By then Ackers and Dave had been holding for some time. I and my CPG, Will, were given the all-clear to go to the flight line and hold. Will was a decent young officer but lacked experience in both flying and in Afghanistan and so would be under my command in Ugly 56. Shortly after, and all still quiet on the ground, we were cleared to head for the first rendezvous point. Ackers updated on the progress of FF before we moved in and he moved back to Bastion.

JTAC Mayhem 08 cleared us to leave our holding position and establish an orbit in the overhead. Everything was pitch black so we needed to be sure of FF troops' location below. Hundreds of feet above us, Cody 47 was silently orbiting. Between the Apache and the drone was Broadsword, a Sea King stuffed with complex sensors. Mayhem 08 had three sets of eyes over the compound areas. And he had a serious array of weapons under his command.

The target compound was in an area of wide, open ground. It wasn't hard to find it or the friendly troops. The assault began on schedule. Teams, split into small groups, stormed strategic sections. From above, it looked like an artfully executed plan. Within around two minutes the location was packed with ground troops. Unfortunately, there was no one else there. They searched, bagged up documents, computers, various items and left. The HVT had been around not long before. They didn't get Bishmullah but the intel gathered helped the net close tighter.

The troops departed for the helicopter pickup point about 2 kilometres away. I advised Will we would wait for a time to ensure that they were well clear of the area.

'All callsigns. Cody 47. I have visual on three males who seem to have come out of some form of hide to the south of the target compound.'

This was set to change the game. The men, the UAV's flying crew said, did not appear to be armed. But they were moving in the direction of the departing troops. I told Will we'd need to get eyes on these guys as soon as possible.

'Okay,' he said, 'I have them on TADS. Three moving slowly but definitely towards the area of the pickup point.'

Despite the deep dark of the night, the men seemed to be moving easily, as if aided by night-vision devices. Other than suspicious activity, we had nothing on them – no sign of weapons, no clear suggestion of hostility. It could be they were simply curious about the visitors. Yet, as we watched for some more minutes, as they seemingly tracked the friendlies for a full kilometre, they came to a sudden stop. All three crouched behind a wall.

'Ugly 56. This is Broadsword. We have now moved into position. We also have them visual by the wall.'

'Roger. Thanks.'

We broke away temporarily, moved our focus to FF, watched each step as they closed in on the extraction point. We turned back to the unknown trio. I had to reposition to secure a good view of the stored grid, their location behind the wall. The wind had been getting stronger. It took an effort to hold things steady between the friendlies and the suspected insurgents. A lot of turning, adjusting and moving around just to stay eyes-on.

Mayhem 08 was keen to know every detail. Cody 47 could now see what looked like a cylindrical object in the hands of one man.

He said a second had some form of sack over his shoulder, that its shape suggested it contained a weapon, but still there was not enough to go on.

Will advised Mayhem 08 that if he felt his men were in danger, if the LS itself was at risk, we would fire warning shots.

'Ugly 56, Mayhem 08. We are okay at the moment. Good eyes on all the area. Unless you spot a weapon, you are to just observe.'

The extracting Chinooks were approaching from the north. Once loaded, the plan was to head south. But were these three, out for a wander at 03.35hrs, going to get in the way of that?

The Chinooks were getting close. I advised all that I was changing location, that I wanted to be in pole position to take on this trio if things went haywire.

Broadsword advised he had just spotted two more heat signatures moving from the village area towards the three men at the wall.

'Oh mate,' I said to Will, 'this is not right. Something's definitely going on here.'

We were looking at a situation where five men, all possibly armed, could leap into action as an air asset arrived. A helicopter and its crew, as well as the personnel it is dropping off or collecting, are never more exposed than when taking off or landing.

Will advised he had eyes on the two new men, that there was about one minute until all five were together.

'Roger,' I said. 'Chinooks five hundred metres from landing. Any weapons, Broadsword?'

'Negative.'

'Shit.'

Twenty seconds until landing, twenty seconds until the group of men formed up around 700 metres from the LS. I took a breath and held the aircraft as steady as I could. The two men joined the three as the first of the big helicopters was seconds from touching down.

'One has a weapon. Repeat, one has a weapon.'

It was Broadsword – urgent, clear. The man with the sack over his shoulder had stood up and pulled a gun from it, was getting into position. We couldn't see in the same detail as Broadsword, but we had eyes on the five, one of them a little further away from the others. It was all we needed. The thumps beneath the floor as the heavy gun delivered a chain of 30mm rounds. The gunman took the first of it, rounds slicing through him. Job done. Two ran for it, two tried to hide. Sights went in search of the next target.

'Ugly 56, Broadsword. I have two running south.'

Now the other two, springing to life, dashing from the scene, heading towards trees in the direction of the compound. Each was now clutching a weapon. Tremors as more heavy fire hailed down from the night sky. The pair had met with the other two. All were about to run into the compound when everything around them was ravaged. The building's wall, the trees, the ground, three men – all pulled apart in a second. Just one man moving now, a make-or-break sprint through smoke and dust towards trees. The gun tracked him but he vanished.

At the LS, the Chinooks loaded the waiting troops as Cody, Broadsword and Ugly 56 scanned the area. The engagement had taken less than ten minutes.

We learned later that a Taliban ambush team had been in place waiting for just such an assault on the compound. They had figured their revered guest might draw some fire. It was a well-planned operation on their part but they hadn't factored in the view from above. When it came to keeping an eye on Bishmullah, the Taliban were pulling out all the stops. Unfortunately for them, we were doing the same.

Chapter Twenty-Two

'BISHMULLAH. CONFIRMED.' AFGHANISTAN, 2008

ONE DAY LATER. 10 July. By now we knew that ground forces had missed Bishmullah by minutes. Dickers (watchers), on alert around the clock, had spotted the Chinooks land and their man fled. But fresh intel was in on his latest location. Another plan was developed to capture or kill this HVT.

He was holed up in one building within a sprawling compound of some fifteen structures, including a hospital facility for wounded Taliban. Again, troops would be dropped off some distance away, take control of entrance/exit points and launch the assault. A UAV and AC-130 Spectre gunship would be above in case it all went kinetic. And if it was to get up close and personal, an Apache would be on standby out of earshot.

The UAV was sent over the location many hours before the assault to establish comings and goings. I'd been involved in the previous three SF operations and was glad to hear I'd be needed again on this one. By now, like many others, I wanted Bishmullah's head on a stick, albeit not literally. I crossed my fingers that tonight he would wake up with a British gun barrel in his face or an Apache tapping on his roof.

As it turned out, I and Will R 'Rousy' launched earlier than planned because the AC-130 would be delayed. Transit to the holding point gave me time to calibrate to optimal internal lighting, needing to be sure the multipurpose screens didn't blind new guy Rousy in the back.

Progress on the ground was good. Mayhem 08 requested we come directly overhead and issued pre-assigned key building numbers in the western sector of the complex. Cody, the UAV, watched the central area including the main target building, and the late-arriving AC-130 took the remainder. When it all kicked off, we were to pick off 'leakers', known enemy who exit an area of interest.

Troops with night-vision gear formed a cordon below before, with precision timing, surging forward, breaching the wall and storming the compound. Yet, with my NVGs on and eyes wide, I could see no leakers. There was no sign of anyone at all. After thirty minutes all but one building had been cleared, an 80 x 80-foot structure with its own perimeter wall and high gate. Mayhem 08 advised we could call it a night. I was okay for fuel and said I'd hang on for the final clearance.

'Last time around,' I said, 'five men appeared from nowhere in the last minute.'

'Roger.'

Below, an instant explosion of action, maximum aggression, men bursting through the gate, smashing into the building in seconds. And again, no one around. The attackers were inside the hospital and surrounded by bundles of bandages, surgical equipment, X-ray slides, training manuals, books on various weapons. After breaking into one back room, they found men tucked behind furniture and inside cupboards, but offering no threat. All were arrested and taken in. They needed to check whether Bishmullah was among them. He was not. He had slipped the net again.

A few days later and we were advised in the morning briefing that heavily armed Taliban were taking over compounds occupied by civilians. As families were forced into one room to wait it out, the fighters chained up the gates. They took to the vantage points ahead of launching attacks on FF. It was part of their cat-and-mouse attempts to smudge the intel we had on where they were, on which properties were likely to pose a risk. And they knew that if we hit the compounds, civilians might be among the casualties. Engineering civilian deaths was part of their plan. They would use any such deaths as propaganda to help drive a wedge between us and those ordinary Afghans who were fed up living under the iron fist of the Taliban, an organisation that publicly executed those who assisted Coalition forces. It all seemed to indicate that we were winning, that the hearts and minds of many everyday locals were being won, that the Taliban were getting desperate. No wonder the intel from local sources kept coming.

On 12 July there was new information on Bishmullah. He'd been spotted in the area of two compounds at Now Zad, several kilometres south of that last location. Cody showed that there was little around, that the property was set away from other buildings, and that the closest wood line was 100 metres away. This could be an easier watch for ground troops and air assets. I wasn't on duty on that night but tuned in from Bastion. As before, an Apache on standby, ground troops with night-vision devices, the stealthy approach, the cordon forming. Three armed men, spotted by Cody, bolted from one of the buildings towards the wood line and disappeared. The UAV dropped a laser point, visible only to the ground forces, onto where the trio were thought to be. Part of the cordon broke away to make a cautious approach to the hiding men. As they came within hearing distance, the insurgents opened up. Gunfire was returned, but more accurate, more effective. The trio died with their fingers on the triggers.

Again, the area and buildings were clear as the bodies were

searched and photographed. And as the operation was winding down, there came some unexpected, quality news.

'Bishmullah. Confirmed.'

They'd got him. He was one of the trio killed in the firefight, the others being his two bodyguards. My feelings were a strange mix of delighted and pissed off. The bastard was dead, but I hadn't been there.

The determination put into taking him out was not wasted on the Taliban. While they were playing mind games, we were playing some of our own. They knew by now that when your name is high on the list, we will come for you again and again until the job is done.

Bishmullah wasn't the first chief to be hunted down and he wouldn't be the last. And it was no secret that the next name on the list was Mullah Rahim.

Daily Mail, 23 July 2008:

TALIBAN LEADER SURRENDERS AFTER HE HEARS BRITISH SF ARE 'CLOSING IN'

The most senior Taliban commander in Afghanistan's war-torn Helmand province has given himself up because he feared being killed by British SF.

The news will be a massive blow to insurgent forces.

Mullah Rahim surrendered to authorities in Pakistan, the Ministry of Defence said last night.

Rahim — thought to be one of the five main Taliban commanders — is reported to have handed himself in to Pakistani police near the border and is being held in the town of Quetta.

The surrender of Mullah Rahim is likely to plunge Taliban militants into disarray.

The success of a NATO campaign directly targeting the

Taliban leadership has led to hopes that a power vacuum at the top has weakened the group. Hours after Rahim turned himself in, British forces killed their third senior Taliban leader in little more than three weeks.

Top British commanders said Rahim's surrender was a massive breakthrough that would plunge militants in Helmand into disarray.

Forces spokesman Lieutenant Colonel Robin Matthews said last night: 'The Taliban's senior leadership structure has suffered a shattering blow.

'They remain a dangerous enemy, but they increasingly lack strategic direction and their proposition to the Afghan people is proving ultimately negative and self-defeating.' Gulab Mangal, Governor of Helmand, urged militiamen to join the Government side.

He said: 'I advise all those Taliban who are engaging with terrorist actions that the fighting has no benefits. Choose a good, bright and honourable way.'

The three Taliban chiefs killed by British troops include Abdul Rasaq, known as Mullah Sheikh, who died in a precision missile strike after Rahim surrendered.

It came eight days after the death of an associate of Rahim called Bishmullah, and 24 days after leading bomb-maker Sadiqullah was killed in a helicopter missile strike.

Chapter Twenty-Three

AMBUSH THE AMBUSH. AFGHANISTAN, 2008

SIX SINKS FOR about fifty people. Six often filthy sinks just across from the stinking urinals, close to six seatless metal toilets (one reserved for those with the squirts), just by the often-filthy showers. If you're lucky, your shower might have a curtain. And no air-conditioning at all in there. Taking a dump, even taking a breath, could be a truly grim, sweaty experience. Closing the door for a smidgin of privacy was like closing an oven door with you inside. We called it going for a RES – a real emotional shite.

'This is,' I said to myself many times in there, 'my last Afghanistan tour.'

A tasking. Ugly 52 requested to provide overwatch for a platoon-size patrol in Musa Qala. Within five minutes of getting airborne, I and Rousy were told of an Amber callsign alert in Marjah. They had spotted dickers and feared an ambush might be imminent. I knew the layout down there, knew a lot of roads ran alongside each other, that the place was jammed with dense tree lines and sprawling compounds, and that the Taliban had good reason to regard it as fertile ground for their campaign.

The radio was not secure. We'd need code again, which I knew would slow things down. On the plus side, the area on the map was well marked with coloured spot numbers. Amber 44 was a six-vehicle mobile patrol. I opened comms and was advised they were in the area of Blue 7. It was easy to see on the map.

Rousy flew us over. I could see several static vehicles on the side of the road, a couple of troops gathered outside them. I slaved the TADS, the sights now tracking my eyeball, allowing me to see the finer details. I had first to establish that they were the friendly vehicles in question. Then I would search – culverts, rat runs, buildings, trees. Troops had gone static due to concerns about a compound on their left. We looked over the lot but could see nothing.

Silicon 11, another mobile ground callsign, piped up on the radio. It hoped Ugly 52 could check a route further along. We moved to the new point, checked it out and confirmed all was well. Amber 44 came back to say it was moving to the next junction.

'Roger. I have eyes on and you are cleared to move.'

'Moving now.'

'Rousy,' I said, 'eyes on the junction ahead.'

'Roger.'

He positioned the aircraft parallel to the road. This allowed me to keep the TADS just ahead of the convoy.

'Steve,' he said, 'when are they going to move? They haven't even got back on board.'

'I thought they were already moving.'

'Amber 44, this is Ugly 52. Confirm you are already mobile at this time.'

'Ugly 52. Amber 44. Confirmed.'

What?

A terrible feeling, an instant, heavy nausea.

'Jesus Christ,' I said. 'Are we with the right patrol!?'

I checked the map. The features below matched up. Yet now I

could see a slight bend in one of the junctions that wasn't the same on the map.

'Steve,' said Rousy, 'what is it?'

I roared it, 'Fuck! I'm looking at the wrong patrol. Go north Rousy, go north one road over.'

We had been looking at Silicon 11. The right junction was 300 metres away. And seconds later I could see the Amber 44 patrol, safe and sound. The relief was immense. The lesson was salutary. I'd made an assumption because I knew the area. I should have checked that map properly. Christ knows how bad that could have got.

Now we had eyes on both patrols as they planned to move from junction to junction. As Silicon 11 boarded, Rousy called, 'I have a motorbike on the other side of the bank moving fast away from the patrol.'

I slaved the TADS. A lone motorcyclist driving away at speed. There was nothing unusual about a motorbike, typically a 125cc, in the area. It was the most common form of transport, often with two, three, four or more passengers.

But they were also the dickers' vehicle of choice – quick, small, versatile. The intricate business of war among civilian populations is all about the circumstances, timing and evidence.

Unseen and unheeded by the male rider, we watched as he approached the next junction up from Silicon 11. He stopped, looked back towards the convoy. His interest in the patrol was ensuring our interest in him. He moved off again, turning south, tracked by TADS, pulling up near a wood line beyond the entrance to a compound. He was now about 200 metres from the junction. Now another motorbike appeared, approaching from the other direction. It stopped in the same place as the first guy. A man dressed in white emerged from trees, signalled for both to dismount and enter the compound, all three disappearing under a canopy as they entered.

'Keep us to the west, Rousy. Let's keep them thinking we are still looking at the patrol.'

A man in black emerged from the compound, walked to the middle of the road. He put binoculars to his eyes, looking towards the approaching convoy.

'Silicon 11, Ugly 52. Remain in position until we can confirm the intentions of individuals further along.'

'Roger.'

The man in black disappeared. We'd need to get around the other side to get a better view into the complex, but I didn't want to give the game away. I needed them to feel they could begin something to allow me to end it.

'Rousy, come further to the east then turn south.'

'Roger.'

As the TADS slaved to the wood line, five figures came into view within the shadows. They appeared to be sitting in a small trench among the trees. One stood and began moving towards the compound, ducking low. Another followed. We couldn't confirm any weapons. But the line of sight from their location would have revealed the position of FF up the road, around 200 metres further north. The male in black from earlier came back into view from under the tree cover. The two men from the wood went to him, gathered around as if for a briefing. Then a third arrived. As the remaining two got to their feet in the woods, something important became clear for the first time.

'RPG.'

'Got it,' said Rousy. 'Possible AKM also.'

The weapons were picked up, carried over. As all the men joined together, we could see another one had a long-barrelled weapon.

Gotcha.

'Silicon 11, Ugly 52. I have several armed males near the area of Red 7. Am observing but this may be an ambush, remain static and will inform.'

'Roger. Let me know. All friendlies are in my location, no friendlies further south than me.'

That was good to know. Other men appearing now, about ten altogether. Intense conversations and hand signals, the man in black leading the show. They left as a single group, exiting the compound to walk alongside a low wall in preparation for their ambush. The path would take them through woods, passing beyond Silicon 11's position. It seemed the intention was to attack the patrol from the rear. Friendlies were now in imminent danger.

I actioned the gun.

'Silicon 11, Ugly 52. I have armed males to your south repositioning to the rear of your convoy. I can see a tree line that they are able to follow all the way to your location. My intention is to engage. Confirm again no friendly forces south of your position.'

'That is affirmative. Clear to engage.'

Recoil as the cannon spat ten rounds into the centre of the group. Chaos on the ground, injuries, panic, death. Those who could, ran for it. Some dashed further along the same path by the wall. More raced back to the compound. I picked the larger group. The man in black was among them. Crosshairs were on them as they ran, as if coming towards the gun. Two bursts of twenty rounds. A quick adjustment. Then forty more. The ground was blown open, lumps of earth and tree splinters flying up, a fog of dust all around the impact points. It would take time to clear. I moved the sights back to the first firing point. Two or three dead. Moved the sights again, in the direction where the smaller group ran. No sign of them.

I swung the weapon to the compound. It was possible that the dust might have given cover, that some might have made it back. Sixty explosive rounds sliced through the air, ramming the walls, the roof, the doors.

Knock knock.

A Hellfire missile would be a better choice for this job. Yet I felt there was no need to risk tearing down other buildings. Those sixty rounds would be enough to clip their wings, and at least scotch the ambush plans.

Silicon 11 advised its crew had spotted a remote-control IED (RCIED) partially buried in the road ahead. It was confirmed later that the enemy had planned to trigger it before engaging the patrol with small arms.

Marjah ops room asked Ugly 52 to get eyes on Amber 44, to ensure they were covered for the route home. For some bonkers reason, the patrol had split. Two groups were going in two different directions. Worse than that, we lost comms. As light started to fade, this felt like the beginning of a nightmare.

We were low on fuel. We had ten minutes at this location before bingo fuel, when we would have to get out of there or we wouldn't make it back. We could see both sections, about 1 kilometre apart, yet couldn't communicate with either.

Nine minutes.

Eight, seven, six, five.

'Amber 44, Ugly 52. Receiving?'

Nothing.

Four minutes.

'Ugly 52, Amber 44. Radio check.'

'Amber, Ugly 52. You are loud and clear. I am visual with your convoy, both sections. You are about a kilometre apart.'

He advised he was in the rear section. He had been trying to contact the lead section 'to tell them to slow down'.

'Roger. I have three minutes to bingo fuel then I have to depart.'

'Ugly 52, this is Marjah ops room. From our watch towers we are visual with the lead vehicles. Will be sending out a mobile patrol to meet them. Estimating with them in ten minutes.'

'That's good to hear Marjah ops. And in that case, we can get going.'

'Roger.'

It was great news.

We landed with exactly the required minimum fuel amount

and sighed for a long time. An ambush ambushed, FF potentially saved from injury or death. Yet the debrief on the successful day would begin with bleak news. Another UK fatality: a British Army dog handler and his dog killed in another part of Helmand in the previous hours.

Chapter Twenty-Four

THE N BOMB.
AFGHANISTAN, 2008

INTELLIGENCE overview 19–25 July:

Overall increase in EF activity. The southern MSQ wadi has reportedly been reinforced with fortified defensive positions and a Warrior patrol having been fixed in place for 24 hours following an IED strike was engaged by indirect fire, small-arms fire and RPG. A new tactic has emerged where the enemy place IED/Mines where FF are likely to take cover during any engagements.

More effort was directed towards ensuring re-supply convoys made necessary following numerous engagements of civilian convoys passed without incident.

Threat to Aviation – more Intelligence has again suggested that EF are keen to shoot down a Chinook. Dicking Aviation and threatening to engage assets whilst both airborne or wheels down is assessed as credible but as no major leaders were known to be in the area a degree of bravado is also probably playing its part.

We were airborne less than twenty minutes after the call. A British patrol south of Musa Qala was coming under heavy small-arms fire from a number of locations.

As Rousy and I in Ugly 50 closed in, Widow 73 informed of ongoing mortar attacks from MSQ district centre. While munitions are in the air, no aircraft is allowed through. We positioned to the east and waited for things to go cold. I urged Widow 73 to focus on the mortar guys, to end that soonest so we could get to work.

'Roger,' he said, and was as good as his word.

Mortars silent, we were cleared to look at buildings ahead of the static FF. There was a potential enemy firing position identified within a compound marked on the map as K4, 350 metres south of Widow 73. I slaved the TADS, scanned buildings, walls and tree lines. Nothing doing.

Widow 73 was sure, saying, 'Definitely small-arms fire from that area. Civilians cleared out some time ago.'

'Roger,' I said. 'I'm requesting clearance to fire warning shots to the east of the building to gauge reaction.'

'Roger. Happy. Call when engaging.'

I found an open area, lined up the sight's reticule, fired off ten rounds from several thousand feet above. In the corner of the TADS, a lone figure running close to the wall, exiting one building and heading towards the doors of another. He was a distance from where I'd been aiming but with no one else to watch, I kept my eyes on him. It looked as if he was standing now at the doorway, maybe attempting to remain hidden in the shadows, yet looking right at us. That entrance had large double doors, which were open, the courtyard around dotted with trees and the complex surrounded by a high wall. Just beyond the main entrance, a small single building joined to a larger building. Beyond that, an entrance led into another courtyard where chickens were running around. Another main building further along. The whole place was a labyrinth. The more I looked, the more confusing it became.

What we didn't know at the time was that the perimeter wall had its own doorway leading outside to the open fields beyond.

As we orbited, eyes on the man, he began making hand gestures. I asked Rousy to move to the north to allow me to see who could see him. Another man came into view, standing where the individual had run from. He too was trying to stay in the shadows, and appeared to be carrying something.

'Keep coming round to the west, Rousy,' I said. More of the scene was unfolding. The new man moved forward, into the shade of a tree. It was only a second, but I got to see him clearly.

'Gotcha,' I said. 'RPG in hand and several RPG heads in the bag over his shoulder.'

He moved again, darted from one shadow to another, ducked between trees, kept going. As he reached the final tree by the wall, he slipped off his bag, put it on the ground. By now I was confident these two had just been involved in engaging FF. The warning shots had made them show themselves. It was worth doing it again.

'Widow 73, this is Ugly 50. Two enemy spotted, one armed. They have now gone firm in the compound. Request further warning shots to provoke a reaction.'

'Roger. Happy. All FF behind hard cover. You are clear to engage with 30mm.'

Flashes in the sky as ten rounds roared out, striking fifty metres to the left of the building. A quick adjustment. I was about to release a second burst when both men ran for it, dashing towards that largest building in the compound. I hit the trigger again but hadn't adjusted enough. The rounds fell just outside the perimeter wall. A third burst, but they hit the wall. I still hadn't moved the reticule enough. I waited for the dust to clear.

'Steve,' Rousy called as I recalibrated.

'What?'

He'd seen two other men running from a small building to the larger, to where the other pair had run. He was sure they had a long-barrelled weapon. But in the messy, dusty picture below, could they have been the same two, running from building to building and back?

'Ugly 52, Widow 73. Intelligence just received confirming the compound area you engaged does indeed contain EF. Intercepted radio calls. Enemy saying "We are under fire, will reposition before shooting back".'

I requested permission to fire a Hellfire. Friendlies were far enough away to avoid risk.

'Roger. Wait out,' Window 73 said, sending the request further up the line.

'Roger.'

Forty, fifty seconds later and, 'Cleared to Hellfire.'

Rousy was already repositioning away to run in for the shot. We were looking at a large rectangular building, a tough nut to crack with a missile. Yet it had just two exits, was very much a contained unit. I realised something. For the first time in my career, a weapon I had never used before would be the best option. The new N-type Hellfire.

N for November.

The standard Hellfire K1 was a fine option in many cases, particularly good against armoured vehicles, but would produce only a limited effect in a large building. The N-type, also known as a thermobaric missile or vacuum bomb, could reach the parts that the K1 could not. Controversial, brutal, decisive, efficient, and not yet used in the war by British military. Ideal for an attack where enemy is holed up in buildings or caves. The weapon punches in, but no bomb blows. Instead, there is a pressure explosion, an enhanced blast forcing air outwards, including the air in people. Victims are essentially vacuumed to death as internal organs collapse in on themselves. Apache missile rails were equipped with the N-type Hellfire by 2008, just for moments such as this. That sturdy big building would take too long to smash apart. And that would give those inside options I did not want them to have, including training RPGs on myself and Rousy. The protection offered to the Taliban by those solid walls and minimal exit points was about to be turned against them.

I selected the 'N', slaved the sight, manually adjusted the cross-hairs to seek out the best impact point. I pulled the laser trigger on the right-hand grip, the beam releasing from the TADS bucket on the aircraft's front, striking the roof. The missile's sensors found it. But only when the range is right and the aircraft is within firing limits could the trigger be pulled. A true test of coordination. And I did not want to bugger up this first 'N-type' shot.

Clunk. Whoosh.

The missile left the rail. I held the reticule on the centre of the target, heart thumping. Those few seconds were among the longest of my life. When the missile hit the centre of the roof I remembered to breathe. It had burst through. The TADS filled with destruction, a building bursting apart from the inside. As the dust cleared, rubble everywhere. Looking at the inside of the remains of one wall, a doorway, unseen before, now visible, exiting into yard. Two men were running in, must have been in the shadows beyond. They began digging into the chaos with their hands, desperately pulling at lumps of shattered building as if searching for something.

My heart crashed.

Had I misread this whole situation? My head filled with images of a father looking for a child, a son seeking a mother amid the wreckage I had just delivered. I knew anyone who had been within those walls could not have survived, that they would have died fast yet horrifically. Christ knows what kind of carnage was buried under the dirt. My gut felt hollow.

'Rousy,' I said, 'those two men had weapons, right? Definitely?'

'Yes definitely.'

'Be honest. Please. Are you sure?'

'Yes. I am sure, Steve.'

So, what were we looking at here? Two men dashing to the scene of a missile strike, putting their lives on the line to dig for people who could only be lost to them? I needed to see the tape.

Rousy maintained a tight orbit to the north as I rewound the HI8 video to the guy with the RPG and heads at the tree. No doubt about it. And fast forward now to the two Rousy saw running from the smaller and into the larger building. A long-barrelled weapon in the lead guy's hand. No doubt. I paused the tape. Stared at the image.

'Thank fuck for that,' I said.

We watched as the men dug further. Then an answer. Not people, but weapons. As the picture cleared further, another four men by the doorway, maybe more. One of the guys digging passing something back to the next guy, then doing it again. We continued the orbit, manoeuvring to the opposite side. Two of the men were dusting down freshly recovered PKM machine guns. Faces turned our way. Maybe they had not seen us before. Maybe they didn't realise the missile had been sent from an Apache, maybe they had assumed it was a Javelin type fired from the ground, maybe they thought it was from a fighter jet, maybe their hearing had taken a hammering. But now they were in the picture. They ran from the scene, dashed towards another large building where earlier a man had lurked in doorway shadows, one of its walls alongside the perimeter.

Widow 73 on the radio. Troops receiving small arms from the area, gunfire from portholes. These guys were outnumbered and unfathomably outgunned but they were fighting on. I admired their fortitude, but only for a second. It was time to end this.

A second Hellfire engagement requested and permitted. Rousy lined up, switching the attack heading for the northern side of this building. A K1 clunked and whooshed, pierce the roof of the building just above the doorway. Dust poured out from the large hole like chimney smoke, havoc delivered deep inside. Small-arms fire ceased. The lull would allow the FF patrol to continue. Our eyes stayed pinned on the building but nothing appeared. The two of us wondered in silence if more gunfire would come.

'Unlikely,' I said to Rousy. He knew what I meant.

'Time for home?'

We had been in the air for an hour now and needed to begin making plans. But. . .

'Two leakers,' I said.

Two men right alongside the freshly bombed building, moving just under the shadow of the perimeter wall. As we repositioned, they ran. One stopped briefly to fire in the direction of the friendly patrol. That was cover fire, designed to allow the second male to sprint from the shadows for the next compound 100 metres south. But for a few seconds they were both in the open. I put the crosshairs on the runner, squeezed the trigger. The juddering floor beneath our feet. Dusty ghosts whipped up on the ground. Yet the two figures came dashing through the haze. They dived through a hole in the wall, tucked themselves in at the other side. We needed to swing around now to get eyes on. As the aircraft moved above, they were gone. But no – appearing again, belting from shadows a good distance further along. These guys were bloody Olympians. And the lead guy wearing flip-flops too, his AK gripped tight. Another ten rounds slammed down and he ran on. Another ten, landing where he had been a split second before.

Rousy asked to fire using his helmet-mounted sight. I agreed. He actioned the gun from the rear, placed the crosshairs on the target and fired. Adjustments now meant only the smallest movement of the head. But by now the leader was at the next compound. He ran under a tree line as twenty rounds blazed down, earth exploding by his feet. Rousy snapped his head back to the second man and fired. His body fell, tumbled forward, his life over.

As we checked back along their path and towards the open field, another body. He must have joined the pair as they fled. I had wounded him moments before and, in the dust, he had continued, made it into the field before falling for a final time.

Widow 73 recommenced the advance forward to carry out a battle damage assessment (BDA) to gauge the impact on personnel or buildings, to see what equipment, materials, maps or weapons could be secured. ANA troops stormed into the Hellfired buildings and reappeared with bundles of weapons in their arms. They moved from there to the body of the man in the field, recovering a weapon and papers.

Widow 73 was getting word of more enemy sightings to the east, but Ugly 50 didn't have time for another search. Ops was informed and a second VHR aircraft would support.

Ugly 51 went on to locate an enormous T-shaped bunker to the east, a 100-metre-long hideout with sandbags and timber frames providing views and firing holes in all directions. A Hellfire missile was sent inside to see what it could do.

That evening we received reports that nineteen enemy had been killed during the day's engagements, including seven within the compound I hit with the N missile. Many weapons and thousands of rounds of ammunition were recovered. We had ended what amounted to at least a company-strength Taliban unit operating against ground patrols.

A few days later I was in conversation with one of those involved in the BDA on that day. I said I had fired the N-type into that building, that I believed it was the best weapon for the task at hand. They agreed it had done the job. Out of curiosity, I asked what they had found among the rubble.

'Do you want me to describe it?'

I wasn't sure. But whatever I was about to hear had been my own work.

'Yes,' I said.

The Times, 22 June 2008:

Army 'vacuum' missile hits Taliban

British forces in Afghanistan have used one of the world's most deadly and controversial missiles to fight the Taliban.

Apache attack helicopters have fired the thermobaric weapons against fighters in buildings and caves, to create a pressure wave which sucks the air out of victims, shreds their internal organs and crushes their bodies.

The Ministry of Defence (MoD) has admitted to the use of the weapons, condemned by human rights groups as 'brutal', on several occasions, including against a cave complex.

The use of the Hellfire AGM-114N weapons has been deemed so successful they will now be fired from RAF Reaper unmanned drones controlled by 'pilots' at Creech air force base in Nevada, an MoD spokesman added.

Thermobaric weapons, or vacuum bombs, were first combat-tested by the Soviet Union in Afghanistan in the 1980s and their use by Russia against civilians in Chechnya in the 1990s was condemned worldwide.

The decision to buy the Hellfire AGM-114N missiles was made earlier this year following problems attacking Taliban fortified positions.

British Apache pilots complained that standard Hellfire antitank missiles were going straight through buildings and out of the other side. Even when they did explode, there were limited casualties among the Taliban inside, particularly when a building contained a number of rooms.

'We no longer accept the term thermobaric [for the AGM-114N] as there is no internationally agreed definition,' said an MoD spokesman. 'We call it an enhanced blast weapon.'

The redefinition has allowed British forces to use the weapons legally, but is undermined by the publicity of their manufacturer, Lockheed Martin, which markets them as thermobaric.

The laser-guided missile has a warhead packed with fluorinated aluminium powder surrounding a small charge.

When it hits the target, the charge disperses the aluminium powder throughout the target building. The cloud then ignites, causing a massive secondary blast that tears throughout any enclosed space.

The blast creates a vacuum which draws air and debris back in, creating pressure of up to 430lb per sq in. The more heavily the building is protected, the more concentrated the blast.

Jim Gribschaw, Lockheed Martin's programme director for air-to-ground missiles systems, said the thermobaric Hellfire was 'capable of reaching around corners to strike EF hiding in cases, bunkers and hardened multi-room complexes'.

The MoD said: 'We are conscious of the controversial aspects [of this weapon] but it is being used sparingly and under strict circumstances where it is deemed appropriate by the commander on the ground.'

Chapter Twenty-Five

THE LONGEST DAY. AFGHANISTAN, 2008

THE BADLANDS BETWEEN Bastion and Kandahar. No British troops had deployed there before, the area considered too deadly, too wild yet to tame. But the time had come.

Then 3 Para had arrived in numbers to begin a major search operation, to barge most unexpectedly deep into enemy territory, a targeted hunt for people, weapons, training materials and other resources. We arrived later in the day, 6 August, receiving updates advising that guns had been found and arrests made. But no kingpins had yet been nabbed and those captured weapons stashes were believed to the tip of the iceberg.

I was holding out of earshot of the enemy to the west as a company from 3 Para moved towards two large compounds just before dawn. They would reach the first in about twenty minutes and the second some ten minutes after that. Leakers, especially at the further compound, were anticipated as news of the Paras' arrival spread.

Nowhere 51 cleared us into the overhead of the compounds

when the troops were 300 metres out. As Rousy positioned us to the south of the first, I slaved the TADS in the hope of spotting any runners. It made sense that they would run to the south, aiming for the cover of trees and other buildings. Running in any other direction would put them in open desert.

As the chopping of Ugly 50 was heard in the buildings below, doors opened, people came out to look up, began dashing from place to place. A human chain seemed to form close to a small building. Seven or so people, possibly a single family, were moving goods towards a larger building. It appeared that the goods were being brought up from a hole in the ground, a possible hide, that was appearing as a hotspot on the TADS. We couldn't tell what they were shifting. Within about three minutes, the people and their cargo had disappeared into the bigger building.

No enemy had yet been encountered on the ground. Several men were seen leaving in a group earlier before splitting up and scattering. With improving light, I advised that a search of the suspected hideout area might be in order. Nowhere 51 agreed, sending troops forward, asking me to direct them in from above. As the ground commander got close, I said, 'Two metres to your left and there it is.'

'Roger,' he said, 'but there's nothing here.'

'Are you positive? That's where I saw this happen.'

'Positive,' he said. 'No hideout. It's all solid ground, just gravel and dust.'

'Roger,' I said. 'Let me review the gun tape. Stand by.'

'Roger.'

The review caused me to rethink. They were bang on the right area, but no hole in the ground. It struck me that the goods, whatever they were, may have been under a blanket of some kind, that the warm stash itself had shown up as a hotspot.

I advised, asked if there was anything to suggest something had been recently moved. The ground commander looked over the area again before confirming colour contrasts on the ground. Something had been there for sure.

'Roger,' he said, 'carrying out a full sweep of buildings. We'll be bringing in the sniffer dogs soon. If there is anything, we'll find it.'

With no activity after that, we were cleared to head off to refuel. I was feeling shit after wrongly identifying a hide, cursing myself for no good reason. I had to look ahead, to make a better fist of the rest of the day.

We filled the tank at Bastion and headed for FOB Ink, north of Sangin, to watch over a foot patrol. Widow 70 advised everything was delayed there and all was quiet too. In the meantime, we moved on to FOB Gibraltar, where Widow 53 had intel about enemy activity near his mobile patrol south-east of the Green Zone. The patrol's intention was to search isolated buildings alongside the Helmand Canal that paralleled the Green Zone. But the Taliban were onto them fast.

Widow 53 briefed of suspicious activity around one building within a compound. I slaved the TADS onto a long east-to-west structure. In its large courtyard was a lone male and a motorbike. Rousy spotted movement near by. I slaved the TADS, saw a guy running for the tree line, a second man moving into the shadows. Widow 53 advised of an interception on Taliban comms: 'We are now in place and ready.'

The transmission, we were advised, came from the compound I'd just been observing. I looked over it again. No one around. But I was sure that the dense tree line was packed with Taliban. Seconds later, a woman and a child walked into the courtyard. This added a new and difficult dynamic. The Taliban knew we would hold fire. And if we didn't, they didn't care. Injuries or deaths of women or children made for great propaganda.

A further intercepted message relayed by Widow 53: 'Get the big gun and we will attack.'

That attack was likely to be aimed at the foot patrol. Yet it had gone static, taken hard cover. The chances of the insurgents engaging with an Apache overhead were limited. Yet clearly something was about to happen. We were sure the enemy was locked and loaded. We needed to encourage them to get on with it.

We were cleared to leave, to fly five miles and return in the hope that our absence induced movement. Five miles took us beyond JTAC radio range but I was still just about able to keep sights on the compound. On our return, we heard of fresh intercepted messages referencing that the enemy had eyes on the patrol.

Bullishly, Widow 53 chose to make the next move. The troops began a cautious move towards base, as planned, with the assurance that we would keep close watch.

A lone man in black now, walking by the wall within the compound of interest. I zoomed in. He was staying close to walls, electing to stay in shadow when he could, even ducking down on occasion as he went. Outside the compound, other people were walking, occasional civilians going about their business. Another complicated picture in this complicated war.

The man was outside the compound now, heading towards the canal some 200 metres away, still keeping low. He didn't know he was being watched. FF were on the other side of the water, on the move once more. The man went quickly towards them, striding through long grass, crouching down and stopping as he came to a small wall. He pulled a radio from inside his clothing, sun glinting off its long antenna. I asked Widow 53 if they were getting a further interception.

'Ugly 50, Widow 53. Yes. We have a communication saying "Patrol is now moving, bring up the big guns and get ready to fire."'

'Roger. I think we have spotted your dicker.'

We agreed we would need to check the timing of another interception to confirm. I watched as our man got back up and returned to the compound. He met a man in the courtyard, pointed towards the troops. He left again, dashed back out, ducked as he made his way to the little wall again and peeped over. Rousy had smartly brought us to the north side, giving a better position to see him from the front. He lifted the radio and began to speak.

'Widow 53, Ugly 50. He just made a call on his radio. Did you intercept?'

'Yes, just now. He's saying the patrol is moving further away and they should attack now.'

'Roger. Request clearance to fire under Card A.'

'Roger. Will confirm with ground commander. Stand by.'

Firing under Card A meant acting on imminent threat to life. I had no doubt this guy, although seemingly armed with only a radio, was Taliban, no doubt that he was controlling the ambush. And we had him right in the open with no other people around.

'Ugly 50, Widow 53. You are clear to engage.'

'Roger. Stand by.'

Gun actioned. Ten rounds selected. But the dicker was heading fast back towards the compound. And then he vanished in the blink of an eye. It took me a moment to work it out. He had jumped into a culvert.

'Jammy bastard.'

'Yep,' said Rousy, feeling the same annoyance.

The top of the man's head just visible now as he moved towards the building, only this time by a different route. He popped up in full view by the entrance, went in, met the same man, pointed once more and, seconds later, ran into the trees.

'Ugly 50, Widow 53. Just received further that Taliban will engage as soon as reinforcements arrive from the north-west, estimating within a few minutes.'

'Roger. We have lost the dicker. Just waiting for him to move into a clear area then will engage. He has maybe moved into the wood line to meet with reinforcements. We are at present unable to see the ambush but will engage the dicker which may be enough to disperse the attackers.'

He reappeared from the woods, heading for one of the open fields 50 metres from the compound. As sights settled on him, he crouched to send a radio report. Now or never.

Kickback in the Apache as the rounds rocketed towards him. Five seconds to impact from this distance. And in one of those seconds, he stood. In another, he walked off fast, further into the field. If ever a man had a sixth sense, he did. He froze as bullets drilled holes right behind him. He turned, worked it out, ran. I followed with a burst of twenty. Something fell from his hand as he disappeared into a north-south line of trees.

'Ugly 50, Widow 53. We have an intercept saying "They are shooting at me, will run towards reinforcements."'

Good news. He had led me to the ambush team.

'Roger.'

I put the sights on the trees, right where he had vanished. I pressed the trigger, the aircraft jolting again and again as I drew a long north-south line with that M230 chain gun, shredding wood all the way to a junction.

'Ugly 50. Widow 53. The dicker is saying "The rounds are getting closer and they are nearly getting us all."'

More good news.

'Roger.'

I scanned for movement. Some of the wood line was thin, even thinner now than it was a minute ago. I hoped I'd be able to spot something. But the enemy was likely in the denser sections. Crosshairs now on some of the heavier greenery. The underfoot tremors as the gun growled again, stitching a line of deadly fire into the woods. Twenty, thirty rounds.

'Widow 74, Ugly 50. Any word?'

'Negative Ugly 50. Just static.'

'Roger. Will continue to look into the wood line and compound as you move towards the FOB.'

'Roger. We'll be there in around ten minutes.'

No more movement, no more radio calls came. The patrol made it home without incident. A later look at the video tape showed that the dicker had dropped a handgun when I fired at him. No attack had taken place on the building, but its location went up the intel chain.

Back at Bastion an hour later, as we were about to climb out after refuelling, a groundie approached to say that a TIC was ongoing, and we needed to contact the ops room right away. We got back in.

The area was Marjah, fifteen minutes out. I'd been there twice before, fired many rounds. Right now, Silicon Zero A, a joint UK and ANP patrol on search duties, was coming under mortar and small-arms fire. All firing ceased as we arrived overhead. I got eyes on FF including the long line of ANA soldiers moving along one of two parallel roads to form up ahead of a planned push south. These parallel roads were a bloody nuisance for us, the ground between often a mass of ditches, trees and buildings, with civilians here and there. And now we had static friendlies.

I swept the area for over ten minutes, yet knew I would not be able to say I was certain that all was clear. It was hoped that just having a Mosquito overhead would be enough to deter the insurgents for now. I was close to passing that thought on when I spotted four men walking at speed away from the area of FF. Zooming in, I could see they were not armed but there was something about their demeanour. They crossed into a field towards a large crossroads about 1 kilometre south of FF and disappeared into the tree line at a road junction. Now Rousy spotted three more individuals moving towards the same junction from another direction. Soon after, all seven met up and walked further to meet another ten or so individuals. They were coming from everywhere. But would active enemy fighters meet so publicly like that? I'd never seen a Taliban group of that size in Afghanistan before, if they were Taliban. And still no visible weapons.

As Rousy reported our findings, the group split in two. The

original seven moved further south along the road and the rest moved east, almost paralleling the FF. Both groups were attempting to move stealthily now, making use of walls and ditches for cover where they could. Their behaviour had switched. Alarm bells rang louder in my mind. I opted to follow the bigger group. I was sure that all had been unarmed but I hadn't taken a good look at that group of ten. They reached another wood line and split further into two. So now I was having to decide which one of that lot to track. I went with the group closest to FF, about 800 metres from them.

The FF advance was slow. The ANP were stopping every man and his dog they met, seemingly searching every culvert, building and behind every tree. The search couldn't be faulted for its thoroughness, but concerns were mounting that the pedestrian pace of this was ramping up the danger and giving the enemy time to set up an ambush or lay RCIEDs.

The five I was following moved into an open area between wood lines. That's when I saw weapons for the first time.

'They're armed,' I called out to Rousy.

One at the back had an RPG just visible under a cloth over his shoulder. One alongside him was cradling an AK. They had become overconfident while unaware they were being watched. But something told me there was still a chance these guys were maverick ANP.

'Silicon Zero A, Ugly 50. We have several armed men visual about 700 metres to your south. Confirm you have no ANP patrols in that area? Also confirm are all ANP in uniform?'

Silicon Zero A knew of no patrols in the area and confirmed all patrolling ANP were uniformed. Yet he too could not be certain whether or not a rogue patrol was somewhere out there. I said I'd fire warning shots to try to clear this up.

Rousy repositioned. I slaved the sights to the thin wood line, to where the suspected EF were now walking. Ten rounds rammed into soil. Immediately the three others pulled out weapons. All ran for the trees. It seemed none of them knew the shooting came from the air. They were likely now keen to begin taking on ANP they knew were in the area, Taliban believing their own police were a soft touch. Because by now Rousy and I had become confident these guys were enemy. I fired again along the line of advance. They were running right into the line of fire. The guy in the middle of the group, wearing a backpack, was lifted from his feet and flung a distance into the field. He basically exploded, his backpack, loaded with RPG rockets, having been hit by one of the rounds.

Some 100 metres away, where the wood line ended before the road, Rousy spotted a large minivan braking hard. Two men dived out and into long grass. We figured they could be civilians seeking cover after spotting the attack.

Back at the wood line, four were dashing back the way they had come. I swung the weapon to the far side of them. One individual dived into the trees, turned, aimed at us with his AK and opened fire. I answered with twenty rounds, pummelling him into the ditch then blowing the others away. As the foggy cloud of dust and smoke faded, we could see no sign of movement at all from any of them. Start to finish, the action had taken three minutes.

Silicon Zero A reconfirmed no FF presence near by. We were told that ANP were now standing on vehicles to watch the Apache engage the enemy at the wood line. They were, of course, sitting ducks for any Taliban sniper, but 200 relatively undisciplined men aren't easy to control.

Another scan of the wood line, looking towards the road, and just the two men in the long grass, the guys who had leapt from the van.

'Silicon Zero A, Ugly 50. Two men moving towards the scene of the explosion,' I said. 'Might be trying to recover weapons.'

I'd seen the same pattern before, men taking huge risks to charge in and secure guns. Weapons were truly precious to the Taliban. These two were crawling through the long grass. They reached the bodies and we saw them collect the RPG and AK. I was sure these weapons would get turned on us sooner or later if we didn't end this now. The big gun burst to life once more, rounds blanketing the ground. And that was the end of that.

We had been up since 3 a.m. It was now 4.30 p.m. My longest, busiest day in Afghanistan, with just over 500 rounds fired. And it was also the final sortie Rousy and I would fly together. He was heading back to the UK in two days. And within just a few short weeks, I was gone too, my final duties completed. In three tours of Afghanistan, I had personally fired 18 Hellfire missiles, 273 rockets and 10,132 rounds of 30mm.

I could not wait to get home once more to the partner I loved. In November, Tracey and I married in a simple, lovely service at a register office in Nuneaton, Warwickshire.

Chapter Twenty-Six

TRAINING A PRINCE. HAMPSHIRE, 2010

A LAD NAMED Harry Wales wanted to fly Apaches. That couldn't be right, could it? Yet I had every reason to believe it was right because, by chance, I heard it from the horse's mouth.

There had already been a whole lot of noise about this dashing young Blues and Royals officer since he joined the army. His regiment had been called up to serve in Iraq in 2007 and, when the British media found out, a massive debate had ensued. Should Harry really risk his life on the front line? Wouldn't he be a high-value target for insurgents? Would that mean he and those around him would draw more fire and face increased danger?

From a soldier's point of view, we were talking here about a Sandhurst-trained professional who, if his granny had been anyone else, would have been off to Baghdad without anyone batting an eyelid. At the end of the day, his career choices were no one's business but those of the then Second Lieutenant Wales and the British Army.

But neither you nor I are naive. Young Harry was, at this time, pure gold in terms of the tabloids. He was the single biggest royal talking point in the world, one of the biggest celebrities alive. And, with no offence to stately-looking Prince William, the charismatic, fiery-haired, fun-time Harry was the only high-end blue blood whose antics (including frequent run-ins with the paparazzi) had the attention of a nation.

In February 2007, after no doubt taking the thoughts of a few million self-appointed experts into consideration, the Ministry of Defence confirmed the prince was off to war. The then head of the British Army, General Sir Richard Dannatt, signed off on it. Harry would deploy, it was reported, in May or June with his regiment as part of the 1st Mechanised Brigade. His duties would involve patrolling the Maysan Governorate, a formerly hardline Islamist region in the south, bordering Iran. Young Wales was quoted at the time as being raring to go, saying, 'There's no way I'm going to put myself through Sandhurst and then sit on my arse back home while my boys are out fighting for their country.' So, more debate ensued while, presumably, Iraqi insurgents were taking copious notes and passing Harry's picture around.

Then, in May, General Sir Richard Dannatt updated on the deployment. Like a twist in a soap opera, millions gasped when he said there had been a change of plan. All that HVT stuff had been chewed over and it was decided Second Lieutenant Wales (the rank is also known as a cornet in the Blues and Royals) would wait out the war at home. Clarence House, the then home address for Harry and his immediate family, said the lad was disappointed but would duly abide by the decision.

And that, it turns out, was all a bit of a bluff. The next twist came in June when it was leaked that Harry was deep in training alongside Canadian military near Medicine Hat. The army said this was in preparation for a tour of duty in Afghanistan where the second phase of the NATO-led conflict was ending. So, was that right? Or was he actually going to Iraq instead? Very few people knew for sure. But something was happening.

In February 2008, one year after that initial announcement about Harry heading off to Iraq, it was confirmed he had in fact been to Afghanistan. German newspaper *Bild* broke the story (and broke a media blackout too). It said Harry had completed a ten-week stint as a forward air controller in Helmand, and the MoD, having by that stage got him safely home, confessed it was true. The UK's most eligible bachelor had called in airstrikes and helped Gurkhas repel a Taliban assault as part of his front-line duties. The tabloids couldn't get enough of it. His posting to a war zone had been the first for a member of the Royal Family since 1982. Back then it was Prince Andrew getting shot at while flying helicopters in the Falklands (after which, unexpectedly, he never sweated again).

So, considering all that, it seemed pretty clear that if Harry Wales was now to apply to fly hunter-killer Apaches, the press would have a field day. Given it was no secret what the aircraft had been doing in Afghanistan, would the MoD even allow his application? Would it want all that attention on his movements around something so secret yet so crucial to the war? And why on earth would he want to put himself through the wringer in that way? I didn't have all the answers and didn't especially care, but on that last point I had an understanding.

Let me put it like this.

Harry would already have known that of those who apply for Apache training, most got nowhere near one. He would already have had some sense that of those who do get over that first hurdle, the intensity of the course sorts out the wheat from the chaff sharpish. And he must have considered that, if successful, the subsequent duty was no picnic. It's no exaggeration to say the impact of what might lie ahead can take its toll. He'd have surely known that fighting an Apache is a colossal responsibility in terms of protecting and defending your comrades, and that everything you do could get examined at any point in the future at the press of a button. Those high-intensity decisions can strip a layer or two from a person – and add a few new ones. Those of us who have gone ugly, who have fought, killed, saved, won and lost on those things don't forget a second of it.

Lieutenant Wales, promoted from second lieutenant after his 2008 Helmand tour, must already have had all that in his mind and decided it was still right for him. So, it seemed to me that this young man's time in theatre had stoked up something formidable inside. It could well be that, regardless of being born with blue blood in the veins and silver spoon in the mouth, the guy was the Real McCoy in terms of soldier material. The British Army's highest-value human target seeking to pilot the British Army's highest-value technological target? It certainly looked like Harry Wales had balls. Maybe this young man was another one searching for a place to leave normal behind, somewhere to push the limits, to seize control of the elements and go higher, faster, further, harder. Maybe he too was a dreamer who knew dreaming just wasn't enough. I was getting close to finding out.

After leaving Afghanistan in 2008, and after fifteen years of flying, I'd felt it was time to gather up what I needed to apply to become an army flying instructor. The QHI course placed me in RAF Shawbury, Shropshire, with the follow-on of the competent to instruct (C2I) course moving me back to Middle Wallop, Hampshire. It was there, in the October of 2009, that my sister called with news of our mother. She was terminally ill. It all happened very suddenly. Just two weeks before, she had been taken into hospital for a routine leg operation but X-rays had found shadows on her lungs. My sister and I, along with my brother who lived in the USA, rallied around while Macmillan nurses and loved ones, including Tracey, spent many days at her bedside. At first, I'd opted to stay on the C2I course, to visit her often but she was growing weaker with each visit. It became impossible just to switch off from loving my mother and revert to loving flying. I asked to be removed from the course for the foreseeable future. Testimony to the fact that I wasn't in a good place was being pulled over by police while doing 95 mph on the way to see her in hospital, knowing she was close to the end. Under the circumstances, the cop kindly let me off with a warning. By the time I arrived at my sister's house on the way, Mum had died.

It all left me distressed and empty, as if I'd played it all wrong and let her down, let myself down too. In some kind of response to that, I put on my running shoes and entered the Great North Half Marathon, running on behalf of Cancer Research UK. I'd never done such a thing before yet ended up doing the following three in a row. Anyway, three weeks after my mother passed away, I was back at AAC HQ in Hampshire and, although deeply melancholy, finished up C2I.

My new role, now as 673 Squadron Sergeant Major, would be to teach part of the CTT course for the Apache to new students, to handle some of the admin, to manage discipline where needed. My aim was to achieve the hours to allow me to complete an instructor upgrade. After that, at some point down the line, I'd look at going back to a squadron to become their QHI. That was the plan anyway.

I was already aware that Harry was training at Middle Wallop, although it wasn't widely known. Talking about his presence was subtly discouraged. I'd become aware he was there after spotting him. In fact, I'd seen him several times the year before, too, when our time overlapped at RAF Shawbury. He'd been taking the tri-service rotary course at the Defence Helicopter Flying School at the same time I was attending my QHI course. If I'm honest, it had all become a bit awkward.

The first time I saw him at Shawbury was when he was filling up his car at a local garage near the base. I saw him, recognised him, nodded, said something like 'Enjoy your weekend' and he nodded back. Standard enough sort of over-the-pumps thing. I've no idea if he knew I was military or not.

I remember feeling a little uneasy when I pulled into the same petrol station a couple of weeks later. I had started filling up before I realised he was there again and doing the same. And, once again, he was just across from me. Again. Another little nod and that was it. Still no idea if he knew who I was.

And then, about three weeks later, the same bloody thing. I pulled into the same filling station and there he was at the pump. Jesus Christ. This was starting to get embarrassing. On that occasion I looked over and gave the now familiar nod. And short of saying, 'Look, mate, honestly, I'm not a stalker, I'm just going to drive away now,' I instead joked, 'We'll have to stop meeting like this.' He smiled, nodded, paid his bill and went on his way. Harry Wales might genuinely have thought at that point that I was actually a stalker. Same time? Same place? Three times? I couldn't blame him if he was getting suspicious. The most worrying bit was that, naturally enough, he was being shadowed by an armoured black Range Rover, his no-nonsense protection team forever close by. I'm pretty sure my face and number got logged on MI5's nutcase files. It was time to find another petrol station after all that.

Anyway, back to Middle Wallop in 2010. I knew he was on the base but, as with most of the military, had no interest in him. He was there to learn, to develop his skills, to do a job just like the rest of us. I'm a patriot and have huge respect for the Royal Family, but in the camp, it doesn't matter what kind of position you or your people hold on the outside. Army life is the best leveller there is for people from all sorts of places with all kinds of backgrounds. And that's the right way of things. It teaches you the value of the team.

During the warm August of that year, I was planning one of the many training sorties in one of the briefing rooms. The windows were open. I could hear chit-chat coming and going as people passed by outside. One speaker lingered for a while right by the window. And the voice was unmistakable. Harry had not chosen his location wisely when it came to having a significant phone call.

A few words in and it was clear he was talking to his dad. He asked him if he thought he should try to get a place on the Apache course, because that's what he was thinking about doing. I don't know what happened from there because I stepped away, echoes of those petrol pump meetings on my mind. I mean, this accidental stalking sideline of mine had to end. I kept that exchange to myself, but I knew then there was a fair chance he might apply for CTT.

Whatever was said, whatever advice was offered that day, the then twenty-five-year-old had a big decision to make. As I've explained, selection itself is no mean feat. This would not be a sideways move for him, but a vertical one in every way. Everything any soldier had already achieved in uniform, and everything he'd screwed up, gets raked through not just by senior instructors but also by those further up the food chain. Every known detail about attitude gets explored, and any unknowns will not stay that way for long. Important to remember that everyone coming forward with Apache dreams is someone who wants to get their hands on a £35-million state-of-the-art war machine. If there's a question hanging over you about your motivation, some suspicious gap in your background, then forget it.

A few weeks later and all became clear. It seemed Harry did get his dad's blessing. We were advised that the young prince had applied, got the green light and was all signed up for the new CTT intake.

What did I know about him? Not much. His military record seemed solid, he was apparently a capable helicopter pilot and his family were quite well known. And, apart from what kind of car he drove and the kind of mileage he was doing, not much else. I had, however, met both his parents in years gone by. Prince Charles, as Colonel-in-Chief of both the AAC and the Paras, had also visited my dad's barracks when I was six or seven. The most memorable thing about it was that Diana came with him, complete with her warm smile and big bright blonde hair. I'd never known as much fuss over one person before and remember feeling a little shy about the whole event at the time.

She had leaned down to say hello to me and asked, 'What's your name?'

Overwhelmed, I can't recall saying anything in reply. I hope I at least mumbled 'Steve' but it's possible I stood there gawping.

Twenty years later, and, as already mentioned, I was briefing and then flying Prince Charles around Brunei in a Bell 212. He was being wined and dined at the Sultan's pretty bloody breathtaking palace on the banks of the Brunei River. I was tasked with taking him for a look at the property and its 300 acres of gardens from above. To be honest, it made Buckingham Palace look like a cottage, although I didn't say so. Before we did that flight, I had landed us in a densely forested area being used by the SAS during ATAP Hurdle, the jungle training phase of their selection course. HRH was briefed on warfare courses taught there and I was tasked with briefing him on all the safety features of the 212.

So, from there I took HRH to the Brunei capital, Bandar Seria Begawan, for the overflight of what's reasonably said to be the world's most spectacular palace. I'd been advised at the time to take care because word was that the joint was equipped with its own air defences in the form of Rapier missiles. Pretty alarming, really. I asked around for confirmation, but no one could tell me much more than that. So, basically, I flew nicely, didn't get too close and didn't tell the Prince of Wales.

While I was doing the aircraft safety brief before take-off, I had to tell Mr Windsor to roll his sleeves down. It was just a simple, standard aircraft precaution in case of fire. Experience has advised that flames, although unlikely to appear, don't mix well with exposed skin. I asked him politely and he did as he was told. By the way, both crew were presented with a leather wallet on behalf of the Sultan that day. I still have mine. A nice keepsake.

So now I was one of only four Apache instructors, under a

senior instructor, who would be imparting our wisdom to the then third in line to the throne. I would be co-leading daily meetings attended by him and the other students, helping to oversee pretty much everything the trainees got up to and, of course, teaching the course. From the outset, as instructors, we made sure we were all crystal clear about the situation. Absolutely everything to do with Harry and his performance on our course would be top secret. The everyday media interest in him, already immense, would intensify with his move towards the sharpest, most fearsome mechanised end of the military. We knew that, sooner or later, either officially or otherwise, the story would get out. We pledged that not one word of the story would come from us. It didn't take a genius to know that any titbit, any image of him, any rumours coming from the camp could literally be front-page news in the UK and beyond. And a pretty penny could be made by any enterprising snitch willing to feed that ever-hungry media. From that day onward we considered it part of our job to ensure nothing whatsoever leaked on our watch. And we made it known to everyone taking the course, to anyone who had any insight into our work, that there would be hell to pay if it did.

The heart of the course involves flying regular sorties to create habit from good practice. All that repetition and adaptation enhances the airman mindset and progressively pushes students to the edge of their limits. When each sortie is complete, they get a verbal debrief backup with a colour grade on each sortie report. At the lowest end the grade is Red, signalling Fail. Then it's Brown, for Below Average. After that, Green, which is bang on Average. From there it's the good stuff, the Blues. Light Blue translates as High Average, and Dark Blue signals Above Average. Even the leak of one or two of those recorded scores could get the press juiced up. So those and any associated commentary, we agreed, would be stored in a secure filing system. Access would be strictly on a need-to-know basis. At the outset, I didn't need to know. Harry was teamed up with a colleague for day flying and I would be taking over after the mid-stage test. And so off we went with teaching CTT.

As a student, Harry was quiet at first, cautious and measured as he settled into the new regime and got to know the new faces. And, of course, that's typically the case for trainees trying to find their feet. But then things changed. Within a couple of weeks Lieutenant Wales began rapidly coming out of his shell and showed no sign of going back in. He had by then clicked well with his fellow students and a few of them really started to enjoy themselves in the mess bar. Perfectly natural, of course. But he was going at it hard, perhaps harder than the others. He was a fan of the redoubtable yard of ale, very willing to get one down his neck when the glass was produced. Most of the rest of us, and certainly myself, didn't exactly jump at the chance to slam two and half pints into our systems in as short a time as possible. But on the few occasions I witnessed it, Lieutenant Wales was typically first in line. Fun-time Harry indeed . . . but given the guy was just in the door, it gave us instructors something to think about. In fact, taking all the boozing into account, the amateur shrinks among us had a sense that this young man, unlike his colleagues, was showing all the signs of carrying an extra burden. Or was it just that we all knew so much about the tragic manner of his mother's death that we felt we had some insight into the man he was? I'm not sure. One thing I did consider though was that Harry could be facing an issue that no other student would face. It seemed to me that if he did not bring what he was doing to a successful conclusion it could be blasted all over the media. And not in a good way.

Back in 1987, Prince Edward, Harry's uncle, pulled out of the Royal Marines. Edward had put in four months' commando training after graduating from Cambridge but withdrew. Basically, the Queen's youngest son, then twenty-two, couldn't hack it. And he got absolutely slaughtered in the press. It was truly brutal. He wasn't 'tough enough', it was reported. *The Sun* said the prince had 'cried for three hours' after making up his mind. It said Prince Philip had 'shouted at Edward and told him to pull himself together to spare the Royal Family embarrassment'. It said the Queen and Duke of Edinburgh had pleaded with him to at least finish the twelve months of training but that he could not face it. It must have been shit for him, especially since older brothers Charles and Andrew had both served. Edward's decision, the press gravely reported, had broken a century-old tradition of princes serving tours of duty. Her Majesty was reported as being 'deeply upset'.

Harry knew, like we all did, there could be trouble ahead. The situation wasn't so bad because he had already served, yet his profile was so pervasive that failure on his part – either by withdrawing or by not passing – would not be something he could just forget about. It's hard to imagine that, having made the Apache decision, he was so much as allowing himself to consider failure an option. So, who could blame him for knocking back a few from time to time? It wasn't as though he was often able to really let his hair down outside the base.

But we would still need to keep an eye on the partying. No one wanted rumours about the prince getting out. And, worse, no one within a very large radius wants to hear rumours of someone having a drink the night before they pilot an Apache. For the record, that didn't happen, and I will add that it never would in the Army Air Corps. Anyway, enough. What happens in the mess stays in the mess.

Eighteen months of graft lay ahead. The first part involved learning how to operate the aircraft in a day environment. Each day starts with a briefing from the duty instructor and is typically followed with hands-on training in sims and the aircraft. Things were a little different by 2010 from how they had been when I learned the ropes, mainly because, thankfully, some of those burdening the world with their massive egos had moved on. By this stage there was more room for camaraderie between the students and the process was perhaps more enjoyable and productive than it had been. This was a good time to learn to fly an Apache.

I'd often sit at the back of the room making observations and taking notes about the students as the day briefings went ahead. It wasn't long before I was noting that Harry Wales, as well as being front and centre in the mess, was also trying to mould himself into something close to the class joker. To be blunt about it, he tried a little too hard at times to get a laugh from everyone around him. He'd answer questions in a way that might seem immature, even though he knew better and could do better. To be fair, he was funny now and again, a bit off-the-wall and certainly spirited. He'd sometimes cause a few laughs and earn himself some instant witty feedback which he seemed to relish. No prizes for guessing that most of it was about his ginger hair. He genuinely took it all on the chin, which was good.

Yet this business of ours was a serious one. It wasn't healthy for a new recruit to carry on like that in a learning environment where rank is vital and respect must be constant. Even if some of his jokes raised a smile, the behaviour itself did not. We were teaching control, mindset, grace under pressure. We're looking to find and develop something close to an indestructible situational awareness that would make our students worthy to pilot something truly exceptional. Harry needed to have a think to himself, work it all out and calm the fuck down.

After the mid-course test, and with fourteen sorties under their belts, the students were allocated new instructors to take them through the next phase – night flying. I was taking Harry for this, assigned to get him through one of the toughest parts of the job. All being well, after that he would go ahead for the final handling test in April 2011. Without passing that, there was no next stage and there would be no Apache for the prince.

I felt a little nervous about what lay ahead. I didn't want this guy, of all trainees, to fail while under my instruction. It would reflect not just badly on me, but badly on him and perhaps even on the Army Air Corps itself. The whole bloody world would know about it. Yet while my head was annoyingly coming up with things to worry about, I couldn't wait to get started.

The trainees would dip their toes in the night-flying waters in daylight, via the cockpit blackout system (CBS), aka the Bag. As discussed earlier, it strips away all daytime reference points and forces the pilot to rely on instruments, chiefly the FLIR. It uses heat signals to create a picture of the world outside and differs from night-vision goggles in that it builds the image using ambient light. People get disorientated and claustrophobic, including myself. I did not like the Bag phase one little bit. I can honestly say that if you'd advised me I could skip any single Bag Phase sortie on condition that I slammed my nuts repeatedly in a sock drawer, I'd have taken the drawer. Every time.

The plan for each sortie is mapped out in advance, shared with the trainee and uploaded to the aircraft. That means, as I told each student, they needed to swot up ahead of time. They needed to know what sort of thing to expect. In a chat with them all, I said they should arrive well prepared for the briefing or not bother arriving at all.

'So, Harry,' I said in a one-to-one, just as I was outlining what was expected of him. 'Do you remember me? We met before a couple of times?'

He looked at me, shook his head. 'No,' he said. 'Sorry. Where was that?'

'Forget it,' I said.

He looked at me. I had to tell him after saying that.

'It was at the filling station near RAF Shawbury,' I said. 'I think I said hello to you there a few times.'

'Oh,' he said, and a smile formed, then a little nod.

'Yeah,' I said. Wish I'd never mentioned it.

It takes, they say, something like £3 million to train and place a pilot in an Apache to the point that they're combat ready. The equipment in each helicopter is tailored to suit each user. Chief among this is that heavy helmet, with a unit price tag of at least £30k. The sensor systems it holds allow for the pilot to read the outside world and, in turn, for this heavy headgear to read the pilot's responses and react accordingly. It's a strangely close relationship where man and machine feed off each other to help ensure both have the best chance of handling whatever the mission requires.

Within the aircraft we have the pilot night-vision system which uses infrared heat energy to create a sharp, richly green image of the territory. And there's the FLIR image, which is beamed back onto the helmet-mounted display and viewed through the monocle by the right eye. The left eye sees the night view and part of the training involves getting used to something that, at first, the brain is not at all happy with. It depends on the settings, but as well as the world in green, the monocle typically displays speed, velocity vector, height, attitude and power reading. It all ensures that the amount of time a pilot needs to spend looking at instruments is slashed to the minimum.

Yet more overlaid data – ranges, weapons information, selected sight, cueing dots, direction detail – is scattered around the edges of the MPDs front and centre of the cockpit. Learning to get comfortable with all of that takes time and patience. At first, it's information overload. Yet sortie by sortie, day by day, night by night, it falls into place.

But first the Bag. Harry was eager to put the work in from the start and, given the tales that had leaked from the mess, that was a good sign. Overall, first impressions chimed with what I'd read in the reports. His handling skills were, most of the time, pretty good. Yet, observing from my daylight cockpit, I was soon finding he was at times too slow to manipulate emerging information from the ground, too slow to input and amend data where necessary. I told him so, said after that first Bag sortie that he was some distance from getting himself a Dark Blue grade and that I'd be ramping up the focus around his responding to data. He agreed with me that this was where a weakness lay.

Ahead of the next exercise, I pressed home the point. I said the Apache needs to work hand in glove with forces below and very often at critical times, to prowl around, to hunt and destroy armoured vehicles, to defend, save and take lives. Without swift transfer and response to emerging details, the edge is lost. And losing that edge can mean losing a great deal more. My pep talk freshly delivered, Harry disappeared again into the darkness and we headed skywards once more. An hour later and we were back, two out of three completed. It was, I told him, nothing special. He could, I told him, do better.

'Third time lucky,' I said.

Off we went on that final Bag sortie, some real determination obvious in my student's demeanour. I told him I wanted to see something a little special, to know that he was progressing and not just plodding along. Unfortunately, once again, it didn't go so well. That third sortie was, I decided, moderately poor. In fact, there had been three average sorties, with a Brown, or moderately poor, as his last one. He still wasn't responding well enough or fast enough to circumstances. There was too much weight on the FLIR image, not enough on the symbology. Among the nitty-gritty of it all, he needed to understand that at times it can be better to come up with a Plan B instead of pushing a bad situation too far. There was no sign of that kind of thinking going on and I was, I'll admit, a little concerned.

We spoke again. I said an Apache night pilot needs to strike an even balance between FLIR and symbology because they complement each other. I said that with application he could get himself some consistent Greens, that there were even a potential above average Light Blue coming his way. But there was no Dark Blue in sight.

But it didn't matter so much, at least not as much as I made out that it did. This was only the beginning. He was three sorties in. There was plenty of time to do better and I had a feeling he was good enough and ambitious enough to get there. I suppose I just wanted him to think about it all the time, to really refine what it was he needed to fix. I wanted him to think about it before and after he was strapped in, to think about it at the weekends, to think about it when he was dining with the Queen, when he was partying, driving, exercising. The big goal was to fly the Apache, but I needed him to keep thinking about the details that would get him there. Three months of real night flying lay ahead. I didn't let the doubts win. First, he would have to pass the Bag check, which would be completed with another instructor.

As part of the first night sortie, Lieutenant Wales had to lead the pre-flight briefing. This meant he needed to take the room and run through the mission ahead. He would need to identify, depending on the scenario, what problems might crop up. And, happily enough, he arrived rested and relaxed, seemed prepared and confident. He ran through a recap of the meteorology, aircraft details, air traffic information, a few bits and pieces of general admin and then a broad sortie profile. It was the sort of thing I'd expected, the sort of detail I'd briefed on, and been briefed on, dozens of times. I remember thinking that I really needed to tune in on exactly what he was saying by way of preparing myself for what I might have to do in the couple of hours ahead, just in terms of compensating for errors on his part. Yet I also remember zoning out and missing a good deal of what he was on about. My mind had started to wander into the facts of this unusual situation and away from the matter at hand. It wasn't like me. Yet I couldn't help thinking that here was this royal now seeking endorsement from me. I suppose it felt a bit like a sort of reality TV where a major celebrity shows up to be taught how to fight battles. I don't think my mind had ever wandered like that before.

'Do you have any questions?' he asked.

'Ah, no,' I said, hoping he had not just been standing there talking gibberish. 'Thanks, Harry. That all seems fine.'

I took over, picked up on some aspects of the sortie details I'd drawn up earlier. From there I fired a few questions at him about circuit heights, speeds and other parameters to make sure his brain was in the right gear (and mine too). After that, we made our way out into the night and across to the dispersal where our helicopter waited. Harry got stuck into his aircraft checks, including weapons checks, and they were nothing less than comprehensive. In fact, that might have been the first time I was actually impressed by his take on some of the lesser-known aspects of the Apache and its hardware.

The first night sortie was a reversionary flight, one in which the pilot uses no night vision other than his own eyes. During which we would move on to the basics of ground taxiing, hovering, circuits and more before the following sortie of running take-off and landings. My plan was, along the way, to introduce him to a few power limitations which would involve my simulating a single engine failure. All the aircraft's parameters need to be not just understood but really ingrained. No pilot should ever bite off more than they can chew. But it didn't happen that way.

Inside the aircraft, during an early standard pre-brief, Harry started to lose his way a little, as if becoming distracted. He missed a few things on the map, failed to fully advise me of what lay ahead at our planned destination, failed to identify all potential obstructions. In a true rookie error, he didn't even zoom in on the map as he was reading from it. He was briefing me from the wrong scale. He could not have seen all he needed to see. Ten minutes ago, he'd been across his brief and all of a sudden, he seemed to have lost his way. This was already going tits up. I was disappointed.

I got to addressing this fast, to telling him that it had all been a bit hit-and-miss so far. And it was then that a meteorological update came in. Things were getting a little bullish in the area, including

331

right over the airfield. The wind was whipping up, the rain was coming in. It was all pretty much out of the blue and, on receiving more specific data, I knew we had to bear it in mind. On the upside, it was an opportunity for a nice little test.

'So, what do you think?' I asked. 'What should we do?'

He checked the details, had a think and said he was pretty sure we were still on track. But, he said, it might be wise not to do the longer-range work we had planned. This was, after all, his first night flight and there were other aircraft around. I was chuffed to hear it. As a direct follow-up to his wobble he had made a sound call. Best of all, he hadn't bottled it when given an opportunity to do so. We made a new plan to stay low and close and use the purpose-built 400-metre HALS . It wasn't ideal but the same principles and techniques we were planning would be in play. And it wasn't being used by anyone else.

We set off on wheels with no issues and got ourselves established on the HALS. That first take-off went well, suggesting some good technique, even suggesting he was a little more relaxed inside the real night than inside the Bag (and I was familiar with that feeling). His first circuits were not great, maybe average at best, but there was nothing to be concerned about at this stage. I checked in to remind him to anticipate wind drift and he responded he would do so. And in terms of the rest of the flight, while everything he was doing could be improved upon, nothing was dodgy to the point that I had to take control.

And then the running landing, or what you might call the tricky bit. To get that right, the pilot needs to meet the correct speed and height gates and have the aircraft configured for landing. Planning is crucial. Timing is crucial. Awareness is crucial. There are, of course, no emergency brakes on this kind of vehicle, or at least nothing as efficient as an emergency stop you might execute in a car. If you're too fast on hitting the runway your only hope in an Apache is aerodynamic braking. That means pulling the rotor disc back via the cyclic to reverse the lift thrust, and using the aircraft brakes all in one go. It slows the Apache but, even when not fully loaded, it is one heavy flying fortress. Stopping like that takes absolute self-assurance that you know what you're doing. It also takes quite a bit longer than you might expect.

On the other hand, if you come in too slow you need more power to arrest the descent when you're near ground to save you and the aircraft from a hard landing. And all that necessary power might not always be available. In fact, that's the very reason why simulated limited-power exercises had been introduced in the first place, to maximise safety to man and machine in the case of drops like that. The exercises had already proved very useful in Afghanistan where aircraft, stuffed to the gills with weapons, had been maxed out in terms of weight. But there was an art to it.

And now a suddenly complicated picture was emerging on this first intense night sortie with Lieutenant Wales. As he turned his attention to landing, he made a small error. I was checking in on what was what when another small error followed. And then another. And then a sort of complex spiral began to appear in which, in order to arrest the previous error, he was not attending to the other errors.

He had not cross-checked his symbology, nor correctly aligned with the centreline. So now he was too low. And worst of all, it occurred to me he was coming in way too fast. As I took it all on board, it seemed clear that this guy was again more focused on the imagery instead of a balance between imagery and symbology. As the Bag had shown, he needed to put more faith in what the aircraft was telling him. But he had left all that too late.

All of a sudden it hit me. I'd somehow let it slip from my mind. We were not heading for the runway landing for which he had trained, instead we were on course for the 400-metre HALS. That wasn't going to be long enough, not with this current approach. My gut told me that without an abrupt change of just about everything, mostly speed, there was going to be a problem. To land this machine he was going to have to hit the very start of the runway. We really were going to need every inch. I tensed, cleared my throat and stayed as calm as I could. I was going to have to hold my nerve here, and hold my tongue too. I told myself to consider there could be some real value in letting this unfold, in waiting to see how long it would be before Harry worked it out, aborted and flew around for another circuit. That was, by this point, pretty much the only remaining option. If he didn't realise, he was in the shit, I'd have to step in fast and fix this. Yet I kept on telling myself to sit tight, to put him in the position where he would have to realise his own error, to admit it and take a decision he didn't want to take.

We closed in, closer and closer. Still too fast, still no sign of him even thinking about a Plan B. I was seconds from calling a 'go around'. But Harry wasn't even considering it. He surely knew by this stage there was going to be a hell of a thump and some high speed on a short runway. I wondered if it was because I wasn't saying anything that he wasn't backing down.

And somehow, without either of us saying a word, that belting Apache passed the point of no return. Lieutenant Wales and I were going to slam down hard onto the airstrip and zoom along too fast for too long. Urgent calculations ran through my brain. The helicopter, I hoped, could handle it. And, I hoped, I and this Harry guy would survive. But this was going to be one badly graded sortie. Time to ride the tiger. I could only hope that the wheels had been bolted on good and tight.

I braced. We hit that HALS as hard as I've ever hit the earth, the pair of us jolted like crash dummies. And off we went pelting towards the end of our minuscule runway. I was still saying nothing. Maybe I didn't know what to say. But I wanted to be sure Harry was giving those brakes everything he'd got. Hard to tell if they're full on when it feels like you're in a land rocket.

But sure enough, I'm glad to say, that big, heavy, shook-up

bird came to a stop just a couple of metres before the wet soil beyond.

Thank Christ.

'Congratulations,' I said, taking a deep breath. 'You have thoroughly tested the undercarriage of the aircraft. Almost to destruction.'

I think I was laughing.

He said nothing in return. He was either still catching his breath or he'd fainted.

'So,' I said, 'what did you think of that?'

Another moment passed.

'Sporty,' he said, gasping, chuckling.

'Sporty? More like being a crash-test dummy in here.'

I never did let him know that I'd slammed on those brakes in my cockpit too. Between the two of us, we saved that Apache from a mud bath.

Chapter Twenty-Seven

'THIRTY MINUTES BEHIND...' HAMPSHIRE/FRANCE, 2011

SEVEN NIGHT SORTIES followed and every running landing was an improvement on the one before. By the time we were finished, Harry had fourteen day sorties, two instrument-only flight trips, those eight night sorties, multiple simulator sorties and five hours in the Bag to his name.

In among it all, there were many calls for him to get back home, to be present at one or other official event, to perform some or other official duty. While he was always in training for the Apache, at the same time he was always a fully qualified royal. I don't know how many times he was called on, how many times he was spirited away for some engagement or other with barely an hour or two to spare. After the third or fourth vanishing act, when Queen and/or country had again demanded his presence, I remember nicknaming him the Ginger Ninja – there one minute, gone the next. Yet despite it all, I know of no one who ever saw, heard or even got the slightest sense that, deep down, Harry didn't want to do his best as both soldier and prince.

As anyone passing a newspaper stand would have known, he was dating a woman called Chelsea Davy at the time. Unsurprisingly, when he did get a chance to break free on his own terms, his minders would swing by, he'd jump in and off he'd go to see her. It was very clear he was not a single man. But without a ring on his finger, he was still considered the most eligible bachelor in England and beyond.

That side of things came into sharp focus on one occasion when, as a group, we all got into civvies and headed off base for a few drinks. There was a quiet pub near Andover, a few miles away, which was friendly in terms of hosting off-duty military. We figured it might be discreet enough for our royal colleague.

The place was close to empty when we arrived. We tucked ourselves discreetly into a corner, ordered a few beers and got on with enjoying ourselves. Over the next hour or so, the bar began to fill. And the new arrivals were almost exclusively young women. Word had got out. It seemed as if the most ambitious singletons of Andover (or maybe not so single) had slipped into something less comfortable and made their way over. There must have been several dozen or more there by the time we were on our third or fourth round. Had Harry been single and seeking company, he could have had the night of his life. But that wasn't how it was. As a result, unexpectedly, the whole situation became nothing less than bloody awkward.

Looks were getting fired our way all the time. Every move Harry made was being watched. Going to the bar or the toilet for any of us, especially him, took on a new element of complication. The girls, in separate groups and at different tables, were drinking and looking and talking and smiling and some of them seemed to be slowly moving our way.

Harry's unspoken take on all this was along the lines of 'Here we go again.' He didn't comment, didn't want to get into it. It was the rest of us who watched it all unfold, who turned to each other to say, 'Have you noticed how this place is now wall-to-wall young women?' (Or words to that effect.)

In the grand scheme of things, of course, this situation was no big deal. No one there wanted anything other than to enjoy themselves. No one there meant to cause him any trouble at all – quite the opposite. But, jokes aside, it became a pain in the arse. We couldn't tell these people not to take pictures if that was what they were doing. We couldn't ask them to stop whispering and pointing and staring and to mind their own business because they were, of course, free to do whatever they liked. But it mucked things up for us. Something simple had become complicated. It meant we had to keep an eye on the time, to plan an exit, to have to think about not getting drunk, to ensure our royal colleague didn't do anything rash, to remember to remind each other that, although off-duty, we were on-duty in terms of ensuring everyone from us, to the Army Air Corps and the Royal Family, did not end up in the papers. We had a responsibility we didn't want, yet the reason we were there in the first place was to step away from responsibility. I had on that night very clear confirmation that it was much more than just journalists who were forever trying to get closer to this guy.

So how long would it be before a snapper was camped out in the car park? How long before an enterprising or undercover reporter was working their way towards us?

It wasn't that the microscope this man lived under had been switched on once more, it was that it was always on, that it had always been on and would always be on everywhere in the world. No wonder Harry Wales wanted to get into the sky.

Speaking of which, his training was going well. I had a sense he was on target to get through CTT and begin the next phase, CTR, to finish up with flight and get specific with fight. There was a way to go but by now I understood he had the kind of command of detail which suggested he was aiming right at his goal. His learning had come a long way. His best qualities were surfacing nicely, among them his respect for the machine, for the sky, for the ground. He'd listened when I'd told him he needed to know that any one of these things can act against him if he doesn't give them proper acknowledgement. I'd said that when you're up there the only enemies must be the ones you want to fight, the ones seeking to kill you and your friends. I'd said it was his duty to be at ease with the aircraft. I think he had the feeling by then that he was getting there, that he could well be in action in the not-too-distant future. But he couldn't get complacent.

By now the MoD, forever fielding questions from the British media, was working in tandem with the Royal Family's PR machine to issue updates on Harry Wales's progress on the course. Such a thing was totally new to me, and I didn't like the idea. My thinking was that any ongoing commentary about someone on any course is a little unhealthy. And it could still all end badly for him. If so, what then? After the whole thing had been built up so much, the public expectation could only be that they would see him don an Apache helmet in due course. If that didn't happen, what was Plan B?

While the MoD and Royals did work with the press for understandable reasons, we stuck to what we agreed at the outset. The more I got to know Harry Wales, the clearer it became that he saw the media, from the tabloids right through to the BBC, as a malign force in his life. Yet it was one that he knew he could not avoid completely. He never actually put that into words, but it didn't take a genius to work it out. Although at times high-spirited, there was very little about Harry that suggested he was anything other than a private, decent and, apart from the obvious, regular guy. To the best of my knowledge, while with the Army Air Corps, he never talked about his father or mother, about his grandparents or his upbringing. He never talked of his duties, his then girlfriend, about that very public and immense loss he suffered after his mother was chased through Paris by the press and the extraordinary funeral that followed. He was never rude or angry or cowardly or aggressive. The guy I got to know was nothing less than a good soldier and a good man. And it was in getting to know him that I came to know that the discussions we had about keeping him beyond the media's range were welcomed. When we did what we could to shield him, he was thankful. Just as with any other blue beret, or any other colleague in the British military, we had his back.

I wondered once, due to being a close colleague and being part of that shield he enjoyed, if he might do me a favour. My mother-in-law was an avid royalist and, with her seventieth birthday coming up, I thought I might get a signed picture of the prince. A doddle, surely? I brought it up after one of the sortie briefs.

'It really would make her day,' I said.

And I knew then it wasn't going to happen.

'I don't,' he said. He was as nice as possible when he explained he didn't sign anything for anyone anywhere. It was, he said, a personal rule that he would not break.

It was a shame as it really would have meant a lot to her. Yet it was probably a wise decision on his part, and certainly one that I respected. (I didn't even allow it to affect his grading.) So, if ever a signed Prince Harry picture pops up on eBay, now you know it's a fake.

After the initial night-flying phase, Harry's training continued on simulator sorties, chiefly to advance his weaponry skills. I was routinely hearing he was doing well in mock engagements, that he was comfortably above average when it came to arming the systems and verbalising the various commands. Things really were looking good.

In terms of our training together, we would now move on to night formation – two-aircraft operations in the darkness. It's an Apache fundamental, to fly in often very close proximity to the other half of your callsign. If you can't fly with full mental awareness of the guys near by you shouldn't be flying at all.

Initial formation sorties are designed to show students which references to use while working closely with another aircraft. It is at first a daunting thing to experience another Apache just two main rotor widths away from you in the dark of night. Your head fills with 'what-ifs' and 'holy shits', and staying calm and collected is a mission in itself. As a student, your job in this section is mostly to maintain position and navigate everything in your charge while bearing the lead aircraft in mind. The rest of it is just to hope like hell that that lead aircraft does what you're expecting it to do. No surprises, please.

Harry would be moving from the rear seat, where he had been acting as pilot, to the front seat, where he would now act as aircraft commander and co-pilot/gunner. It was a move of only a few feet for a man but one that put him front and centre with the weapons in a more visceral way than a sim can.

But ahead of learning to get the feel of the guns, Harry and the rest of the students would be required to lead error-free, pre-flight briefs. In terms of the teaching theory, the idea was that trainees with talent at this point needed to develop their ability to work off initiative not instruction. That needed to come out nice and clear in the pre-briefs. Those would show, or not show, that the student really was starting to think independently. Pre-flight briefs at this level include a rehearsal of concept (ROC) drill. That boils down to a more enhanced walk-through of what's lined up for the sortie ahead. This is the point where each flight commander must share their plans, take on board anything that arises and adapt accordingly. As instructors, we liked to throw in a few curveballs here and there to put pressure on each student, to force them to think on their feet. There were times when these little sessions got a little complex, where the pressure started to show, when we learned a little more about each of the trainees. It was all useful stuff. Basically, from our point of view, if there was an umbilical cord between the student and the instructor, this was when the initial cut came.

Harry's first delivered briefing was a little shaky because he seemed, once more, to be trying to get a few laughs going. Let's just say that, at this advanced stage of the game, it wasn't appropriate at all. I was disappointed. That awkward, clownish behaviour wasn't what he was really about at all. Was it that he was so buoyed by his night flight success that he was getting complacent? I hoped not. Anyway, off he went, playing the joker in the pack. I remember being intrigued when he threw an obscure comment into that drill about having to watch out for 'armament factories and elephants' as his flight would be making its way towards enemy territory. That was a reference to a quip from the classic 1989 *Blackadder Goes Forth* comedy series with Rowan Atkinson: in the front-line trenches of the First World War, a clownish upper-class officer paints a romanticised image of German defences ahead which, as Blackadder comments, in reality may have had 'a few more armament factories and not quite as many elephants'. Harry seemed to be making a niche joke about his own interpretation of the sortie.

His briefing left me with the sense that if, in the air, Harry was compelled to change his plans fast, he might not respond as well as required. Call it instinct, but I felt that if his jokes were springing from discomfort, even from self-deprecation, if they were some kind of go-to response for when he felt overwhelmed, then what happens when he's really in the thick of it? He had not done himself any favours. I had been clear with him before and felt I was going to have to say it again. I wanted to see focus, clean decision-making and leadership. I was getting to see it in bursts, but how could I know it would be there when it counted? We were moving into the last stage of this phase, and he had to hold his nerve. For all our sakes, Lieutenant Wales, no more jokes.

When the time came, he knuckled down once more. In fact, it was characteristic of him to bounce back from difficulties or errors and refocus on the job. That was good to see, good to know he could, when he worked for it, aim himself at winning the moment in front and not let the one before drag him down.

Over the following formation sorties I took it on myself to insert faults into the plans, to slow down here and there and veer off course, but he caught me every time and redirected as required. I complicated his objectives, muddied the waters, forced him to bear an increasing number of things in mind beyond targeting and navigation. I was heartened again, becoming confident once more that he would find inside what he needed to get through CTT. But that's not to say he had earned himself a Dark Blue grading for any single sortie. He had banked the Greens and the Light Blues and that was no mean feat, but the Dark Blues were staying beyond his reach. But only just.

I would not be with Lieutenant Wales for the Final handling test which assessed his handling/gunnery and command skills. But, as with all my students, I wasn't far away. I arrived just ahead of him and a fellow student launching into their brief and, with not a single joke, it seemed pretty good to me. When all the timings were confirmed, he headed out to the aircraft.

He nodded my way, poker face.

'Good luck,' I said.

Another nod. I got the sense he was in the zone. He would need to be.

Minutes later, before a rotor had even turned, some seriously annoying news.

'Can you believe this?' I said to anyone in earshot.

'What's the problem?' asked one of the instructors.

The squadron radio had announced that Harry's aircraft had gone unserviceable on start. A delay would have to be added to all the timings. He'd have to wait. This meant all that confidence he was carrying would need to be locked in place while the Apache was reset and restarted. It's known as 'going cold steel', which is our way of saying CTR-ALT-DEL. So, everything was rebooted to iron out the glitches and then he was ready for . . . nope. Still no success. Another reset, another ten minutes or so and . . . nope.

For fuck's sake.

I knew he must be seriously annoyed. I certainly was. And that wouldn't do either of us any good. All I could hope for was that he wouldn't start cracking jokes, that his mindset would hold strong. I put in a call to see if there was, by any strange chance, a spare Apache knocking around but no joy.

Meanwhile, Harry Wales was heading for his fourth cold steel restart. He must have been very close to calling the whole thing off. It was his flight and if the aircraft was having this much of a strop, then maybe it would be wise to let it alone. And if he did call it a day, it would mean he'd have to repeat the whole lot another time.

Then, after forty-five shitty minutes, the good news. That fourth cold steel start had done the trick. The grumpy Apache was ready to play. The serviceability call came over the radio and it was action stations. Thank Christ for that. My mind eased. There was hope. But Harry would need to remember to delay all his timings by forty-five minutes. And given this was practice for the real world, he'd also need to inform the other crew of the situation with the right lingo – Rolex plus forty-five. And, without me knowing whether he did or not, off he went.

Two hours later and I heard his callsign on squadron radio, him calling to say he was inbound. This was great news. The Apache hadn't needed to come home early for whatever reason. I waited in the ops room like an anxious parent. On sight, I gave the thumbs up, seeking a response in return. He replied with a shaky fifty/fifty. I nodded. So be it.

Off he went to the briefing room. Everything hinged on this sortie, this examination of the product of my instruction, in order to get him to the next stage. It took an hour. The door opened. I walked right in before he walked out. I looked around, looked him in the eye. It wasn't good. Shit.

'Well?' I said. Whatever it was, I wanted to hear it from him.

'It's fine,' he said, a smile appearing.

'You're a twat,' I said. 'The look on your face. I thought you'd failed.'

'Nah,' he said, 'just winding you up.'

I was genuinely delighted. I was delighted when any of my students got through, but I'd have kicked myself bloody hard if this one hadn't worked out. There had, the report said, been some struggles at the outset but once airborne he had got into his mission bubble just fine. Weaponeering went well and there had been no problems with captaincy. Even the running landings were said to be of a good standard. Again, not a Dark Blue but he was bloody close. I remember chatting with him afterwards, how he said that his only disappointment had been that he had come all this way yet never bagged himself a Dark Blue. I told him it didn't matter.

I said, 'You should forget it. The simple fact that we never had to re-fly any sorties says it all. You've done well. Your average is above average.'

He and I would have one more instrument sortie together before he moved on to mountain flying. The only reason for that was to ensure his skills were kept sharp due to a pause between the test and the next stage. It's important always, for obvious reasons, that pilots have flown as recently as possible. We set off with no issues, flew for ninety minutes with no issues and landed with, I'm glad to say, no issues. It was a relaxed, controlled and robust bit of flying. Perhaps because I hadn't been banging on about a specific mission, perhaps because it was all instinct and zero anxiety, he really did hit his stride. I'm also glad to say that quietly confident young Wales managed to get himself a well-deserved Dark Blue for that sortie. Safe to say he was chuffed.

So, it was full steam ahead for the prince, into the Alps in the south of France where he would face the kind of environmental complications he had never faced before. I would be squadron sergeant major for the students now in the last key phase of the CTT course. What lay ahead was one week of Exercise Panther's Peak. Squadron members, along with several Apaches, would be based at Le Luc in the south of the country, a truly breathtaking location where the French and German military train Tiger attack helicopter crews.

Ahead of crossing the Channel, I got down to the work of putting everything together. And right from the outset it was clear the international press were already all over the place. They had been tipped off that the prince would be training at Le Luc and, I was informed, worked out it was inevitable he would be refuelling at one or two airbase facilities there in the days ahead. The cameras were out and there were rumours that staff at the refuel stations were being approached. The hunt for Harry, or for any scrap of information about him, was on. And once again I wanted to make sure I'd be spoiling the party. We were taking part in a military operation involving high-speed flying through the French Alps. Aside from everything else, this just didn't seem to be the place for a celebrity photoshoot.

I would be going over as part of the first flight, and by flight, I mean two aircraft and four airmen. I was flying with a sergeant while Wales and Rich, the OC of the squadron, would be in the other Apache. Before we set off, I got the four of us together. We needed to get the prince over there, through Panther's Peak and home again with as little bullshit as possible. Harry heartily agreed it would not be a good thing to have him plastered all over the papers while under our watch in France. We all knew it might be a bit of an uphill struggle to ensure we got what we wanted, but we were a resourceful bunch.

So where were the weak points? I did some more digging. I confirmed that refuel crews, all local French civilians, were indeed being approached by press seeking information. Not only that, but they were being offered cash too. In fact, a liaison there was able to advise that money was being offered to people in bars and clubs too. That seemed a bit speculative and I felt confident we could find a workaround if we were planning a night out. It didn't concern me.

What did trouble me was those more finely targeted promises of cash being made to refuelling staff.

It wasn't essential but it was good practice for a crew to disembark during refuelling. And typically, while training in the area, that's what our pilots would do. I advised we stick with that, that when our flight arrived the four of us should get out of the two aircraft. We would avoid showing ourselves clearly to the fence lines, where I'd heard the paparazzi were gathering, and stand closely together at the side of the aircraft. We should take the helmets off – they had obvious name tags – to further avoid suspicion, yet keep our heads down and faces difficult to photograph. Basically, we would linger as much as possible on the far side of the aircraft and, if there were images to get, the best of them would be those of a couple of guys, helmets on, climbing into a helicopter. We wanted to make it complicated for anyone, refuel crew or otherwise, to identify us. This would, I hoped, dampen down any suspicion that Lieutenant Wales was there at all. And for good measure, I asked that we all remove name badges too. If Harry was to make a misstep, we didn't want anyone with a powerful enough long lens to zoom in on 'WALES' and have their hopes confirmed.

As a final thought, I said it might be an idea to say 'thirty minutes' if anyone asked about Harry. In the event of any refuel crew wondering out loud if he was on board, one of us (not Harry) would give them a friendly answer.

'Prince Harry?' they should say. 'He's on the next flight. It'll be here in about thirty minutes.'

Something like that.

Harry was front-and-centre in all our minds on the day we departed. That wasn't ideal. The training should have been front-and-centre. All of this was an extra layer of shit to handle, but it was nobody's fault.

Our bags and equipment were laid outside the squadron lines and we stood around waiting for everything to get loaded.

Harry wandered out from the briefing room to join us. He nodded towards a battered-looking blue bag among the cargo. His hand went up, his finger pointing.

'Whose mangy bag is that?!' he said, laughing out loud.

I didn't take it well. It was an asshole comment. No real malice in it, but I thought it was bad form, the only smidgen of snobbery I ever saw from him. And anyway, it was my bag.

'Hey,' I said to him. 'That's my mangy bag. And it used to be my mother's. She died recently, right? It's sentimental to me. Is that okay with you?'

His cheeks flushed redder than his hair. He was lost for words. It was my bag but, in truth, the bit about it being a keepsake from my mum wasn't true. I never told him that. Wouldn't do him any harm to stew a little.

Over in France, the 'thirty minutes' plan worked like a charm. Curious eyes were on us as we touched down across the week, curious helpers emerging to ask if Harry might be along some time soon.

'About thirty minutes,' we said.

On the first set of occasions, word quickly reached the paps. They swarmed close to the wire and waited to get their man on the next flight. And, lo and behold, about thirty minutes later the next callsign pair arrived and, nope, the royal could not be spotted.

Unfortunately, due to the secrecy of what we were doing and who with, that initial following flight had not been briefed on our plan. Both aircraft landed to see the beaming faces of massively eager refuel crews as distant paps gave them the Hollywood 'A' List treatment. A mean trick, but it worked.

Across the week, while out and about, we couldn't avoid getting caught up in all the fuss about Harry being in the small town. He chose to keep a low profile from the start. But as soon as the rest of us were identified as British military, we were routinely approached and asked the same thing.

'Is he coming out tonight?'

'Does he have a girlfriend?'

'Will you give him my number?'

We did our best to try and get a laugh out of it. After a lot of interest in one club, I was dared to approach the manager and ask him to keep it quiet and advise that Prince Harry was on the premises. The man's eyes lit up. I said the young royal was having a great time and that he had expressed an interest in wanting to personally tell the manager just that. The guy seemed excited, maybe a bit taken aback, almost confused by the whole thing. But he nodded and said that was 'no problem', that he'd be happy to meet him.

I escorted him to where we were sitting and watched as he looked at all our faces. There was no Harry. But one of our guys had already accepted a dare to do his best to impersonate the prince. He was roughly the same build, although looked nothing like him. Yet confidence can take you far in this world. The lad stood, reached out and firmly shook the manager's hand. In a (fake) posh accent, he said, 'Thank you for your hospitality. Grandmother would be most appreciative.'

We were, of course, by now pissing ourselves laughing as this bemused man was smiling and nodding at the lad, unsure whether to bow or not. It seemed pretty clear he either didn't have a clue what Harry looked like, or if he did, he didn't want to tell this fella that he was nuts. From that moment we were expecting a bouncer to appear and ask us to get the hell out.

But no.

Two minutes later champagne arrived – on the house. The waitress said it was to be enjoyed by the young prince, his minders and British Army colleagues. Our laughter continued for some time. And then we laughed some more. As squadron sergeant major, being fully aware of my duty, I drank the first glass. I'm sure that, as our fake Harry had said, a certain grandmother would have forgiven us. Her grandson certainly did, anyway.

The training itself introduced the prince to up- and downdraught winds, advanced formation flying and route selection. All the students came away with something close to a renewed understanding of the aircraft's capability. The exercise went well, with no hiccups, and the press never got a single frame of Lieutenant Harry Wales.

As the week came to a close, I got stuck into writing my final report, which was then to be sent to the conversion-to-role course senior instructor. I wrote of a bright and capable young officer who was eager to learn. I said he liked both to work hard and play hard and that he had a way of finding a good balance between the two. From what I had seen, I knew he was a quality team player and at the same time he was a confident, good-natured individual seeking to make his mark. In terms of recommendation, I wrote that I thought Harry Wales was best suited to the front seat given that his gunnery skills were perhaps his most impressive. If I was sending him into battle, I said, I'd be comfortable knowing he was manning the weapons.

We were into 2011. Lieutenant Wales had passed eight months of CTT training. He was awarded his Apache badge by his squadron OC on Thursday 14 April, effectively marking the end of one section and the beginning of another. Between times, he was promoted to captain, not due to passing CTT but because of the time he had served as a lieutenant. What lay ahead for Captain Wales in CTR would involve a further eight months learning to fight the aircraft in specific environments. He would be instructed on the intricacies of electronic warfare, tactical formation flying, advanced weaponeering, and he'd move into live-fire training situations, and emerge combat ready. Basically, he was off to be trained for operating where his fresh skills were needed most – Afghanistan.

The final part of his CTR had moved away from Oman and would now be a challenging two-month operation based in the USA, known as Exercise Crimson Eagle. It was just after completion of that in 2012 that the press finally made a breakthrough, if that's what you want to call it. Pictures were secured of him buck naked and living it up at a boozy pool party in a £1,000-a-day chalet in Las Vegas. The whole thing, just two weeks before he was due to deploy to Afghanistan, was a bit of a scandal. The leaked pictures showed the third-in-line to the throne surrounded by near-naked women, and one or two bare-naked ones as well. I suppose it was clear once again that he couldn't always trust the people around him. It was also clear that, every now and then, temptation is going to win. He really did look like he was having a hell of a time.

As one of his instructors, I've been asked many times whether he had some extra leeway or advantage during training. The answer is no. That never happened. Not for a second. He was a student like all the others. He worked hard, played by the same rules as everyone else, put in the same hours and earned his stripes.

He went on to a twenty-week posting at Camp Bastion in Helmand where he was a fine Apache gunner. He told afterwards how he had been involved in casevacs and had protected troops. He told how he had saved lives and taken lives, saying, 'If there's people trying to do bad stuff to our guys, then we'll take them out of the game.' One Afghan warlord had labelled him a 'jackal' and made it clear he was a prime target for his band of insurgents. I'm happy to say Harry did more damage to that individual's standing than the other way around.

In 2014, just ahead of him leaving the British Army after ten years' service, Prince Harry founded and launched the Invictus Games. It's a truly international sporting event for injured military personnel and is nothing less than an astonishing, uplifting, tears-in-the-wide-open-eyes spectacle. In terms of its scope, success and sheer bloody human value, there is nothing like it. If ever a man gave back . . .

Captain Wales left service in 2015. His private and public life have continued to fill newspapers and phone screens, and fire up debate on both sides of the Atlantic. His marriage to Meghan, the later decision to step aside from his royal role and what he has said, and said about his family, since have had immense impact. His life is controversial, but I don't believe he ever wanted it that way. I don't think, if the choice was his to make, he'd want you even to know anything about him at all. What's maybe most significant about this guy is that he is and always has been an ordinary man in an extraordinary situation. It seems to me that he reached a point where, to be true to himself, he could no longer be the man he was expected to be, and acted accordingly. The instructor in me likes the idea of him having the balls to go for Plan B when things weren't working out.

Whatever passing views I might have on whatever he says aren't views that stand the test of time. As any soldier will tell you, what lasts is the respect we have for each other as military comrades. What matters is that Prince Harry will always be one of us.

Chapter Twenty-Eight

CIVVY STREET. UK, 2014

WHEN I JOINED up, most generally left the army after twenty-two years' service or on reaching their fortieth birthday. Things began to change after the idea of routinely ditching highly trained professionals with much yet to offer was seen to be ill-advised. Extensions became commonplace, typically offering another fifteen years to those with specialist trades.

After serving twenty-six years, I made plans to leave and begin a second career aged forty-four. I had done my bit and achieved all I could have hoped to achieve in the military in peacetime and otherwise. I felt confident I would be able to find that new journey and keep on flying for twenty or more years, all the way to pensionable age. It was, still, all I wanted to do. As a result of some forward thinking back in 2004, I already had a civilian pilot licence. From flying soldier to flying civilian would be an easy transition. Or so I thought.

In early 2014, the oil and gas industry was on a roll. Global economics, on something of an upswing, meant the price of a barrel of black gold was hitting as high as $125 and rarely falling to less than

$100. That was getting on for double what it had been just a few years before. With business booming, offshore aviation companies were loading up on helicopter pilots.

I was watching all this unfold as a serving soldier across 2013. By the end of that year, I responded to a recruitment drive at Bristow, one of four helicopter companies operating out of Aberdeen. I got a call back from a man called Matt. I was a good candidate, he told me. No problem with the licence. All I needed was to gain an Instrument Rating (IR).

To fly legitimately, a pilot must hold a valid medical, an aircraft type rating and, in some circumstances, a valid IR. The latter was needed in this case as the work was likely to involve flying in poor weather and within cloud. As such, I'd need to be able to rely entirely on instruments. I'd have to get to a training flight school to do the necessary, though, given my experience, it would be a short course. But it would still cost me over £20,000.

Bristow academy was a flying school at Staverton airfield in Gloucester. I was under no obligation, but I decided to sit the course there. It began in early 2014, with me taking it alongside Paul F, a fellow ex-Apache pilot. His plan was to go on to secure a flying position with the police in his hometown of Glasgow. My plan involved taking on the all-new territory of the North Sea.

The course was tough. I needed to learn a whole new set of aircraft limitations and a whole new set of procedural instrument flying procedures. If I failed, I'd have to fork out for a resit and potentially limit the opportunities ahead.

The final test, which took about seventy minutes, was led by an ex-Navy pilot called Nick G who, I discovered, didn't like to talk. That didn't help when it came to getting feedback because there wasn't any. But he had to in the end and surprisingly began speaking at length, going methodically through everything I had done. Then he told me I had passed. It was quite an emotional moment, as it happens, perhaps because the whole bloody thing had been so expensive. Although Paul had required an extra training sortie prior to his check, he had passed too, which was great. Then I was handed an additional bill for £220 from the flight school. This was because, I was told, while I was waiting for traffic to clear so I could cross a runway (Nick was piloting) and get back to the flight school, I had hovered for an extra twelve minutes, clocking up the extra charge.

I called my family first to tell them the good news, and then called Matt at Bristow. My application was progressed, and an interview was lined up in Aberdeen. This would be the first job interview I had sat in twenty-seven years. I studied hard, learning the firm's history, the names of key personnel, practising answers over and over.

I arrived early that morning on a flight from London and, with a few hours to spare, sat in my rented car near Bristow's offices, re-read my notes and practised my answers some more. The interview itself went quite well and included stuff about key personnel, company history and general aviation questions. It also involved a flight test in a Super Puma flight simulator and, although modelled on a very different kind of machine than I was used to, it went well.

Waiting at reception afterwards, ahead of meeting someone from HR, Pete Barnes walked past. He had been the civilian instructor who twenty years before had instructed me on my Bell 212 course before I went to Brunei. We had a good catch-up before HR informed me I should head off home and that I would be advised about next steps later. I was feeling pretty good.

Ten days passed without a word. Finally, a large white envelope with the company logo.

'We are pleased to confirm . . .'

I was delighted. I would be starting in ten months. It was a distance away but the company was confident of good times ahead. Besides, the army does like a year's notice and Tracey and I had to get ourselves moved to Aberdeen.

Signing off as a soldier felt like a whole new adventure. It was sad in the sense that I had loved my career, yet at the same time it was like having a weight lifted from my shoulders. A whole new world was waiting.

As the months ticked by, I continued on various military duties but made sure to keep in contact with Matt. I was keen to get as much information as I could ahead of time, to know what I would be flying, to prepare myself as best I could. Tracey and I spent a hectic week in Aberdeen viewing twenty-one properties, settling on one, and getting an initial sense of the area. Aberdeenshire itself caught our imagination with – like Co. Durham, where Tracey had grown up – its stunning, rolling open countryside. Although those vistas were interrupted every now and then by the grey, gloomy charms of Aberdeen, the Granite City.

Indeed, there had been something of a gloomy cloud hanging over my plans to work in Scotland from the outset. Back in 2011, the Scottish National Party had won the majority of seats in the Scottish Parliament. Its mission was independence from the UK, to harden up the border with England and go it alone. I hadn't paid much attention to any of this, fairly sure it was a lot of nationalistic bluster albeit with an at times anti-English, anti-British Army tinge. But when, in 2013, a date was set for a referendum, I sat up and listened. It was hard to believe that a 300-year-old union between our close-knit nations could be coming to a close, but it began to feel like we were at the beginning of the end. I watched the results of that September 2013 referendum come in while teaching the CTR course in the USA. Fifty-five percent voted against independence. It was a little tighter than I would have liked but I was chuffed all the same. As a proud ex-member of the UK armed forces, the thought of moving to and living in a newly independent Scotland did not appeal.

In my final couple of months in the army, I looked over some of the courses being offered to soldiers making the transition to Civvy Street. One of them was a two-week DIY course at Colchester.

I thought it would be just the thing for me, given I was setting up in a new house. During that fortnight I put in a call to HR at Bristow over some minor matter.

'Ah yes, Mr Jones. Can you hold for a minute please? I know Matt wanted to have a word.'

'Okay,' I said. It seemed unusual.

'Hi, Steve. It's Matt. I have some bad news. Due to the downturn, I regret to inform you that we have no job for you.'

I was due to start there in six weeks. We were moving house in four. Bristow had been fully aware I'd ended my army career, that I'd rearranged my whole life to take up the firm job offer in Aberdeen.

'Matt,' I said, 'tell me you're joking.'

He wasn't. He talked some more but I was too busy trying to control my rage to know what he said. I had some thoughts to collect, and they weren't good ones.

'I'll speak to you later,' I said, and ended the call.

I took a breath, tried to calm myself and returned to my DIY course.

On the way back to base that evening, I called Tracey. It was an emotional conversation. After that, I called our solicitor to see just how deep in the shit I was. The advice was that I could pull out of the house purchase but, in Scottish law, if the property was then sold at cheaper price, we would have to make up the difference. And the seller could seek compensation too.

Just about in control of my fury, I called Matt.

I was, he explained, one of forty-seven people he had called that day with similar news. Over about an hour, we talked it all through. He said things can change rapidly, as I was now well aware, and assured me he would continue to review all options and update me weekly.

That mid-2014 downturn had been a result primarily of a global drop in the demand for oil. The 70 per cent tumble was one of the three biggest declines since the Second World War, and the longest lasting since the supply-driven collapse of 1986. Much as I had wanted to scream at Matt, it wasn't his fault. I called him at one point to say I understood the position he had been in, that I wouldn't have liked to make those forty-seven calls. There was little point in holding it against him.

In one way, though, this was a lesson in civilian loyalty. I had committed to Bristow early, put all my cards on the table, applied nowhere else, attended the company flight school, began to emotionally connect with this excellent aviation firm. Yet its only interest all along had been in the bottom line. There was nothing to be surprised about of course, I wasn't naïve. Yet there was an unmistakable mismatch in that one of my most unassailable characteristics had been given in return for nothing at all.

Tracey and I chose to push on. We would move to Scotland as planned, keep our eyes open and fingers crossed, see how things worked out. Every week I hoped hard for a call from Aberdeen to say it was all systems go once more, that there was an opening after all. But it didn't come. And no one else was hiring pilots. On the contrary, they were being let go all over the place. I know that because I sent out thirty-five CVs and got thirty-five responses saying the same thing. My timing couldn't have been worse. I had, just weeks before, been at the top of my game, teaching students to fly the most advanced helicopter in the world. Now I was heading nowhere fast.

So, what to do? Sign back on with the army? I did contemplate this but had by now already resigned myself to leaving, I was mentally and physically ready. The other option – being unemployed – was not something I would ever want to experience. I was a highly driven individual and my skillset was very much all about flying, and there was that short DIY course too. I reckoned the best I could do was pitch myself as an active, honest, reliable and disciplined sort of guy with a very strong track record. And, emphasising those qualities, after a few days of interviews I had my first job offers – a manager's position at Sports Direct; a senior leader of a team of twelve with SSE; an area manager for Rentokil. Good offers under the circumstance, I thought, even though none of them involved helicopter flying. But would I stick them? Would they challenge me, fire me up, bring out the best in me? I was seriously doubting it. That's when I had the idea about the police. Alas, as explained at the beginning of this book, that didn't exactly work out either.

On the very day I came to consider ditching my four-day-old Police Scotland career, I received an email from Cobham Aviation. I had attended a video interview with the firm a few weeks before and assumed nothing would come of it. Yet here they were, apologising for the lateness of the reply, telling me I had been successful, asking if I was still able to take up a civilian flying instructor's position? The only issue was that the job would be at my old stomping ground of RAF Shawbury, so I'd have some lengthy commuting to do.

The distances ran counter to what my retirement from the army was meant to be all about. Yet Tracey agreed it was the best option so far, understood where my real passion lay and that I would not settle until I was flying again. I told Police Scotland I was out of there.

RAF Shawbury in Shropshire, home of the Defence Helicopter Flying School (DHFS), trains around 1,000 students a year from across the UK armed services and international partners. The base had three squadrons, all of which had a mix of tri-service instructors, but in essence each represented a service. 670 Squadron was Army, 705 squadron Navy and 60 Squadron RAF. I was very happy to be attached to 670.

Amongst its many global services, Cobham also provided aviation support to DHFS. As there was a shortage of military QHIs due to front-line commitments, Cobham took on ex-military instructors to fill the shortfall. The last time I'd been there was for three months back in 2009 during my QHI course. I had spent the last five years teaching already qualified pilots. Those I would train at DHFS were new to it. A specialist course taught me how to teach a student right from the start, and after taking on my first students I learned it would be as much as learning curve for me as it was for them.

We have a saying in aviation – 'I learnt about flying from that.' It applies when things go tits up yet you get through it. One of those came early on when, being flown by a student called Phelan, the aircraft suddenly yawed through 120 degrees and pitched up 20 degrees. Luckily, I knew what to do.

'I have control,' I called, looking over at one very pale Phelan.

And then I went pale myself. I couldn't bring the helicopter under control. It was as if the controls were jammed, taking a mammoth effort to budge them. I'd never known this to happen outside of a pre-planned emergency test run. The aircraft pitched and rolled, and my mind began playing out the worst scenarios, all of which involved us crashing. And then it struck me that none of the controls had hydraulic power. A quick check. Somehow Phelan had managed to switch it off. I knocked them back on. With a thump, the aircraft stabilised. I have no idea how we didn't at least suffer a tail strike having rapidly pitched nose up then down. It had been my mistake. I hadn't tracked everything he was doing, my mind wandering while a competent student was in charge. It had almost cost an aircraft, or worse. I learnt about flying from that.

For months I was commuting back to Aberdeenshire every second weekend, a very long one-way journey. If I didn't get away before 15.00 on a Friday, I'd hit heavy traffic and the journey would become an epic voyage, and not in a good way. So, when I received a call about a recruitment day for an air ambulance job closer to home, I fired over my CV.

Specialist Aviation Services (SAS), based in Staverton, Gloucestershire, provide support to the emergency services and other organisations that rely on aircraft as part of their own operations. I knew the firm because it had previously offered me the job but

I'd committed to Bristow at the time and turned it down. This time around it was recruiting for a new contract it had secured for The Children's Air Ambulance (TCAA) charity on the new AW169, a ten-seat twin-engine helicopter. The work, largely transferring critically ill children from hospitals to specialist paediatric centres across the UK, sounded fantastic. I would be based in Doncaster. It wasn't quite Aberdeenshire but it certainly wasn't Shropshire. I made the grade and sat the AW169 course in Sesto, Italy, the home of Leonardo Helicopters. And, of course, I said a fond farewell to Cobham after thirteen months in post there. Entering January 2017, I was on my third job (fourth if you count Bristow) since leaving the army eighteen months before.

Sesto was a real education, my first full insight into the civilian flying stream in which even the terminology was different. For example, in the military the person flying the aircraft is the handling pilot, now it was the pilot flying. One of my trainers was Joanne, who I knew had been part of the army's Apache force. She lived locally and invited a few of us for a bite to eat and a drink in an eight-hour downtime period between sorties. We all had a little too much sauce and, when back in the cockpit, I was startled to hear a BANG out of the blue. The helicopter, with three on board, had decelerated from 120 knots to zero in a split second. My heart almost exploded. We had crashed! Fortunately, we were in a simulator. All three of us had fallen asleep. It was the first time in twenty-five years of flying this had ever happened to me.

Ahead of beginning work, a rework of the rules would place TCAA crew in the temporary role of technical crewman (TCM). Up to that point this role of TCM had been conducted by the paramedics in the aircraft. Yet they had limited training, flying permanently in the left-hand seat to assist the pilot with navigation. The new policy freed up paramedics and ensured the TCM was a qualified pilot whose primary role was safety. This left-seat job would be my role and would continue to be my role until I received the line training that allowed me to captain the air ambulance, the job I had been hired to do. It wasn't ideal and it certainly wasn't what I had joined the company to do but it was, very nearly, flying.

At a later induction in Kent, I was shown around the MD902 NOTAR (no tail rotor) helicopter by Budgie, who had helped instruct me on the Lynx many moons ago. The NOTAR eliminates all the mechanical disadvantages of a tail rotor, including long drive shafts and 90-degree gearboxes. Added benefits included reduced noise and reduced pilot workload as the Coanda Effect (where air stream clings to a curved surface) helps with tail boom lift makes everything more stable and therefore easier to control. As we headed off for a brew and a chat about aerodynamics, a call on the base's emergency line. It was a case of just getting on with it. Budgie dashed for the aircraft and I darted off to get info. A doctor scribbled down location, nature of accident, injuries. I grabbed the flight iPad and my helmet. The iPad displayed the route, airspace and communication information so I could advise Budgie. It was a road traffic accident (RTA).

'Okay, Steve,' he said, 'tell me what you know.'

'An RTA to the west of Oxted.'

I strapped in, he set off and I attached my iPad to the aircraft screen mount, bluetoothed my flight information to his iPad. With medics on board, we were airborne in just over ten minutes from the call. The scene lay somewhere between the M25 and A25. The M25, regardless of time of day, could be seen for miles as its traffic snaked around various towns orbiting London. The A25 lay to the south paralleling the M25 from Chipstead to Godstone.

'Okay, Budgie, Sevenoaks straight ahead, western side is a large junction, west of that is the A25 going west with the M25 laying to the north of it.'

'Seen.'

'Follow the A25 west until you come to the next largest town, approximately three miles. That's Westerham.'

'Seen.'

'On the western side of the quarry is a small road orientated north to south before the town of Oxted. Along that road is where we should be looking.'

'Okay,' he said, 'happy with the rough area. Slowing.'

Moments later in the back, the paramedic called, 'Okay I have eyes on two ambulances in between a small road junction, in our three o'clock now.'

Location identified; I did the landing checks as Budgie touched down in a farmer's field. With a bergen on each of their backs, the two crew departed to the scene 400 metres away. Budgie shut down the aircraft and we got out to stretch our legs. After a moment, I wandered towards the scene. Two cars, one of which seemed to have pulled out of a junction in front of the other. Pieces of it were scattered for metres up the road. The second car had travelled thirty or so metres after impact before finally coming to rest against a stone wall on the other side of the road. Some passengers were being treated for, primarily, shock. The two elderly folks in the vehicle that pulled out were in a serious condition and still trapped in the vehicle. The fire engines were en route but had been delayed due to traffic. Annoyingly, adults and kids from a nearby estate were gathering, forcing the police to push them back.

Firefighters arrived. It was quite something to witness their hydraulic cutting device slide through metal like the proverbial hot knife through butter. The roof was peeled back finally providing access for medical crews. One passenger would need to be airlifted to the Royal London Hospital in Whitechapel. Once fully stabilised the doctor, paramedic, ambulance tech and I carried the patient on a stretcher towards the aircraft.

I found London mesmerising from the air, vast to the point that it becomes the horizon itself from miles out. Finding the capital was easy, although finding that seventeen-floor hospital wasn't as simple. Luckily Budgie knew the layout well. At 284 feet, the helipad at the Royal London is one of the highest in Europe, almost the same height as Big Ben. The slow approach towards the rooftop helipad was like something I had never experienced before. Then we were out of the aircraft again, a team waiting to meet us. And once the doctor briefed the new medics on the patient's condition, we were away again.

We returned to base and as I went, finally, to make that brew, another call. This time we were off just south of Canterbury. A farmer had sustained some form of crush injuries. We landed on a school football pitch on this occasion, and although it was the weekend, local people swarmed towards us. I got out and spoke with a few face-to-face, including offering a few stern words to the kid on the bike who went whizzing under the tail boom. He was so close to clocking it with his head. If he had, we may have lost this aircraft until inspected by a maintenance team. It was a stark reminder for me about having eyes in the back of the head especially when distracted. In the end, we weren't required to fly the farmer anywhere. We set back for base again and even before we arrived, footage of us in that football field had been uploaded to social media.

It was because I had so much experience that I started to get frustrated. Weeks passed by and I was still a TCM on the AW169 while I had been employed to captain. And still there was no sign of the line training promised that would allow me to captain. I felt compelled to fly but could not fly. It was troubling me day and night. Yet others didn't need to carry this burden of mine. I made only occasional check-ins about line training and tried not to let it bother me.

An RTA, a motorbike hit by a car. The rider was in a bad way. With the casualty in the back, and just before getting back on board, I was approached by one of the road ambulance team. He gave me the biker's wallet and watch. I assumed I was to take them with me and, once at the Royal London, pass them to staff. I asked

Budgie about it on landing. He was startled, even a little angry. I was baffled.

'You should never accept any of a casualty's possessions,' he scolded. 'Give them to the police if in attendance or put them in a bag strapped to the casualty, but never take them.'

Jesus. I'd somehow hit a nerve.

He went on to explain that some patients have gone on to claim against the charity. Some had said that money had been taken from wallets, that watches had been stolen, that those watches had been on occasion a Breitling or a Rolex. This kind of crap had caused many problems for the air ambulance people who were doing nothing less than working hard to save lives. I can't believe sometimes how low people can go.

Another month passed by. I was itching now, getting very pissed off. I should be in a different role on a specific aircraft type. Did the words on my contract not count for something? I asked again when I would be earmarked for further training. It seemed I was starting to annoy people. There was, at this stage, no sign at all of a date. I was bluntly told I should wait. So that's what I did. Again.

The call-outs were primarily RTAs, very often heart attacks and on one occasion we had to land at a harbour to deal with a very sick passenger on a cruise liner. A high point came when one patient visited the charity some time after being airlifted to hospital to voice their appreciation to the crew involved. A low point came when I was advised to ensure no one ever got a chance to sneak up to the aircraft because they might steal, as had happened before, medical equipment or whatever else they could get their hands on. A yet lower low came when, while close to medics at the scene of an RTA, a large brick was thrown at them from over a nearby wall. Like I said, I can't actually believe sometimes how low some people can go.

Was the company trying hard enough to get me trained? I didn't think so. It wasn't even updating me as to why training kept being delayed. I had been told the TCM duties would be temporary, yet by now I'd been there ten months and was getting seriously fed up with travelling the 601 miles to Kent (and 601 back) for the four-day duties.

I looked into the situation offshore once again. Someone tipped me off about one company. I put in a call and got speaking to John. It turned out that not only had we been in the same squadron when I was in Germany in the late eighties, but he lived just three miles from my current address. There were no vacancies, he said, but recommended I keep in contact. He called back one day, asking if I might want to have a look around the company when I was back at the weekend. I jumped at the chance. And three days after that, I was asked to attend an interview. The company had just won another contract and required an uplift in crews as soon as possible. If I was successful, I'd be required to start in two weeks. I called SAS and explained, said I was not being used in the role for which I had been hired. They said, if needed, they would let me go with two weeks' notice. I got the job and they did.

I was sad to leave having never got to fly the AW169 or even start that TCAA contract. The exposure I had was on a par with the excitement of flying in Afghanistan, the not knowing if or when or why the phone might ring. It struck me that I had gone from taking lives in Afghanistan to saving lives in my own country. But if I didn't move on from it, I was going to need an ambulance myself. Not flying was doing my head in.

Chapter Twenty-Nine

A NEW WORLD

THE OFFSHORE industry's aviation sector had experienced major changes in recent years due mainly to several tragic accidents involving the 225 Super Puma. The latest at the time, in 2016, was off the coast of Norway. The crash took the lives of thirteen people, including one UK citizen. In response, Norway and Britain suspended commercial flights involving this type of helicopter. The aircraft had been the workhorse of the industry for many years, yet now offshore workers and their families understandably demanded that they not be used again. With Super Pumas grounded, a new mid-sized or 'super medium' would have to be found. The Airbus H175 was an ideal contender. I would need to get to know it because I had just landed the job I'd been seeking since leaving the military.

There had been an interview and a deep-digging psychometric test measuring intelligence, attainment, aptitude, personality, values and motivators. That had been followed up with securing the H175-type rating at Airbus Helicopters in Marignane, France, then back to bonnie Scotland ahead of line training.

And before that, I was launched into the annual sessions covering fire, first aid, emergency aircraft door exits, dangerous air cargo and the helicopter underwater escape trainer (HUET), aka the dunker. HUET boils down to a practice run at getting out of a submerged helicopter in daytime or night. It is bloody awful. But I'd already done it a few times so wasn't overly troubled.

Ahead of that main submerging, you get practice by way of being turned upside down by divers on what is known as the witch's chair. The idea is to teach you to stay calm underwater, to retrieve the short-term air supply system (STASS) breathing equipment and put it on. Incidentally, I can tell you from experience that it's seriously important to blow hard into the mouthpiece first to clear it of water, because you may well gag on it the first time you take a breath. Trust me, when in the dark, upside-down and disorientated, and under water, that is not nice.

The dunker machine itself is a large metal rectangular hollow structure divided into two – cockpit and rear compartment – each with basic metal seats and harnesses. When submerged, the water comes at you like you're in an alien world, a swarm of crazed bubbles crashing into your face and forcing their way up your nose and into your mouth. You take a breath as it covers your head, pulling your helmet upwards as you descend 8 feet (2.5 metres), your harness tightening with the air trapped in your survival suit. It is a test of endurance, of self-control, to get a firm grip of the door, to unfasten the harness and get to the surface. Once there, you have to do it all over again. Only this time, when submerged, it will rotate 180 degrees and so the floor becomes the roof. If you ever fancied something truly challenging on your bucket list, I recommend it.

Dunker training is invaluable. The one main difference between offshore and onshore flying is water. When onshore, you have options. When offshore, whatever reason it might be that stops you reaching the platform, you can only go into the sea. Some of the platforms are hundreds of miles from land. Other safety aspects, not least the management of fuel load, are of paramount importance.

I wasn't sure what I would feel when I began my first training flights over the North Sea. One of the first things to strike me was that even from 3,000 feet I could make out the white tips of colliding waves, that a rolling, indifferent hostility was everywhere below. And the familiar colours were gone. Here the baked brown deserts were replaced by icy grey seascapes; flashing towns and cities replaced by the lights of isolated oil rigs. Flying in driving rain would be something close to a constant, low cloud would become standard. Reduced visibility, and therefore reliance on aircraft automation and procedural systems for an airborne radar approach (ARA), would now be typical.

There is a lot of air traffic on these routes, each aircraft strictly flying at specific heights depending on direction. Radio, at times patchy over land, can be more so over water because there is nowhere to place communication towers.

I remember the weight of it all dawning on me when I was about 130 kilometres beyond the coast with nothing to see in any direction. Emergencies out there in the hard winds and unlit, turbulent panorama require a different way of thinking, almost a different way of being a pilot. I had been trained to the highest levels on high-end aircraft in the British Army, and yet here I was in an utterly new danger zone. And it thrilled me to the core.

The rigs themselves have astonished me. The first one I saw on that first training flight appeared like a hidden city, as if from nowhere as I dipped below the cloud level of around 1,000 feet. It was a mass of structures, a confusion of pipes and towering cranes all on one colossal, giant-legged tripod like some futuristic metal god rising from a furious sea. I was mesmerised.

In the past I had carried a maximum of eight passengers cramped in the back of a Lynx, while now I would routinely carry sixteen. The rear cabin is a fair size, but so are some of the guys who work offshore so I'm used now to seeing it fill up fast. Ahead of flights, each person gets weighed and security checked as standard, which wasn't exactly what I was used to while in combat.

It was with a full load of sixteen during my line training check flight with Markus, one of the company's line trainers, that, as I touched down in Aberdeen, I heard a grinding from the nose wheel. The aircraft then lurched to the left. Markus and I looked at each other, baffled, my hands already ensuring we had lift-off again, bringing us into the hover.

'Bad landing,' some smartarse in the back said, which proved he knew diddly squat about flying helicopters.

It turned out the nose wheel had somehow loosened and was literally hanging off the helicopter as we had touched down. I had to wait for ground staff to pile up sandbags and land the nose on those instead. It reminded me of a similar situation back in Afghanistan in 2008 when a Sea King had to land after accidentally tearing off its left wheel. Low on options, we had to dismantle a sangar a kilometre away and, like the evacuation of Dunkirk, get any wheeled vehicle we could to shift the sandbags and materials to the landing site to stack them and so prop up the aircraft.

Now, ten years on, and during my line check, I had to land onto the rear wheels, maintain the delicate balance of holding the nose up while passengers disembarked, before lifting again and then landing with the sandbags as support. By that point a bus, hastily arranged by management, was already racing to collect the passengers. The fear was that the press would be arriving fast to get pictures from just beyond the fence 50 metres away. It seems that the media are forever poised to pounce on any stories linked to offshore workers. And, sure enough, within minutes three cars pulled up and the cameras came out. By then, having been through the experience of keeping Prince Harry out of the papers, I was pretty sure their likely snitch was one of the passengers.

It entered my mind afterwards that this nose-wheel incident had been a real-life test beyond the actual test. Letting the nose fall with the rotor spinning could have been catastrophic. So, I think it was fair enough that I passed the line check. I did wonder for months after that if it had been me who buggered up that wheel in the first place. But only until an investigation ruled, as reported in *Energy Voice* in July of that year, that overworked engineers had failed to spot the problem in advance.

'If it wasn't for the quick reaction of the pilots when the nose dipped and they heard a crunching noise, the consequences are unthinkable,' it read.

After two years in the role, I applied for the deputy chief pilot role with the company, a key management position underneath the Chief Pilot. I felt I needed to keep the momentum going, that I could gain experience in the position. At the end of the interview, I was startled to be asked by Harry (ex-Dutch military and head of flight operations) if I would consider the chief pilot role instead. I declined, saying I didn't think it was, at that point, the right move. A week later and I was asked again by Harry my now boss, to consider the chief pilot role on a temporary basis. And then I agreed. The position was confirmed, and I was told my deputy would be Marco, an ex-Italian Army pilot. He had recently returned from flying fixed wing, leaving his post with Thomas Cook before it went into liquidation. Now combining office days with flying the line, I was wondering exactly how temporary this post was going to be when I was informed it was permanent. And, I'm pleased to say, I was glad to hear it. I had been stitched up in the nicest possible way.

I work these days in the thick of the mercurial, dynamic and vital oil and gas industry. Everything we do can be impacted by the ever-fluctuating price of oil, with huge contracts getting won and lost on the strength of fast-moving market forces. Offshore firms are constantly reviewing arrangements, always looking for the most cost-effective way forward and aircrew numbers are instantly impacted by the decisions. It's a brutal rollercoaster we're on in this industry and all the indications are that the ride will only get wilder.

I had been in the job for just two months before it fell to our department to let several people go. I've faced some hard situations before but this was a new one and something that sat uncomfortably with me for a long time. Our department would not only be delivering the bad news, but also had to select those who would be packing their bags.

And after that, the Covid-19 pandemic hit, compelling us to develop and enforce a whole new set of rules at breakneck speed. We had, as had many other industries, to manage the risk, ensure everyone could be social-distanced, ensure everything was as safe as possible for all of us. It wasn't like any of the aircrew could work from home. We had to bring in newly designed screens to separate crew, initiate temperature tests on passengers, source and manage the logistics of supplying personal protective equipment, set up special flights for workers who showed symptoms while offshore.

During all that I was pleased to learn there were already a great many experts on the transmission of Covid-19 in the aircrew fraternity. They already knew which rules to bend, break and even to enforce themselves, and such information has been no end of help. At time of writing, I'm glad to say, we have managed to keep cases to a minimum, for which I can only thank the flying virologists whose constant and conflicting advice has been invaluable.

Management is no easy game, very often a thankless task. My work is helped by the incredibly professional pilots I have the privilege to call colleagues, and I just wish I could hire many more. That said, I have to say too that there are several assholes with wings out there. The soldier in me says these are people who overrate themselves and often don't know how good they have it, that most of them would burst into tears if they found themselves staring at a TADS in an Apache while men below rush to kill.

And I do miss it, those long seconds and hard minutes and fierce hours in conflict, those explosive VHR duties, the incalculable importance of racing to the aid of a patrol or a single fellow soldier. There is nothing like drawing a literal line in the sand from above, nothing like interrupting those who mean imminent harm to your fellow countrymen, nothing like the honour of being entrusted with immense power and being sure that, while in your hands, you did the right thing with it. I signed up to reach the extremes in the air, and an army career took me to the extremes of my existence, to meet people I would never have known before and see places I would never have otherwise seen. That part of my career has been the greatest part.

Now I'm settled on home ground, the father of a wonderful young woman who serves as a fine police officer in Germany, the husband of a wonderful woman who has been everything and more, who has been there for me each time I returned from wherever the extremes have taken me.